History of
West
Nottingham
Academy — 1744-1981

Magraw House

History of West Nottingham Academy — 1744-1981

Scott A. Mills

1985

Maryland Historical Press

Lanham, Maryland

HISTORY OF WEST NOTTINGHAM ACADEMY, 1744–1981. Copyright © 1985 by Scott A. Mills. All rights reserved. Printed in the United States of America by Port City Press, Baltimore, Maryland. No part of this book may be used or reproduced in any manner whatsoever without written permission except in the case of brief quotations embodied in critical articles and reviews. Published and distributed by Maryland Historical Press, 9205 Tuckerman St., Lanham, Maryland 20801.

FIRST EDITION
First Printing 1985
Second Printing 1993

Designer: Ann Feild

Library of Congress Cataloging in Publication Data

Mills, Scott A., 1924–

   History of West Nottingham Academy, 1744–1981.

   Bibliography: p.
   Includes index.
   1. West Nottingham Academy—History. 2. West Nottingham (Md.)—Schools—History. I. Title.
   LD7501.W3838M54   1985   373.752'38   85-60118
   ISBN 0-917882-17-2

To the principals, headmasters, and teachers of West Nottingham Academy, who have served their students faithfully since 1744.

Contents

Illustrations	ix
Acknowledgments	x
Foreword: West Nottingham's 250th Year	xi
Prologue: Presbyterian and Scotch-Irish Roots	xiii
Map	xviii
1 The Founding, 1744	1
2 Early Days at West Nottingham, 1744–1761	9
3 Role of Early Alumni in Founding the United States	21
4 Samuel Finley at Princeton, 1761–1766	29
5 Decline and Transition	35
6 A New Beginning, 1812–1820	41
7 James Magraw as Principal, 1820–1835	51
8 Continuity with Samuel Magraw and Rev. George Burrowes, 1835–1850	57
9 Frequent Leadership Changes, 1850–1862	63
10 George Bechtel and Samuel Gayley, 1862–1887	71
11 John Conner, 1887–1902	91
12 Eleven Principals, 1902–1924	103
13 Growth as Boarding School under Paul Slaybaugh, 1924–1949	115
14 World War II and Bicentennial	143
15 Hard Times and Rescue by Rev. Charles Blaker, 1949–1961	157
16 Continuity with Norman Farnlof and Kenneth Dietrich, 1961–1981	181
Appendix A. Board of Trustees, 1811–1981	211
Appendix B. Alumni in World War II Military Service	219
Appendix C. Principals and Headmasters	225
Bibliography	229
Index	231

Illustrations

1. **Rock Presbyterian Church** (Located eight miles northeast of academy). Built in 1761 when Rev. James Finley, brother of founder of West Nottingham Academy, was pastor. The current pastor of Rock Church is Rev. Allen B. Yuninger who teaches at West Nottingham. 11
2. **Rev. Samuel Finley.** Founded West Nottingham Academy in 1744 and conducted it until called to the presidency of Princeton in 1761. 13
3. **Benjamin Rush** (In 1802). Student, 1754–1759, Signer of Declaration of Independence, distinguished physician, and founder of Dickinson College. 27
4. **Wiley.** Room and board for West Nottingham students at Wiley was advertised in the first issue of the Baltimore Sun on May 17, 1837. Wiley now serves as dormitory for West Nottingham girls. 59
5. **Old Academy** (Now Student Canteen). Built in 1864 by the congregation of the West Nottingham Presbyterian Church which provided the funds and some of the labor. Pastor was Samuel A. Gayley. 77
6. **Magraw.** Constructed 1928–1930, replacing the dormitory at this site which was destroyed by fire in 1927. Magraw now houses administrative offices, dining room, and boys' dormitory. 125
7. **Paul Slaybaugh.** Headmaster, 1924–1949. 145
8. **Old Friends.** Anne Collins of Elkton and Barton McAuley, U.S. Navy (West Nottingham Class of 1943), meet at Navy repair base in South Pacific in July 1945. 149
9. **Rev. Charles W. Blaker.** Headmaster, 1952–1961. 159
10. **Annual Canteen Club Dinner.** Philadelphia, Spring of 1958 169

Acknowledgments

THE WRITER'S first day of research ar West Nottingham Academy yielded a huge four-drawer file cabinet jammed full of material that pertained to the academy from its 18th Century beginning to 1949. I soon realized that J. Paul Slaybaugh had gathered most of this treasure while serving as headmaster from 1924 to 1949, the longest term in West Nottingham's history. Slaybaugh was continuously corresponding with alumni or their descendants to acquire data for a history of the academy. At the same time his staff was keeping excellent records of his 25-year term of office. Dr. Slaybaugh also contributed significantly to the history by relating to me with some gusto the human interest elements of many events in his administration.

For the 1950s, I found an excellent source of information in Rev. Charles W. Blaker, who served as headmaster from 1952 to 1961. He not only conscientiously answered numerous questions but kept my enthusiasm alive when the history seemed a long way from completion. For the period since 1961, a number of the members of the West Nottingham community generously took time to relate some of their experiences and insights.

In addition to the support given by past and present members of the West Nottingham community, I was fortunate in having three demanding editors. They were my sister, Beatrice M. Wall; my friend, Ann Marie Shore; and my former colleague at the National Aeronautics and Space Administration, John J. Sweeney.

Scott A. Mills
March 1, 1985
Arlington, Virginia

Foreword
West Nottingham's 250th Year

WEST NOTTINGHAM ACADEMY was founded in 1744 by Reverend Samuel Finley, pastor of the West Nottingham Presbyterian Church. The members of his congregation built the school house of logs close to the church meeting house and near present-day Rising Sun High School. As they labored in the summer heat, the perspiring church members would have been amazed if they could have looked 250 years into the future—they would have beheld their pastor's school housed in handsome buildings on a spacious campus a few miles to the southeast. They would see that the founding church had also moved and stood across the road from the campus—the church and school still companions but no longer formally associated with each other.

When Samuel Finley began to prepare boys for college in 1744, nobody could even imagine the existence of the United States—the Declaration of Independence was 36 years in the future and Finley would be dead by then. Yet most of Finley's students and his own sons would find fulfillment in the struggle for independence and the formation of the United States—two students, Benjamin Rush and Richard Stockton, signed the Declaration of Independence.

This book brings the academy's history up to only 1981, but developments since then warrant mention. Completion of the C. Herbert Foutz Center in 1990 gave the academy an expansive dining hall and ample space for the administrative offices, student center, and bookstore—it was named for Herbert Foutz, who has been serving West Nottingham students since 1946 when he joined the faculty as a young veteran of World War II. Since 1981 the academy has also started two new academic programs—the Chesapeake Learning Center (CLC) and English as a Second Language (ESL). The CLC helps students overcome particular learning disabilities, such as dyslexia, but is not limited to this alone. ESL has the purpose of improving the English of foreign students before they undertake the regular curriculum. These programs have broadened West Nottingham's appeal, and the ESL program has encouraged international diversity in the student body.

Scott A. Mills
July 1, 1993
Bethesda, Maryland

Prologue:

Presbyterian and Scotch-Irish Roots

THE ZEAL for excellence in education that brought about the founding of West Nottingham Academy had its source in the doctrines of John Calvin, the principal theologian of the Protestant Reformation. John Knox, a pupil of Calvin in Geneva, applied Calvin's doctrines in bringing the Reformation to Scotland as Presbyterianism. Scots from the Lowlands of Scotland carried the Presbyterian doctrines to Northern Ireland and thence to America where the Scots came to be called Scotch-Irish. Once arrived in America, the Scotch-Irish established churches, founded numerous secondary schools, including West Nottingham Academy, and founded Princeton to educate Presbyterian ministers. Among the hundreds of secondary schools that were founded by Presbyterians, only West Nottingham Academy has survived.

John Knox had established Calvinist doctrines in Scotland in the mid-16th Century. By 1596, there were Presbyterian elementary schools in every parish of Scotland. The Scottish Protestant or Presbyterian church that developed under Knox's leadership also assumed responsibility for education at the secondary and college levels. The ministry was trained at the college level, whereas education at the lower levels had the purpose of bringing all children to a better understanding of God in conjunction with learning academic skills.

In accordance with the importance of the pastor in Knox's Presbyterianism, the ministers did not shrink from leading their flocks with a strong hand as the Scotch Lowlanders encountered a succession of troubled conditions in the Lowlands of Scotland, Northern Ireland, and America. The Presbyterian ministers in 18th century America conducted secondary schools in conjunction with their pastoral duties, led congregations to new settlements on the frontier, organized defenses against the Indians, and served as officers, chaplains, and recruiters for the American forces during the revolution.

In 1757, when the Scotch-Irish frontier settlements were open to Indian attacks because of the French and Indian War, Rev. Samuel Finley, then principal of the highly-regarded West Nottingham Academy, urged wholehearted support for the American-British side in a sermon entitled, "The Danger of Neutrality in the Cause of God and Our Country." In 1776, Rev. Samuel Finley's nephew, who was in western Pennsylvania looking after his father's newly-purchased farm, was hotly pursued by Indians and with great difficulty escaped death. Three hundred miles to the east in Cecil County, Maryland, the boy's father, Rev. James Finley, sensed that his 18-year-old son was in danger so knelt down and prayed. After a time, he arose with the feeling that the danger had passed. Rev. James Finley was not able to join his son until 1783 because his Rock Church congregation and the New Castle Presbytery insisted that he stay. Finally he took a number of the Rock congregation with him and subsequently established two permanent Presbyterian churches on the Pennsylvania frontier.

In the 18th Century there were not enough trained ministers to care for the large numbers of Presbyterians migrating to America and forming congregations that were scattered from New York to Georgia. The Presbytery of Philadelphia, pressured by requests from American congregations for supply ministers, sought assistance from overseas, urging the Presbytery of Dublin and Synod of Glasgow to send ministers and financial aid to relieve "the desolate condition of sundry vacant places who have applied to us for a supply of ministers, who express their Christian desire of enjoying the public administrations of the gospel purely." Education of more American ministers would alleviate the shortage, but the expense of traveling overseas, to Yale, or to Harvard for an education that would meet Presbyterian standards was too great for most students who lived in the Middle and Southern colonies. Leaders in the Presbyterian Synod of New York moved to meet this problem in 1747 when they founded the College of New Jersey. The synod provided crucial financial support in the early years of the college to keep alive what was to become Princeton University. In 1761, the

PROLOGUE: PRESBYTERIAN AND SCOTCH-IRISH ROOTS   xv

first principal of West Nottingham Academy, Rev. Samuel Finley, left West Nottingham to become the fifth president of Princeton where many of his students had already gone upon graduation from West Nottingham.

Besides the Presbyterian emphasis on education that led to founding of schools in America, the other principal element in the roots of West Nottingham Academy were the Presbyterian people themselves, the Scotch-Irish. These Scots from Ireland provided West Nottingham with its founder, many of its early students, and most of the supporting Presbyterian congregation. In Scotland, the ancestors of the Scotch-Irish had been regarded by the English as a useful buffer because they lived in the Lowlands between England and the Highland Scots. The Lowlanders had readily adopted the Presbyterian organization and doctrines that had been established in 1560 under the leadership of John Knox. However, Presbyterian dominance was threatened in 1597 when James VI of Scotland forebade assemblies of church representatives. After 1603, as James I of England, Ireland, and Scotland, the same monarch continued to restrict Presbyterians. Conditions became so intolerable that the Lowland Scots were induced to migrate to northern Ireland under an English plan that was instituted in 1610.

The English needed the Scots to solidify their control over northern Ireland after James I had prevailed over the rebellious Irish landholders and intrigues of continental powers in Ireland. The plan of settlement, proposed by Francis Bacon, consisted of grants of 1,000 to 3,000 acres apiece to English and Scottish "undertakers" who were to provide settlers for counties Donegal, Londonderry, Tyrone, Fermanagh, Armagh, and Cavan in northern Ireland.

The number of Lowland Scots willing to exchange their situation in Scotland for the troubles of Ireland indicates that Scottish conditions were indeed miserable. By 1641, there were 100,000 Scots in northern Ireland, including the counties just named and the counties of Antrim, Down, and Monaghan. About 50,000 Scots arrived between 1690 and 1697.

As might have been predicted, the English policy brought "massacres, sieges, and pitched battles" between the Scots and Irish during the 17th Century. Even though the English benefited from the Scots being in Ireland, the English acted to impede the economic progress of the thrifty, religious Scots. A law of 1670 prohibited direct sale in England of woolen goods, the Scots' most profitable commodity.

Probably of even greater impact were laws that sought to destroy the Presbyterian Church and substitute an Irish branch of the Church of England, termed Anglicism. Beginning in the reign of Queen Anne, only members of the Anglican Church, a minority of the population, could hold public office although everyone paid taxes in support of the English-sponsored Anglicanism. In the early 1700s, the Scots began to sail in droves from Ireland to the New World, their second great migration in a little more than a century. Religious dissatisfaction had driven them from the Lowlands of Scotland to Ireland. In Northern Ireland, the economic and religious conditions must have been considered even worse because many Scots were willing to sign papers of indenture that committed them to several years of labor in the New World to pay for their voyage across the Atlantic. There is evidence that the Scots landed initially at New Castle, Delaware. Later, Philadelphia became the main point of entry. Edmund Burke stated that of the 6,000 immigrants who reached Philadelphia in 1729, four-fifths came from Ireland.

The newcomers rapidly took up land in southeast Pennsylvania, northern Delaware, and northeastern Maryland. This flood of Presbyterian Scots was the first large wave of voluntary non-English immigrants to settle among earlier immigrants in the English colonies. The arrival of large numbers of Scotch Presbyterians aroused feelings of hostility and anxiety in some of the people already in America. Such apprehension set a pattern for American experience in accepting immigrants that persists to this day. When hundreds of Scotch-Irish settled in a certain area of Delaware, an Anglican missionary sent out by the Church of England was particularly discouraged because the newcomers were "very bigoted" and not good prospects for conversion. Although Pennsylvania had issued an invitation for immigration of Scots from Ireland, their actual arrival produced misgivings.

James Logan, Secretary of the Colony of Pennsylvania, tried to reassure his employer, the ruling Penn family, about the multitude of Scots arriving among the gentle Quakers by reporting that "they generally settle near the Maryland line." On another occasion, Logan, a Scot himself, called the Scots "bold and indigent strangers" who, when challenged for the title to the land they had occupied, "cannily" replied, "You solicited for colonists and we came accordingly." Nevertheless, Logan established a settlement of Scotch-Irish on the Pennsylvania frontier as a protection against the Indians "because the Scots had so bravely defended Londonderry and Inniskiller in Ireland." Although a Quaker, Logan was a cousin on his mother's side to Presbyterian William Tennent who founded the Log College, an informal school for training the Presbyterian ministers who were so badly needed by the Scotch-Irish. Logan appears to have helped his kinsman Tennent get the Log College started in 1728 with a donation of £5 and a grant of 50 acres in Bucks County, Pennsylvania along Neshaminy Creek, 20 miles north of Philadelphia. Logan's attitude by this time may have been that the growing numbers of Scotch-Irish might be more manageable if shepherded by strong pastors. He may have foreseen that the Penn family and Quakers would not be able to maintain control indefinitely in the face of the Scotch-Irish influx.

In 1758, the increasing numbers of Scotch-Irish in Pennsylvania did result in their capture of political control of the colony. In 1764 a Royalist declared that Presbyterians were unworthy of election to office because they lacked firm attachment to the King or the laws. He went on with some accuracy to ask, "What King has ever reigned in Great Britain whose Government has not been disturbed with Presbyterian Rebellions since ever they were a people?" The worst fears of the royalists were realized as the Scotch-Irish set Pennsylvania on a course that would give strong support to the patriot cause in the coming struggle for American independence.

By the time the Revolutionary War broke out in 1775, many of the early West Nottingham graduates had completed higher education and established professional careers, but like all Scotch-Irish they eagerly supported the American cause, the best opportunity the Scotch-Irish had ever had to free themselves from British control.

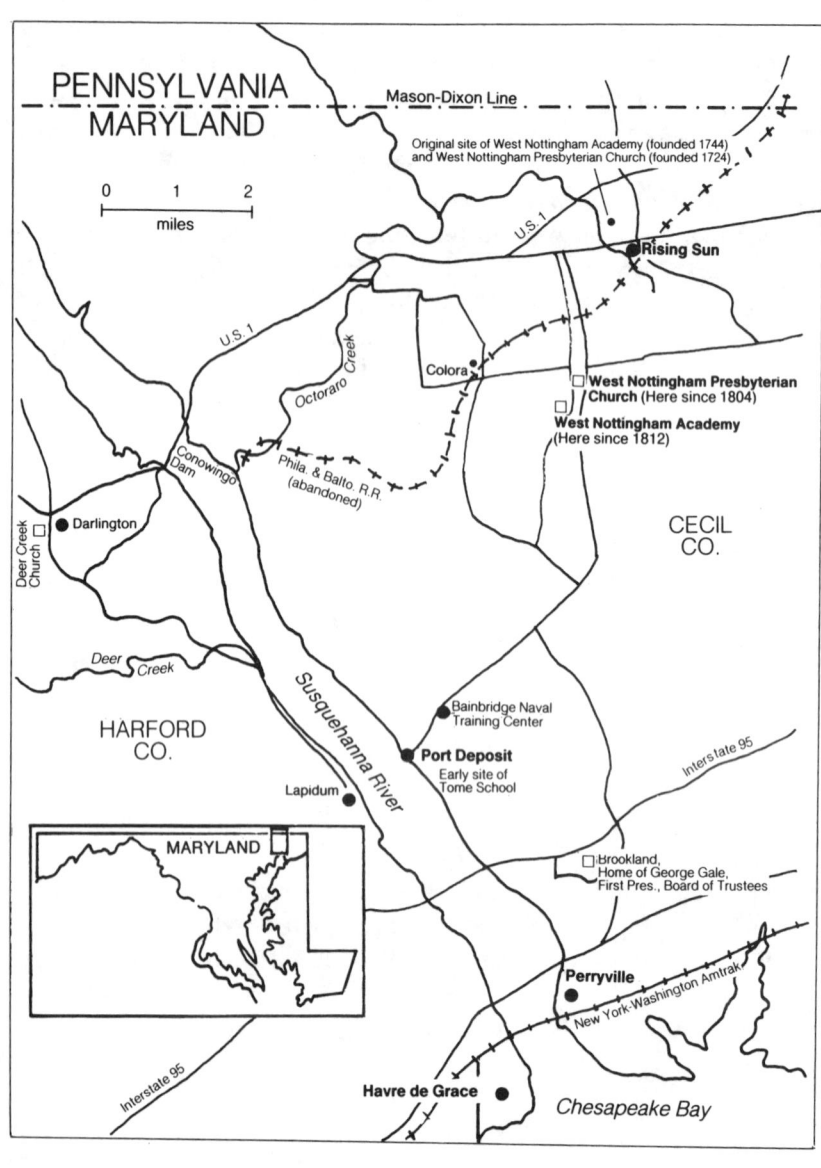

1

The Founding, 1744

WILLIAM PENN and Lord Baltimore did not know that their dispute over the location of the boundary between the Colonies of Maryland and Pennsylvania would lead to the founding of West Nottingham Academy. Astronomical observations in 1682 that could justify Maryland claims northward to Philadelphia induced William Penn to bolster Pennsylvania claims by establishing new settlements as far south as possible into the disputed territory. Penn met the Maryland challenge with two groups of settlers. In 1702 he granted some of his own Quakers an 18,000 acre tract that lay on both sides of the present Pennsylvania-Maryland border, one-fourth in Chester County, Pennsylvania and three-fourths in present-day Cecil County, Maryland. The irregularly shaped tract extended westward about ten miles from Blue Ball Crossroads, Maryland to about one and one-half miles from where Octoraro* Creek flows into the Susquehanna. The tract probably came to be called "Nottingham Lots" because William Brown, the first Quaker to build a house there, decided to name it in remembrance of his early home in Nottinghamshire, England.

Penn's other ploy against Maryland was to encourage Scotch-Irish immigrants to settle west of the Quaker settlers, namely, from the vicinity of present-day Rising Sun westward to the Octoraro and beyond. Not long after the Quakers had moved into the Nottingham Lots, the Presbyterian Scotch-Irish began to settle to the west as Penn had hoped. By 1724 a Presbyterian congregation had formed in the Rising Sun area and placed itself under the jurisdiction of the New Castle Presbytery. Minutes of a meeting of the presbytery directed supply ministers to serve the people at the "mouth of the Octoraro"

---

* Indian for "rushing waters."

on the third Sabbath in April and fifth Sabbath in May of 1724. The New Castle Presbytery continued to send supply ministers to the "lower Octoraro" in the following years but after 1730 "Nottingham" rather than "lower Octoraro" was used to identify the congregation. The presbytery record shows that the Nottingham congregation was reluctant to pay one of its supply ministers but does not give the outcome of the dispute. By 1758, "West Nottingham" was being used instead of Nottingham because of the Presbyterians' location near the western end of the Nottingham Lots.

In 1731, the New Castle Presbytery sent Rev. William Orr to Nottingham where he served as the first permanent pastor of the congregation. By 1735, however, after doctrinal disputes between Orr and a ruling elder of the congregation, the New Castle Presbytery accepted Orr's resignation. West Nottingham's second pastor, Rev. John Paul from Ireland, served only three years until his death in 1739 at the age of 33. In this early period, there were Presbyterians, but no Presbyterian church across the Susquehanna River in Harford County. In order to attend regular services at West Nottingham, some young Presbyterian men of the Deer Creek settlement in Harford County bought a boat which they kept on the south bank of the river for rowing across every Sunday.

Besides the row, the morning trip involved a five-mile hike down into the deep valley of the Susquehanna and a six-mile climb on the other side to reach West Nottingham. Proceeding homeward on summer afternoons spiritually refreshed, the Deer Creek men could easily sense the beauty of God's world as they came upon magnificent views of the great river and the blue hills beyond covered with verdant hardwood forests. When they finally reached Deer Creek, there was no difficulty in getting a sound sleep before starting normal Monday tasks on the farm. Probably at the urging of the Deer Creek visitors, Rev. John Paul occasionally traveled there to hold services. The people at Deer Creek organized a church in 1738.

The early death of Paul brought an end to regular services at West Nottingham in 1739, just as the Great Awakening was beginning to have a drastic effect on American religious life. This spiritual movement has been described as the first great common experience of Americans. Although it reached greatest intensity in New England, the Great

Awakening strongly affected the Presbyterians concentrated in Pennsylvania, Delaware, and Cecil and Harford Counties in Maryland. In the rest of Maryland and generally in the Southern colonies, the predominant Anglicans were less affected by the Great Awakening.

The American movement was part of a worldwide protest against the complacency, formalism, authoritarianism, and lack of emotional fervor that had come to prevail in Protestant churches. In America, the lack of churches and regular pastors in many isolated settlements, such as West Nottingham on the lower Octoraro, made the people very responsive to the messages of visiting evangelists. The American movement split the Presbyterian, Congregational, and Dutch Reformed churches into conservative and popular factions. The Baptists generally welcomed the Awakening and the Anglican clergy disapproved of it.

The foremost American revivalist was Jonathan Edwards, the famous New England preacher. He and the other revivalists preached the stern Calvinistic doctrine that the only souls that could be saved had already been predestined for salvation. In handling the idea of predestination, Edwards taught that one's own salvation could be discovered through an inward revelation of the "divine and supernatural light." Every soul that was to be saved had the capability of experiencing this joy. To assist his listeners in reaching such awareness, Edwards portrayed the torments of Hell so vividly that a dread of sin was aroused as well as a longing for the purification that would permit each saved person to sense God's presence in his soul.

Because of the emphasis on individual experience for salvation in the messages of Edwards and the other revivalists, the Great Awakening generally lifted the hearts of the struggling settlers and increased their sense of worth. The movement also emphasized the idea that spiritual truth could be found by each person in the Bible. This perception reinforced the Calvinistic doctrines of education for all and rigorous training for the clergy. The Great Awakening likewise was compatible with the independent spirit of Presbyterian congregations and the basically democratic organization of the congregation, presbyteries, and synods in which elected laymen shared power with the clergy. Each pastor served only by the favorable vote of his congregation and could be dismissed.

The West Nottingham congregation received much attention from the leading evangelists of the Awakening. In a visit of March 8, 1740, Rev. Gilbert Tennent, son of the founder of Log College and the leader of the Presbyterian revivalists, preached his famous sermon from Mark 6:34 on the "Dangers of an Unconverted Ministry." In it, he described the ministry of that time, "as letter-learned Pharisees, plastered hyprocrites, having the form of Godliness, but destitute of its power." Looking back 125 years later, Rev. Samuel Gayley, pastor of the West Nottingham Church, described Tennent's discourse as "severe, bitter, and wholly unwarrantable as applying to his brethren." On May 14, just over two months after Tennent's sermon, George Whitefield preached at West Nottingham. Whitefield, a famous and powerful English preacher of the Great Awakening, was in America for the second time and would cross the ocean seven times to quicken the spiritual life of Americans. At West Nottingham, Whitefield and the other evangelists in his party were denied use of the Presbyterian meeting house. Whitefield solved this problem as he had many times in England, by holding an open air revival. In his journal, Whitefield estimated that nearly 12,000 gathered under the budding oak, beech and hickory that spring day to be spiritually revived. He may have overestimated because 50 years later the first Federal Census shows a total of 10,000 whites in Cecil County. However, given the climate of religious enthusiasm and the fact that many of the gathering could easily reach Nottingham from Harford County, Maryland and Chester County, Pennsylvania, Whitefield's estimate cannot be dismissed as completely unrealistic. Benjamin Franklin convinced himself by computations that Whitefield could be heard by 30,000 after initially questioning newspaper accounts of Whitefield's preaching to "25,000 in the fields." Whitefield reports about the West Nottingham sermon in his journal as follows:

> As I preached, the influence increased, till at last, both in the morning and afternoon, thousands cried out so as to almost drown my voice. Oh! what strong cryings and tears were poured forth after the dear Lord Jesus. Some fainted, and when they got a little strength would hear and faint again. Others cried out almost as if they were in the sharpest agonies of death. After I had finished my last discourse, I was so overpowered with a sense of God's love, that it almost took away my life. At length, I revived, and was strengthened to go with Messrs. Blair, Tennent, and

some other friends to Mr. Blair's house, twenty miles from Nottingham. On the way, we refreshed our souls by singing psalms and hymns. We got to our journey's end at midnight. Oh Lord, was ever love like thine.

Whitefield visited West Nottingham again in November as did another evangelist, John Rowland, who stayed for some time in 1740 and reported the people to be "particularly favoured . . . by the refreshing influences of the Spirit."

The effect of the evangelists on West Nottingham as on most Presbyterian churches in America was to break the congregation into two factions, the "Old Lights," who remained unswayed by the wave of revivalism, and the "New Lights," who accepted the evangelists' message that a fresh and vigorous renewal of spiritual life should be undertaken. The absence of a regular minister at West Nottingham probably made a clean break easier. In any case, the New Light party built a new meeting house, apparently the same year that the evangelists had conducted their West Nottingham revivals. The new meeting house was located beside a small stream at the foot of the hill on which the Presbyterian meeting house stood that recently had been serving the entire West Nottingham congregation. Members of the Old Light group continued to use the older building. Today, the hill is the site of the Rising Sun High School. In 1740, the two meeting houses were in full view of each other when the trees became barren in the winter. When summer arrived and the doors of both meeting houses were thrown open to catch any cooling breeze, the two congregations could hear each other's hymns.

Soon after the West Nottingham Church divided, the larger and more energetic New Light West Nottingham congregation attached itself to the New Light Presbytery of New Castle and began to apply for supply ministers. A number of ministers were sent as supplies until 1744 when Rev. Samuel Finley chose to accept the call of the West Nottingham New Light congregation among three calls that he had received. Soon after his arrival at West Nottingham, Finley established a secondary school that he conducted in addition to his pastoral duties. This was the beginning of West Nottingham Academy. The New Light West Nottingham congregation had its first permanent pastor and Finley his first church. Finley was 29 years of age when installed.

Born in Armagh County, Northern Ireland in 1715, Samuel Finley had arrived in Philadelphia at the age of 19 with his father, mother, and the eight other children of the family. He was the second child and second of five boys in the family. Samuel's youngest brother James also became a Presbyterian pastor in Cecil County.

Samuel's father, Michael, was born in Northern Ireland in 1683 and had married Anne O'Neill in 1712 in Mullaghabrac, Ireland. Eighteen years later, they and their nine children migrated to America. Michael had shown the same willingness to start over in a new land that had impelled his father, Robert Finley II, to leave Scotland and settle in Ireland. The records show that Robert Finley II was born in Scotland in 1634 and had migrated to northern Ireland around 1678 after selling his land in Scotland. In Ireland he married Margaret Laude and raised a family of five, of whom Michael, Samuel's father, was second-born.

Samuel Finley's early life in Ireland was closely associated with Presbyterianism. According to Archibald Alexander, biographer of early American Presbyterian leaders, Samuel had been heard to say that he was so deeply impressed by a sermon when only six years old that he had never forgotten the experience. Thereafter, he was seized with an ardent desire to become a minister of the gospel. His parents recognized and supported his goal by sending him away to school after local teaching made him proficient in basic learning skills.

In America, it is believed that Samuel became a student at the well-known Log College which was founded and conducted by William Tennent at Neshaminy, Pennsylvania, twenty miles north of Philadelphia, in the same area where Samuel Finley's family first settled. On August 4, 1740, Samuel Finley presented himself to the New Light New Brunswick Presbytery for "trials," and the presbytery licensed him the next day. Finley was starting his life's work at a time and place of outstanding opportunity. His fellow Presbyterians in America were already short of ministers, and Scotch-Irish migration from northern Ireland continued. It was a time of particular need for spiritual leadership because of the challenges the Great Awakening posed to religious life.

Finley's early preaching consisted of filling temporary assignments made by the New Brunswick Presbytery. On January 20, 1741, he preached to the recently established New Light congregation at West

Nottingham. The sermon was published with the title "Christ Victorious and Satan Raging" and was soon reprinted in Boston and Edinburgh, the latter edition carrying an endorsement by George Whitefield. After this promising effort, the presbytery ordered Finley to Dover and Baltimore in August 1741 and then back to Nottingham as a supply minister.

In May 1742, Finley was sent to West Jersey where "his labors were remarkably blessed at Greenwich and Deerfield," according to Richard Webster in his *History of the Presbyterian Church in America until 1760*. On October 13 of the same year, the New Brunswick Presbytery ordained Finley as an evangelist. Sometime in 1742, Finley preached at the Second Presbyterian Church in Philadelphia for six months.

The energetic young preacher spent much of 1743 in evangelistic efforts. He publicly debated Rev. Abel Morgan, a Baptist, for two days in Cape May, New Jersey. The issue was "infant baptism by sprinkling," which Finley defended as valid. Subsequently, Finley published an argument entitled, "A Charitable Plea for the Speechless or the Right of Believers' Infants to Baptism." Morgan countered with his own published argument, but Finley had the final say with his "Vindication of the Charitable Plea for the Speechless."

In August 1743, Finley's presbytery sent him to Milford, Connecticut, "with allowance that he also preach for other places thereabouts where Providence may open a door for him." After he had completed his work at Milford, Finley traveled to New Haven in September to preach for the "separatist" Second Society there at the request of Rev. Pierrepont, brother-in-law of Jonathan Edwards. This body in New Haven, although regularly organized, was subject to a recent Act of the Connecticut Assembly that had been designed to combat the divisive effects of the Great Awakening. The Act made it illegal for itinerants (evangelists) to preach in any parish without the express desire of the pastor. Because the "separatist" New Haven congregation to which Finley had preached was not recognized by civil authority, it was not legal for Finley to preach there.

While going to the Second Society's meeting on September 5, the young evangelist was seized by the constable and confined. The Grand Jury presented Finley for judgment on September 11. The sentence called for the defendant's expulsion from Connecticut as a vagrant.

After being conducted out of Connecticut by transfer from one constable to another, Finley returned to petition the Connecticut Assembly for review of his case, but was not successful. The historian of Colonial Connecticut, Jonathan Trumbull, has criticized the then Governor of Connecticut, Jonathan Law, for supporting the enactment of the Connecticut law that was applied to Finley, a law that was manifestly contrary to developing American ideals.

In June 1744, Finley ended the evangelical phase of his career by accepting a call from the New Light West Nottingham congregation, who three years before had heard one of his first sermons after being licensed.

2

Early Days at West Nottingham Academy, 1744–1761

REV. SAMUEL FINLEY'S decision to accept the call from the New Light West Nottingham congregation brought an end to four years of demanding physical and mental life as a traveling evangelical preacher. It was time to focus his efforts in one place over a period of time. West Nottingham provided him a permanent base for serving the Presbyterian cause. The New Light West Nottingham congregation had been seeking a pastor ever since it had broken away from the original West Nottingham congregation four years before in response to the messages brought by the evangelists of the Great Awakening. Soon the congregation learned that their young pastor planned to conduct a secondary school.

Besides providing educational opportunity for boys living in its neighborhood, the school was well-located to serve boarding students because Philadelphia, then America's largest city, was only 50 miles away and the school's proximity to the Chesapeake Bay made it readily accessible by water for most of Maryland's population and much of Virginia's.

In the summer of 1744 members of the congregation began to hew down trees and haul logs to the building site on the banks of a stream that drained to the Octoraro. Here the school house would be close to the meeting house of the West Nottingham New Light congregation. The school was probably located just across the stream on the north side of the road that leads down the hill and westward from the Rising Sun High School. As the members were constructing the school house in the summer heat, they could not have dreamed that the school and their church would be functioning side by side in 1984, more than two centuries later.

Although nothing remains of the original West Nottingham buildings, the Rock Presbyterian Church, built in 1761, still stands several miles east of Rising Sun and serves its congregation. Its stark, handsome lines and rough stone construction give one a sense of the life and faith of its 18th Century Scotch-Irish congregations.

Prior to embarking on his duties at West Nottingham, Samuel Finley took Sara Hall as his bride. She was of a well-known family in Philadelphia County, Pennsylvania, whose grandfather, Jacob Hall, had migrated to Pennsylvania from Chester County, England in 1683. Sara was the aunt of three Pennsylvania boys who were to be boarding students at the academy that her husband was establishing. Two of the boys, Benjamin and Jacob Rush, were brothers who had lost their father, and the other was Jacob Hall who had lost one of his parents. Benjamin Rush became America's most famous physician as well as a leading patriot and signer of the Declaration of Independence. Benjamin recounted in his autobiography that he and his brother Jacob "were sent to a country school in Nottingham" to study with their uncle by marriage, Rev. Samuel Finley. Their father, a gunsmith, had died in 1751 at the age of 39. Although he left three pieces of property in Philadelphia, they did not provide sufficient income to educate his six children. Mrs. Rush opened a grocery and provision shop on the south side of Market Street. Her success apparently made it possible to send Benjamin, age 9, and Jacob, age 8, to school at West Nottingham in about 1754, three years after her husband's death.

The Rush boys experienced a considerable change in their surroundings and way of life at West Nottingham as they began their studies in the log school house next to a branch of the Octoraro. Instead of the bustling environment of Philadelphia, the young Rush boys could see only a few farms that had been cleared among the forests of immense beech, oak, and tulip trees. Benjamin was convinced in later years that the temptations of hunting and roaming the countryside at West Nottingham had diverted his attention from study.

Instead of living with their mother, three sisters, and an older brother, the two younger Rush boys roomed and boarded with Rev. Samuel

ROCK PRESBYTERIAN CONGREGATION

Rock Presbyterian Church—Built in 1761; Pastor, Rev. James Finley, brother of West Nottingham Academy's founder.

Finley, his wife, their children, and fellow students. In the five years that he was at Nottingham, Benjamin recalled that Rev. Finley's enlarged "family" seldom numbered less than 30. One of Finley's students described the schoolmaster as "small in figure with a round, ruddy face" and remarkable for "his knowledge of the human heart, sweetness of temper and polite behavior." Benjamin remembered his Aunt Sara as being "sometimes irritable because of ill health," but also recalled that she was "industrious, intelligent, frugal, and in every respect a good housewife." In addition, Benjamin found her conversation was agreeable because she was "knowledgeable on many subjects and had wit." For her family of husband, children, and students, she "kept a plentiful table of country food dressed in a pleasant manner." Rush commented "that the appetite is the ruling principle in young people, that students are not open to education without their appetites being pleased, and that bad food is forgiven less readily than other boarding school injustices."

The good food was particularly appreciated when the students helped Rev. Finley with harvesting and hay-making. Benjamin remembered these chores with pleasure even though he suffered a severe cut while learning to reap that scarred his hand for life. Benjamin was convinced that the exercise fostered good health and stated that during his five years at West Nottingham there had only been two or three sicknesses and no deaths.

The curriculum at Nottingham had the basic purpose of preparing students for college. At least 28 of the 39 identified students of Finley continued their formal education after leaving West Nottingham. Incomplete information shows that 22 went to Princeton, 3 to Pennsylvania University, 1 to Columbia, and 5 to Edinburgh University Medical School in Scotland.

In recommending two of his students for study at Princeton in 1759, Finley reported that at Nottingham they had read the common Latin and Greek classics, studied logic, arithmetic, geography, some geometry, and "natural philosophy (science) in a more cursory manner." Benjamin Rush commented that Finley taught "several of the Arts and Sciences usually taught in colleges." The training also included exercises in writing both friendly and business letters.

Besides teaching his students their lessons, Finley promoted good manners in his boys during meals. Rush recounted that

> The slightest act of incivility was reproved. This was done in such an elegant and delicate a manner as not to expose the person who was rebuked. He selected a number of artificial characters with which he connected all the usual follies and improprieties of boys. To these he gave the names of Thomas Broadbrim, Ned Short, Bill Slovenly, and the like. These characters he contrasted by the history of Johnny Courtley, who was an example of all that was proper and amiable in the conduct of a young man. His manner of describing these characters was so agreeable as to fix even the most volatile and desultory of his boys to their

Rev. Samuel Finley—Founder of West Nottingham Academy; Fifth President, Princeton College.

chairs. Sometimes his descriptions were interspersed with anecdotes that excited a burst of laughter. If in his walks and in his study he occasionally overheard an improper expression, or saw an improper act in any of the boys, he never failed to take notice of it at the ensuing meal, but in such a manner as not to excite a suspicion that a personal application of what was said, was intended. One evening I recollect he dwelled chiefly upon the character of Ned Short. Among other things, he informed us that he was of a quick temper, and very prone to give rude answers to the most innocent questions. For instance, if one of his companions asked him if he knew where his book was, he would answer, "Ask about." Here he paused. A blush appeared in the countenance of one of his boys, who had on that day given that answer to a question of a similar nature. The doctor did not appear to be conscious that the rebuke had produced its intended effect. But his table was not made subservient only to this mode of instruction. He made it a constant practice to admit his boys to eat with all the strangers who visited him. The benefits derived from the news, anecdotes, and general conversations which young people are thus permitted to hear are much greater than is generally supposed.

In regard to discipline, the emphasis was on the culprits' understanding of the wrongness of the action rather than on the punishment. When Finley came upon a boy throwing rocks at a fruit tree, he gave him a cuff but explained that though "the offense was trifling, it might lead you to break laws of more importance." Sometimes Finley asked the students' opinions on an offense before he gave his own or "obliged them" to pronounce the punishment before he inflicted it. The normal mode of punishment was three strokes on the palm of the hand with a small switch.

The religious life of the students was integrated with that of Finley's family. As Rush recalls:

> Finley read and explained the whole or part of a chapter in the Old or New Testament every morning and evening before prayers in his family. Many of the remarks that he made upon passages in the Bible, which then passed hastily through my mind, have occurred to me many years afterwards, and I hope not without some effect. He obliged all the boys who lodged in his house to commit the Shorter Catechism of the Church of Scotland to memory, and to repeat it every Sunday evening. He likewise obliged all the members of his family to repeat what they remembered of the sermons they had heard at church. I cannot commend this practice too highly. It created habits of attention and recollection. I was much struck in observing how much we improved in the knowledge

we brought home of the sermon by exercise. Two of his scholars I recollect frequently gave, between them, every idea mentioned in a sermon. The instructions of the Sunday evening were usually closed by delivering in a plain way some of the most striking and intelligible evidence of the truth of the Christian religion. Many of his arguments upon these occasions, tho' cloathed in simple language, were the same which are to be met with in the most logical writers upon that subject, and to the impressions they made upon my understanding, I ascribe my not having at any time of my life ever entertained a doubt of the divine origin of the Bible. I wish this mode of fortifying the reason of young people in the principles of Christianity were more general. The impressions which are made upon their fears, or their faith, by sermons and creeds soon wear away, but arguments fixed in understanding are indelible.

Despite Benjamin Rush's recollection of not being very industrious in his studies, Finley felt that Benjamin was ready for Princeton eight months before his 15th birthday after five years at West Nottingham. Upon arrival at college in the spring of 1759, Benjamin was interviewed by two tutors who then assigned him to the junior class. Rush received his Bachelor of Arts degree in September 1760. Two of Benjamin's classmates at West Nottingham, Joseph Alexander and Thomas Ruston, also entered the junior class at Princeton in 1759. West Nottingham alumni became senators, governors, and leaders of American medical education as well as national leaders of the Presbyterian Church.

For his West Nottingham graduates to have achieved so much, Finley must have implanted something in their minds beyond self-discipline and an excellent knowledge of the classics and the Bible. Finley gives us an inkling of that something extra in the following letter written to a former student:

> You need not doubt but it will still give me a sensible pleasure to hear that you conduct yourself in a becoming, upright manner;—in a way superior to the *mobile vulgus:* and at the same time, while you study to excel, study also to condescend to [keep good relationships with] those whom you excel.
> Seek to have the temper of your mind so framed, that you may be ready for all variety of conditions; as ready to obey as to command; to forgive injuries, as to ask forgiveness; to be despised, as well as to be honourable; and to be poor, as well as rich. Let not the evil dispositions of others

dispossess you of the placid, calm enjoyment of yourself. There is more delight in possessing one's own soul, than in being lord of this earth: It is good, therefore, not to let so large a possession depend on the precarious humours of others. Does any thing trouble you so as to disturb this self enjoyment? Then ask yourself, must this trifle overbalance all my other comforts? Shall this person, or thing, be allowed to have the power of taking away my happiness of pleasure? Can I not be happy without this one's favour, or under that one's frowns? I may allow superiors to dispose of my activity, of my estate, and body; to dispose of my happiness is too much power for any, or all mortals, and mortal things together. If we cannot enjoy ourselves under crosses, we never can in this world; for it is full of them; but, though reason has some force, yet the grace of God only can implant such a happy disposition.

Although the conduct of the academy would seem to be a full time job, Finley also served as pastor of the West Nottingham Church and in at least some periods traveled four or five miles from West Nottingham every third Sunday to preach for another congregation. Finley still had energy left over to serve as trustee of Princeton College after 1751 and to take an active part in wider Presbyterian affairs.

In the early 1750s, Finley was a leader in the formation of the New Light New York Synod from the Presbyteries of New York, Philadelphia, New Castle, and Donegal. Once the New York Synod was established, Finley represented it in seeking reconciliation and union with the Old Light Philadelphia Synod in 1754. In 1757, Samuel Finley and his brother Rev. James Finley prepared the final plan for union of the two synods, which was ratified on May 29, 1758. Thus, Samuel Finley was instrumental in healing the breaches in the overall Presbyterian organization that he had helped create more than 15 years before as an energetic young revivalist.

Finley could not have succeeded so well in his multifarious activities without the whole-hearted support of his wife Sara. Sara not only had primary responsibility for feeding her family and the students but also bore eight children in 17 years of marriage. Mrs. Finley died at the age of 42 in 1760. The high praise for her intelligence and character expressed by her nephew, Benjamin Rush, was consistent with the glowing inscription on her tombstone. No longer legible, it was recorded as stating, "She was a virtuous wife, fond parent, constant friend, lover of God and Saints, grave, chaste, and kind, frugal yet generous, active, cheerful and wise."

Finley received indispensable support from the members of his West Nottingham New Light congregation. They started by building the school house and a manse that was large enough to house 30 or more including Finley, his family, and the boarding students. Once the school began, the congregation helped provide a steady supply of food and helped Mrs. Finley prepare it. In addition, the congregation had to be content to have Finley give only a fraction of his time and energy to pastoral duties because of the school and, as mentioned, his chosen role as conciliator among the Presbyterian organizations in the Middle colonies. The congregation did benefit from the school, however, because it gave their children an opportunity that was rare in the Middle and Southern colonies, namely, the chance to prepare for college while living at home. The actual number of those day students is not known.

Some understanding of the everyday life of the members of the Nottingham congregation can be obtained from George Johnston, who wrote a useful and detailed history of Cecil County in 1880. He states that the first Presbyterian meeting houses were built of logs and had no fireplaces. Joshua Hempstead, a visitor from New London, Connecticut in 1749, reported that the Old Light West Nottingham Church was a large old house with no galleries or sign of carpenter's skill. Although the interiors were cold and poorly lit, Johnston claims that the religious fervor of the Presbyterians was not affected. Conditions usually improved after the original meeting house was replaced by a more permanent structure and a small session house was built near the new building. Johnston states that, "A rousing fire would be made in the session house on Sabbath morning" where the members of the congregation could warm themselves before entering the meeting house. Some time later, probably after 1750, foot stoves began to be used. They consisted of tin boxes with lids that were filled with live coals from the session house fire and placed on the floor under the feet of the worshipers. Even with such comforts, the Sabbath required dedication, at least from our perspective. The program included a morning service and sermon, an hour's break, and then another sermon in the afternoon. Like most of the 18th Century Presbyterian meeting houses in eastern Pennsylvania and northern Maryland, the West Nottingham

Church was located close to a stream to accommodate the needs of members who came from a distance to attend the all-day Sabbath program.

Joshua Hempstead, the Connecticut visitor, reported in his diary that the "minister and people here are very modest as to their apparel." He also stated that the soil, wheat fields, and timber were all generally good. Johnston, the Cecil County historian, writes that the rude log cabins were generally built in a valley near a spring which served both as a water supply and in the summer as a means of refrigeration. The stream in the valley was used to irrigate the valley's flood plain which, thus watered and fertilized to some extent, yielded a good crop of native grasses for hay. Johnston said that the impoverishment of the land that resulted from not using lime led to the subsequent Presbyterian migrations to the fertile valley of Virginia and the Carolinas.

Besides growing hay, members of the congregation cultivated flax and raised sheep from which they made their own clothing of linen and wool. Some also planted apple and peach orchards that provided home-made liquor as well as fruit. Johnston reports that the settlers who lived in the West Nottingham area took their surplus wheat directly eastward for marketing at Christiana Bridge, a town of 400 just inside Delaware at the head of navigation on Christiana River, a tributary of the Delaware. The wheat was carried in sacks holding two or three bushels each that were secured to the backs of horses. One boy astride one of the horses led two or three other loaded animals.

Johnston characterized the Presbyterians as "frugal, industrious, and pious, different in many respects from those who settled in the southern part of Cecil County and Elk Neck." Johnston also points out that slavery was more common south of the Elk River and Back Creek and that tobacco growing came to be concentrated there. However, there were slaves throughout the county. Rev. James Finley, brother of West Nottingham's Samuel Finley and pastor of the neighboring Rock Presbyterian congregation, had a few slaves.

Rev. Samuel Finley had two important decisions to make in 1761. A year had passed since the loss of his wife, Sara, whom he had married when he started his pastoral duties at West Nottingham. Now, 17 years later, he took a new bride, Ann Clarkson of New York City. The other question arose when Samuel Davies, the president of Princeton, died.

Finley had been considered for the post just two years before, but Davies had been chosen, probably because he was a better speaker and his appearance was more impressive. In 1761 Finley's fellow trustees unanimously offered the presidency to him. Finley may have hesitated as he thought of the close ties he had developed with his congregation over 17 years. At Princeton, however, he could influence the education of most future Presbyterian ministers in America. Finley undoubtedly felt the urgency of the call because of the disruption and uncertainty at the college which were associated with the deaths of two presidents in the preceding three years.

Predictably, the West Nottingham congregation wanted their pastor to remain. They probably foresaw the difficulty they would have in finding a new pastor, let alone continuing the successful academy. The congregation's strongest pleas however, could not sway Samuel Finley from choosing the path of greater challenge and service at Princeton where he had been a trustee for ten years and one of the founding trustees. Many of Finley's students at West Nottingham had gone on to Princeton, which would continue to be a favorite college for West Nottingham graduates in the 19th Century.

3

Role of Early Alumni in Founding the United States

T. J. WERTENBAKER, historian of the social and cultural life of the American colonies, praises the founders of Princeton with the comment that "although Presbyterian, they did not think of Presbyterian needs alone. They provided the intellectual training considered appropriate for all professions, Jews, and all Protestant denominations."

Rev. Samuel Finley, a founding trustee of Princeton, applied a similar philosophy at West Nottingham. Of the 35 West Nottingham graduates taught by Finley who had known professions, 16 were clergymen, 12 were medical doctors, six were political leaders, and one was an explorer and mapmaker.

Samuel Finley continued to take a personal interest in his students after they left West Nottingham. An example was Dr. Rush, who had decided upon a legal career after graduating from Princeton in 1760. This choice resulted from his skill as a speaker and writer and was approved by Rush's friends and Samuel Davies, president of Princeton. Accordingly, Rush's mother had arranged for him to study law in the office of a Philadelphia lawyer. Before commencing legal study, Rush visited his old principal, Samuel Finley, for a few days. As Rush was departing, Finley asked him if he had chosen a profession. Upon learning that Rush was going into law, Finley advised that "the practice of law is full of temptations" and that Rush should "by no means think of it" but should study physics (medicine). Finley added, "but before you determine on anything, set apart a day for fasting and prayer and ask God to direct you." Rush recalls that he did not fast and pray as Finley had directed but did turn immediately to the study of medicine rather than law.

A large proportion of early West Nottingham students are now included in the Dictionary of American Biography. That publication contains short biographies of leaders in all major fields of endeavor who, in the judgment of professional historians, have made significant contributions to American life. To appreciate the extent of Finley's achievement at West Nottingham, one must realize that the total number of graduates did not greatly exceed 100 during Finley's regime of 17 years.* Of this total, 15 had sufficiently distinguished careers to be included in the Dictionary of American Biography.

There is no complete list of West Nottingham students for Finley's period. Information on the 39 students who have been identified is given in the following list.

Both the Revolutionary War and founding of the United States provided West Nottingham graduates with opportunities for service and achievement. The following highlights in the lives of some of the West Nottingham alumni were selected as representative of numerous other incidents of historical significance in the lives of the 18th Century graduates. Of the 16 known ministers who graduated from West Nottingham, the careers of Alexander McWhorter and James Waddell are of particular interest. As a boy, McWhorter had a hard time settling down, partly because of having been "awakened to sinfulness by a New Light minister," which in turn had caused him "great distress of mind for a few years." At West Nottingham, McWhorter "was enabled for the first time to rest his soul on Christ." After leaving West Nottingham, he graduated from Princeton in 1757 after less than two years of study. During the American Revolution, he was directed by Congress to win over Loyalists in North Carolina. In retaliation for this effort, the British ransacked McWhorter's manse in New Jersey. McWhorter was present when Washington decided to cross the Delaware, a decision that led to desperately needed American victories at Trenton and Princeton. The doughty minister also served as Chaplain for General Knox's New Jersey Brigade. After the war, McWhorter was influential in framing the constitution of the Presbyterian Church of the United States,

---

* This rough approximation is based on Benjamin Rush's report that six classmates graduated with him in 1759. By assuming that the number of graduates was negligible for the school's first two years, one has 15 graduating classes of seven each from 1746 to 1761 when Rev. Finley departed. This leads to an estimate of 105 graduates.

Known Students at West Nottingham Academy (WNA) 1744–1761

Student	Home	Last Year at WNA	Education**	Career
Joseph Alexander	North Carolina	1759	Princeton	Minister
John Archer*	Harford County, Md.	c. 1759	Princeton A.B., A.M. Penn. Med. School	Physician
James Ashton Bayard	Cecil County, Md.	1756		Physician
John Bubenheim Bayard*	Cecil County, Md.	1756		Merchant, Member of Continental Congress
James Caldwell*	Born in Charlotte County, Va.	1757 or 58	Princeton	Minister, Chaplain of N.J. Brigade
Gerardus Clarkson	New York City	—	Edinburgh U. Med. School	Physician
Charles Cummins	South Carolina	c. 1759		Minister
Samuel Doak*	Augusta County, Va.	—	Princeton	Minister
James Dunlap	Chester County, Pa.	1758?	Princeton	Minister
John Filson*	Cecil County, Md.	—		Explorer, Historian, Map Maker
Ebenezer Finley***	Philadelphia County, Pa.	—	Penn. U. B.A., M.A. Edinburgh U. Med. School	Physician, Captain, Continental Army
John Hall Finley***				Lieutenant, Continental Army
Jacob Hall	Cecil County, Md.	1757?	Columbia A.B., A.M., Yale A.M.	Physician, President of Cokesbury College
William Hannah	Philadelphia			Minister
Ebenezer Hazard*	Philadelphia	c. 1759	Princeton	Publisher, Historian, U.S. Postmaster-General

Early Alumni 23

Known Students at West Nottingham Academy (WNA) 1744–1761 (Cont.)

Student	Home	Last Year at WNA	Education**	Career
John Henry*	Dorchester County, Md.	—	Princeton, Middle Temple (London)	Lawyer, Soldier, Maryland Governor, U.S. Senator, Member of Continental Congress
James Hunt	Virginia	—	Princeton	Minister, Teacher
Alexander Huston		—	Penn. U.	
Thomas King	Somerset County, Maryland			Landholder
William Kirkpatrick		1755 or 56	Princeton	Minister, One of founders of Wash. & Jeff. College
Alexander Martin*	Hunterdon County, N.J.	1753	Princeton A.B., A.M. & L.L.D.	Soldier, Politician, Col. of 2nd North Carolina Reg't, N.C. Governor, U.S. Senator, Member of Continental Congress
Alexander McWhorter*	Newcastle County, Del.	1756	Princeton, Yale, D.D.	Minister
John Morgan*	Philadelphia	1746, 47, or 48	Penn. U., Edinburgh U. Med. School	Physician, Co-Founder of Penn. Medical School
James Powers	Chester County, Pa.	1761	Princeton	Minister
Benjamin Rush*	Philadelphia	1759	Princeton, Edinburgh U. Med. School	Physician, Signer of Declaration of Independence, Founder of Dickinson College
Jacob Rush	Philadelphia	1761	Princeton, Middle Temple (London)	Lawyer, Philadelphia Judge
Thomas Ruston	Philadelphia	1759	Princeton, Edinburgh U. Med. School	Physician

Known Students at West Nottingham Academy (WNA) 1744–1761 (Concluded)

Student	Home	Last Year at WNA	Education**	Career
William Shippen*	Philadelphia	1751	Princeton, Edinburgh U. Med. School	Physician, Co-founder of Penn. Med. School
Archibold Scott	Scotland, Pa.	1760	Princeton	Minister
Jonathan Bayard Smith*	Philadelphia	1757	Princeton 1760	Soldier, Member of Continental Congress
Joseph Smith	Chester County, Pa.	1761	Princeton D.D.	Minister, Co-founder of Washington & Jefferson College
Richard Stockton*	Philadelphia	1746	Princeton	Lawyer, Politician, Signer of the Declaration of Independence
John Strain		1755		Minister
James Tilton*	Kent County, Del.	1761	Penn. U. Med. School	Physician
William Makey Tennent		1761	Princeton, Yale D.D.	Minister, Moderator of General Assembly of Presbyterian Church
William Tennent	White Clay Creek, Pa.	—		Physician
James Waddell*	Connecticut	—		Minister
Eleazar Whittlesey		1747	Princeton	Minister
William Williams	Accomack County, Virginia	c. 1759		Physician

* Biography appears in the Dictionary of American Biography on the basis of his contribution to American life.
** Princeton is used to refer to the College of New Jersey, which was officially renamed Princeton University in 1896.
*** Son of Rev. Samuel Finley, Principal.

composed the Confession of Faith, and served as seventh moderator of the Presbyterian General Assembly.

James Waddell, like his West Nottingham instructor, Samuel Finley, was born in Northern Ireland and emigrated to America with his family. At West Nottingham, he was both a student and a tutor. While active as a minister in Virginia, Waddell lost his sight for a period of eleven years but continued to preach effectively. He firmly established Presbyterianism in Virginia in the face of Anglican opposition. Though firm in upholding Calvinist doctrine, his pleasing personality made possible a friendly acceptance of the Presbyterian Church in Virginia. Waddell was the inspiration for the blind preacher in the popular novel, *Letters of the British Spy*, written in 1803 by William Wirt, who was the prosecutor in the trial of Aaron Burr and later became U.S. Attorney-General.

There were 12 West Nottingham students who became doctors of medicine. Two of them, John Morgan and William Shippen, founded the University of Pennsylvania Medical School. Then two later West Nottingham students, John Archer and James Tilton, graduated in the first class of that institution in 1768. Pennsylvania Medical School was the first in America to graduate students from a medical course of study that involved compulsory lectures. West Nottingham doctors actively supported the American cause in the Revolutionary War. John Morgan left his medical teaching to serve as medical director of the Continental Army, Benjamin Rush served as surgeon general of the Armies of the Middle Department, William Shippen became chief physician and director general of the Continental Army Hospital, and James Ashton Bayard was an army surgeon.

Former West Nottingham students provided a number of political and military leaders for the American cause in the Revolutionary War. Rush and Richard Stockton signed the Declaration of Independence. Alexander Martin, John Henry, Jonathan Bayard Smith, and John Bayard served as members of the Continental Congress. In addition, Bayard served as a Colonel and Martin as a Lt. Colonel in the army. Although a doctor, John Archer served as major in the Maryland militia.

In the postwar period, West Nottingham students were active in state and national politics. Alexander Martin served as Governor and U.S. Senator from North Carolina, and John Henry was the first U.S. Senator

EARLY ALUMNI

NATIONAL PORTRAIT GALLERY, SMITHSONIAN INSTITUTION,
WASHINGTON, D.C.

Dr. Benjamin Rush in 1802—Student, 1754-1759; Signer, Declaration of Independence; Founder, Dickinson College.

from Maryland and was later Governor of that state. John Archer, the Harford County doctor and militia leader, served as Presidential Elector in 1801 and as U.S. Congressman from 1801 to 1807. Ebenezer Hazard became the first U.S. Postmaster in 1782.

Dr. Benjamin Rush was the most versatile and greatest man ever to graduate from West Nottingham Academy. His mother sent him to

West Nottingham at the age of nine, a few years after his father's death, and he stayed until the age of 15. Besides his political and medical leadership in the fight for American independence, Rush took a leading role in a number of fields in the postwar era. He instigated the founding of Dickinson College. He continued an active medical career and was the most popular medical lecturer in America. Rush was also an active social reformer; he helped organize and served as president of the Pennsylvania Society for Promoting Abolition of Slavery, he established the first free dispensary in America, he promoted medical care for the mentally sick, and he condemned public and capital punishment.

4

Finley at Princeton, 1761–1766

IN 1761 SAMUEL FINLEY became the fifth president of Princeton. All of his predecessors had been distinguished, but all except one had very short terms because death cut their service short. The first president, Rev. Jonathan Dickinson, began to "conduct the college in his own home in Elizabethtown, N.J.," but death in October 1747 ended his service just one year and a day after the charter for the college had been granted. The next president was Aaron Burr, father of the future vice-president of the United States. Burr did all of the teaching while continuing as pastor in Newark, New Jersey until the college accepted an offer of land from the town of Princeton to locate there. After the move, Burr authorized a fund-raising trip to England and Scotland that was successful in providing £4000 for the construction of Nassau Hall, the largest college building in America at that time. Burr's service lasted until 1757. The trustees then called upon Jonathan Edwards, Burr's father-in-law and the most prominent American preacher of the Great Awakening, to take the presidency. Unfortunately, death prevented Edwards from officially taking office although he conducted a seminar course in theology from January to March 22, 1758, before dying of the effects of a smallpox inoculation. To succeed Edwards the trustees turned to Samuel Davies.

Davies had been a brilliant evangelist in the area of Hanover County, Virginia, and had served with Gilbert Tennent on the successful mission to England and Scotland to raise money for Nassau Hall. Davies at first declined the job and learning that some of the trustees perferred Samuel Finley, Davies wrote:

> I recommend Mr. Finley, from long and intimate acquaintance with him, as the best qualified person in the compass of my knowledge in

America,—incomparably better qualified than myself. Though the want of some superficial accomplishments for empty popularity may keep him in obscurity for some little time, his hidden worth, in a few months or years at most, will blaze out to the satisfaction and even astonishment of all candid men. A disappointment of this kind [election of Finley] will certainly be of service to the College.

Repeated offers by the Board of Trustees finally changed Davies' mind, however. He became convinced that God willed his going to Princeton so he accepted the presidency after the Synod of New York and Philadelphia approved his transfer from Virginia. Davies began his term of office in 1759 but soon began to experience failing health which ended in his death less than two years later. In his *Princeton 1746–1896,* T. J. Wertenbaker comments on the choice of Davies as follows:

> Modest, lovable, scholarly, eloquent, acquainted with recent trends in education, he was ideally equipped to lead the college. Unfortunately, the trustees had overlooked the important matter of health, for Davies for years had been a sufferer from tuberculosis. In Virginia the incessant riding through forests and fields in his five hundred mile circuit to serve his scattered congregations, had no doubt aggravated his illness. And the confining work at Princeton, where he drove himself mercilessly to remedy fancied defects in scholarship, rising at dawn and seldom retiring before midnight, proved too severe for his weakened constitution. His death in February, 1761, struck the college with dismay and spread a gloom all over the country.

It was probably not unusual for the intensely dedicated Presbyterian clergymen to drive themselves too hard and neglect their health. About 30 years before Davies' death, an excessive desire to excel may have been involved in the close brush with death that was experienced by William Tennent while studying theology under his brother, Gilbert Tennent, the famous Presbyterian evangelist. William suddenly collapsed one day while conversing in Latin with his brother. Every indication of death was soon present so funeral arrangements were made. By chance, a physician acquaintance stopped by and thought he detected a faint sign of life. Rather against the judgment of Gilbert, who said it was foolish to try to resuscitate one who was "cold and stiff as a stake," the funeral was postponed. Efforts to revive William failed, however, and people were assembling for the final rites when the body showed unmistakable signs of life. In about a year William had made a complete physical recovery, but memory of his past life was gone and he could not read or write. In the next few years, however, William Tennent regained his mental abilities. In 1733 he started preaching in Freehold, N.J., where he stayed 44 years and served as a trustee of Princeton.

The early death of President Davies at Princeton shattered the high expectations held for his incumbency. The trustees must have been shaken by the poor survival rate of their choices to lead the college. Nevertheless, they plunged ahead and offered the post to Samuel Finley, principal of West Nottingham Academy, on May 21, 1761, three months after the death of President Davies. The decision to make the offer was unanimous, perhaps because of Davies' own strongly expressed confidence in Finley's ability two years before. Finley departed from West Nottingham on his journey northward in July. He was 46 years of age and would seem to have many years to apply his energy, intellect, and leadership to the development of Princeton. The college officers met Finley a few miles out of town and escorted him to the president's house. After changing to academic gowns, Finley proceeded to Nassau Hall for his introductory address. Finley's low stature and ruddy face contrasted with the slender and well-formed figure of Davies, his deceased predecessor. Dr. Shippen, one of Finley's old West Nottingham students, reported that Finley was "awkward and stammered." Shippen added, however, that he had "all the essential qualifications of a president, more important than being the finest orator in England."

As president, Finley taught Latin, Greek, and Hebrew to the seniors and supervised an "English school" that was established to prepare prospective students for college work. Three tutors taught the other college courses that were offered. After some period in the presidency, Finley wrote:

> Though this institution has succeeded beyond the expectation of its warmest friends, notwithstanding the severe shocks it received by the death of three Presidents, in so quick succession, and its unsettled state, till the chair was filled; yet it still labours under several deficiencies, which nothing but the beneficent hand of charity can relieve. With

mathematical instruments and an apparatus for experiments in Natural Philosophy, it is but very indifferently furnished. The library wants many of the most approved modern writers. It would be also of eminent service had its revenues been ample enough to support professors in some of the distinct branches of literature; who might each make a figure in his own province, could his studies and instructions be confined to his peculiar department. A professor of divinity, especially for the theological students would be of singular utility. At present there are three tutors, besides the President. To these the College funds can, as yet, afford but scanty livings; the tutors particularly, unless they assume a vow of celibacy, are unable to continue in their offices for life. Hence, it happens, that when a young gentleman has, by study and experience, thoroughly qualified himself for the employment, he often resigns it; and the trustees are then obliged to elect another, perhaps not equally fit for it.

Two years after his arrival at Princeton, Finley received an honorary degree of Doctor of Divinity from the University of Glasgow. He was the first American Presbyterian to be so recognized by a Scottish institution. Besides honoring Finley, the award was evidence of continuing support of Princeton by Scots who had helped finance the construction of Nassau Hall.

Samuel Finley's somewhat halting delivery of his introductory address at Princeton was not a good indication of his ability to lead the college. In Finley's five years of service 115 students graduated, of whom 50 became ministers. During the last two years, 1765 and 1766, the number of graduates reached 30 and 31. This level was not reached again until 1792 when 37 received degrees near the end of the administration of the more prominent John Witherspoon, who succeeded Finley and served from 1768 to 1794. In fairness to Witherspoon in respect to the number of graduates, it should be noted that his term at Princeton included the uncertain times that preceded and followed the Revolutionary War as well as seven years during the war when British troops occupied the college.

Finley's success at Princeton was associated with "unremitted attention to the duties of his station" which "sensibly affected Dr. Finley's health", according to the *Missionary Magazine of the Presbyterian General*

Assembly.* Early in the summer of 1766 Finley felt badly enough to seek medical treatment in Philadelphia. The diagnosis was "a fixed obstruction in his liver" that could prove fatal in a month. Finley accepted this verdict with equanimity, considering his fate to be in the hands of God. Bedridden in Philadelphia several weeks later, Finley was informed by his brother-in-law, Dr. Clarkson, that the end was near. During his last days, Finley thanked the friends who had gathered around him saying, "May the Lord repay you. May he bless you abundantly not only with temporal but spiritual blessings." Upon seeing a member of the Second Presbyterian Church of Philadelphia, he said, "I often preached and prayed among you, my dear Sir, and the doctrines that I have preached to you are now my support, and blessed by God, they are without a flaw. May the Lord bless and prosper your church." To a person from Princeton, Finley said, "Give my love to the people of Princeton and tell them I'm going to die and that I am not afraid to die." He spent his last evening taking leave of friends and addressing affectionate counsels to those of his children who were present. At nine the next morning, he fell into a profound sleep in which he remained without changing position until early in the afternoon when he quietly died in the presence of his old West Nottingham student, Benjamin Rush. Rush had been sitting up with Finley every other night for several weeks.

As had been requested by Dr. Finley, eight members of the senior class at Princeton served as his pallbearers. The intent was to bury Finley at Princeton among his predecessors at the College of New Jersey, but the weather was too hot to make the long journey feasible. Therefore, he was buried in Philadelphia beside his fellow evangelist of the Great Awakening, Gilbert Tennent, within the Second Presbyterian Church where Finley had served for six months as a young evangelist before going to West Nottingham. The trustees of Princeton had a monument erected in honor of Dr. Finley at Princeton that summarized his achievements and character in the following words:

> He undertook the pastoral charge of a church at Nottingham, Maryland, May 19, 1744, and was for a long time master of a celebrated Academy

---

* Issue of 1805.

in that place. Being appointed President of the College of New Jersey, he entered upon the office 15th of July 1761. At last, beloved, respected, and lamented by all, he died at Philadelphia the 16th of July, 1766. Skilled in Literature and the Arts, he outshone others, especially in knowledge of divine things. Burning with zeal for the glory of God, he employed all his resources in promoting Religion, by conversation as well as preaching. Patience, modesty, and uncommon gentleness, shone in his disposition and manners. He was remarkable for his kindness, attachment, and watchfulness towards the youths intrusted to him. Frank in his manners and sincere in his Piety, he lived beloved by all, and died triumphant.

5

Decline and Transition

WEST NOTTINGHAM Academy fell upon hard times after its founder and principal, Rev. Samuel Finley, left to assume the presidency of Princeton College. Besides leaving West Nottingham, Finley may have dealt the school a fatal blow by establishing and teaching an "English School" at Princeton. The purpose was to prepare prospective Princeton students for college work. The likely result for West Nottingham was diversion of older secondary students to the "English School" at Princeton who would have gone to West Nottingham if Finley had still been there. The academy may have continued for a time under a Mr. Strain, whom the New Castle Presbytery had ordered to serve the New Light West Nottingham congregation when Finley's departure became imminent. In April 1762, the New Light congregation applied for as much of Mr. Strain's time as possible. If he were the "John Strain" who had graduated from the academy in 1755, memory of his student days might have induced him to continue the school.

During the Revolutionary War and the confused conditions that followed, interruption or decline was typical for colonial schools and churches, especially for Presbyterian institutions because of the widespread Scotch-Irish support for the American cause. This support resulted in the service of a large number of Presbyterians in the armed forces, including 30 Presbyterian ministers who served as chaplains out of the 90 chaplains in the American military service. The principal institution for training Presbyterian ministers, Princeton College, had to close for seven years because of occupation by British troops, but West Nottingham Academy suffered a much more prolonged closure. Unlike the American-wide Presbyterian support available to Princeton, the academy could depend only on the support of the New Light West

Nottingham congregation which barely managed to survive itself. The congregation undoubtedly suffered from the severe economic conditions associated with the war. Extensive fighting in nearby Delaware, Pennsylvania, and New Jersey disrupted regular marketing of crops as did the lack of a stable currency. Cecil County farmers often supplied American forces free of charge or in return for debased "Continental" currency. After the war, the currency situation became desperate because a large part of Maryland's population were debtors whose property was threatened by creditors. There were demands in the Maryland House of Delegates in the 1787–89 period to print more money to provide some inflation for easing the debtors' situation. In Harford County, creditors were terrorized and prevented from bidding on property that had been seized and put up for sale to satisfy debts. In Cecil County, anonymous handbills threatened violence to state officers if they seized property for non-payment of taxes.

The unsettled postwar economic conditions probably increased the movement of Cecil County people westward that was already underway during the war. In 1783, the year the war officially ended, Samuel Finley's brother, Rev. James Finley who was pastor of Rock Church located just east of West Nottingham, led 30 members of his congregation 300 miles westward to the Pennsylvania frontier where they helped found two Presbyterian churches. In 1790, the first Federal Census of Cecil County showed a white population of 10,000. This total had declined to 6,000 by 1800. The county's white population rose to 9,700 in 1810 and finally exceeded the 1790 total in the 1820 census with a count of 11,900. Meanwhile the slave population steadily declined from 3,400 in 1790 to 2,300 in 1820 while the free black population increased from 160 in 1790 to 1,800 in 1820. Cecil County was apparently moved by the same spirit of freedom that affected the states that lay to the north of the Mason and Dixon line, Cecil County's northern boundary. The northern states officially abolished slavery after the Revolution. Because Maryland did not abolish slavery, the decrease in slavery in Cecil County was probably accomplished largely by individuals freeing their slaves. That most Cecil County slaveholders freed rather than sold their slaves southward is strongly suggested by the large increase in the number of free blacks that accompanied the reduction of the slave population. The growth in the number of free blacks in Cecil County was probably typical for the state because by the beginning of the Civil War, Maryland had 83,942 free blacks, more than any other state.

The New Light and Old Light Presbyterian congregations of West Nottingham, which had meeting houses that stood within sight of each other in what is now Rising Sun, remained apart even after their respective synods, the Old Light Philadelphia and New Light New York, had reunited as the Synod of New York and Philadelphia in 1758. Rev. Samuel Finley had been active in effecting this reunion, but his own New Light congregation at West Nottingham had not been ready to act. Local attitudes against reunion remained the same even when the two presbyteries that had supervised the congregations united as the Presbytery of New Castle in 1759.

As the Revolutionary War approached and broke out, both congregations at West Nottingham lacked regular ministers and failed for the most part even to obtain supply ministers. In 1778, the two congregations jointly appealed to the New Castle Presbytery for supply ministers, the first common action since their separation 38 years before. This joint effort was possible only because most of the members at the time of the split were dead. The congregations continued to cooperate after 1778, but were unable to secure a regular pastor. They fully integrated in 1792 when the New Light meeting house was torn down and the Old Light meeting house began to serve the united congregation. The new generation of West Nottingham Presbyterians were entering a more stable era that had begun with the inauguration of George Washington in 1789. The launching of the new government had come only after the long, uncertain years of the Revolutionary War and subsequent trials and errors of the thirteen freed Colonies as they sought to establish a workable union. In 1796, the prospects for peace and stability may have made the West Nottingham congregation decide to build a meeting house. However, it seemed as difficult for the congregation to decide upon a new site as it had been for the former American Colonies to agree upon a location for the federal government. First, a location west of the Octoraro was seriously considered and then rejected. Other locations were likewise turned down after tentative acceptance. Finally, the congregation asked the New Castle Presbytery for advice. Accordingly, the presbytery sent a five-member committee to West Nottingham "to unite the people on a site for the meeting house." The congregation accepted the site recommended by the presbytery's committee, but when the time came to build, the location had changed again to the present site of the church and academy, about two and one-half miles southwest of the original meeting house at Rising Sun and about one mile generally southeast of Colora.

In 1865, Rev. Samuel Gayley, pastor of the West Nottingham Church, described the finally chosen site as the "most beautiful in the whole neighborhood." Today this description still holds true of the high, rolling land occupied by the church and adjoining West Nottingham Academy. The church grounds and academy campus are an unstudied blend of open spaces and towering trees. The surrounding area consists of small farms interspersed with groups of homes at intervals of a mile or less. The well-kept church graveyard, now holding a half-dozen generations of Presbyterian faithful, has a tranquil appearance. Unpretentious posts of gray granite mark the entrances. The unfenced borders and neighboring and overlapping clusters of trees serve to unite the graveyard with its surroundings and create a sense of spaciousness.

In 1800, the West Nottingham Church owned four acres at this site because of gifts of two acres each from Andrew Ramsay and Captain William Johnson, a church elder who had served in the 30th Battalion of the Militia in Cecil County during the Revolutionary War. Although construction began in 1800, the church was not completed until 1804. According to George Johnston, historian of Cecil County, "the work of erecting the new church was herculean because of the poverty of the congregation." The congregation found it necessary to obtain state legislation that authorized a lottery to raise the necessary funds. The legislative act of 1803 names eight commissioners to put the lottery into operation. They were: Samuel Miller, Robert Evans, Thomas Williams, David Patton, James Cummings, James Sims, John Porter, and Jonathan Hartshorn. Samuel Gayley's 1865 history of the West Nottingham Church contains the accounts of three carpenters who worked on the church, James Cameron, William Cameron, Sr., and Captain Thomas Patton. They said that the framed roof timbers were so heavy that a former sailor had to be hired to rig a crane for lifting them into place. Sixty-five years later, Gayley reported that the walls and roof timbers of the meeting house were as strong as when built. It was as though the congregation, reportedly reduced to thirty members in 1800, knew that a fine structure should be ready for a new period of church growth and prosperity. The same year that the meeting house was being completed, Rev. James Magraw settled as pastor.

James Magraw was born in Bart County, Pennsylvania on January 1, 1775. His father, John Magraw, was a Scot who had been forced to flee from his home in Kilkenny, Ireland, because of his membership in a secret political club that was considered subversive by local authorities. He reached America after a brief stay in Gibraltar. Well educated, he taught school at Upper Octoraro for a time before the revolution. When war broke out, Magraw volunteered for active duty with the American forces and served with a Pennsylvania regiment through the war, fighting in most of the battles in eastern Pennsylvania, Delaware, and New Jersey. He married Jane Kerr of Middle Octoraro, who gave birth to James, future principal of West Nottingham Academy. James studied the classics and literature at Franklin College in Lancaster before taking up the study of theology under Rev. Nathaniel Sample, pastor of the churches of Leacock and Middle Octoraro. In October 1800, Sample introduced Magraw to the New Castle Presbytery which accepted him as a candidate for the gospel ministry. Subsequently, the presbytery licensed him on December 16, 1801, and directed him to supply at New London, Chestnut Level, West Nottingham, Faggs Manor, Little Brittain, Chatham, and Deer Creek. He traveled to Luzerne County, Pennsylvania, on a missionary tour in October and November of 1802. On April 5, 1803, the New Castle Presbytery received a call for Magraw from a united congregation in Wyoming and Union counties, Pennsylvania; and the next day a call came for Magraw from the West Nottingham congregation. Young Magraw was not quite ready to settle down after the freedom of traveling and exercising his preaching talent at various churches for fifteen months. He requested four months for choosing the congregation he would serve, but seven months passed before Magraw informed the presbytery on September 27 that he had selected West Nottingham.

Despite a membership of but 30 at West Nottingham, Magraw may have been impressed by the dedication of those 30 who were constructing a sturdy new meeting house and had obtained state authority for a lottery when additional funds became necessary. Or the young minister may have dreamed of reopening the famous academy that had been associated with the West Nottingham Church in colonial times. Once the decision was made, the 28-year-old Magraw married Miss Rebekah Cochran of Cochranville, Pennsylvania on December 6. The following April 4, 1804, Magraw was ordained and installed as pastor of the West Nottingham congregation by the New Castle Presbytery. The roof of the meeting house had not yet been completed so during his first summer, the tall, vigorous young minister preached to the congregation in the grove of tulip, hickory, and oak that stood close by.

The move of the West Nottingham Church from Rising Sun to its present location where Rev. James Magraw was installed increased the distance that the Pennsylvania members of the congregation had to travel for services. The extra two and a half miles seemed particularly burdensome in early spring when the churchgoers were slowed by their horses slipping and sliding in the mud or in winter when the faithful became thoroughly chilled if delayed by ice or snow on the journey from Pennsylvania and back. Accordingly, they organized the Upper West Nottingham Church in 1810 and the parent church in Maryland was renamed the Lower West Nottingham Presbyterian Church. Magraw served as pastor to both congregations, devoting one-third of his time to the Pennsylvania group.

6

A New Beginning, 1812–1820

THE YEAR after Rev. James Magraw assumed the additional pastoral duties entailed by the formation of the Upper West Nottingham congregation, he seized an opportunity that would give him a still wider scope for service. This opportunity arose because the legislature of Maryland believed that its 1810 Act, which granted voting rights to all white male citizens, obligated the state government to make education available to more Maryland citizens. Accordingly, the legislature provided financial support to properly organized academies in most of Maryland's counties to advance the following objectives:

1. To benefit society "by bringing forward a succession of able and virtuous characters qualified to discharge the duties of public and private life."
2. To diffuse knowledge which "is more essentially necessary in a country like ours, the perpetuity of whose happy government materially depends upon the religion, virtue, and patriotism of the people at large, from whom all power in relation to the government emanates, and before whom public men and measures are daily passing in judgment, and who are eligible in one way or another to the most important trusts and offices, both in church and state, trusts and offices that require the utmost extent of human acquisition."

As Bernard C. Steiner, historian of Maryland education, states: the first objective was very like the objectives that governed colonial education, but the second objective embodied a concept that came out of the American Revolution, namely, that because the judgment and capability of individual citizens were necessary for democracy to succeed, education should be as widespread as possible.

To meet state requirements for a secondary school in Cecil County,

41

James Magraw organized a Board of Trustees in 1811 for establishing an academy near the Lower West Nottingham Church. The board in turn satisfied the state requirement for a schoolhouse by having a two-story brick building constructed just east of the manse on an acre lot which Magraw donated to the academy. The 15 members of the Board of Trustees named in the pertinent Maryland legislation of 1811 were George Gale, Thomas W. Veazy, Robert W. Archer, John Groome, Samuel C. Hall, William C. Miller, Robert Evans*, David Patton*, John Troy, James Sims*, George Kidd, James Maxwell, John Cresswell, Henry W. Physick, and Rev. James Magraw. Nine of the members met at the Lower West Nottingham Presbyterian Church on February 24, 1811, to elect officers. After a prayer to Almighty God for a blessing on the institution, George Gale was elected president; Rev. James Magraw, secretary; and Robert Evans, Treasurer. George Gale had fought in the Revolutionary War, was a member of the Maryland convention that ratified the Federal Constitution, and was elected as a representative to the first Congress of the United States. Gale married in 1781 and settled on his estate, "Brookland," where he died in 1815. Brookland still stands on St. Marks Church Road near Perryville. Gale and at least eight other trustees showed their confidence in the school by sending their sons or by persuading their relatives to attend. Dr. John Groome of Elkton had two sons at the academy in 1817, and a student roll book, apparently dated 1816, lists three Magraws, two Archers, and one boy each named Gale, Veazy, Cresswell, Maxwell, and Evans. In 1834, George Kidd's son, George Washington Kidd, graduated from the academy. All six of Rev. James Magraw's sons would eventually attend the academy.

West Nottingham Academy reopened for classes in the fall of 1812 and has operated without interruption in the same location ever since. Finley's famous colonial school had sprung to life again through the initiative of Rev. James Magraw and the financial aid of the state government. Immediate events, however, threatened the high hopes held for the revived academy: the reopening coincided with the beginning of the War of 1812 with Great Britain. On May 3, 1813, a

---

* Was one of the eight commissioners who were authorized by Maryland in 1803 to conduct a lottery for raising funds to build the West Nottingham Presbyterian Church.

British fleet under Admiral George Cockburn shelled Havre de Grace and burned or damaged most of its brick buildings. The next day the British moved closer, sailing two miles up the Susquehanna and burning a warehouse belonging to John Stump that lay less than a mile directly across the river from Port Deposit, a busy port just five miles south of the academy. The British foray into the upper Chesapeake aroused Rev. James Magraw to instigate construction of fortifications at Port Deposit. When the British appeared across the river, Magraw was at the new fort, bolstering the spirits of the American soldiers. His actions were reminiscent of the Presbyterian ministers who had inspired the Scotch-Irish in their struggles against the British for over two centuries in Scotland, in Northern Ireland, and in America during the Revolutionary War.

After burning Stump's warehouse, the British decided to mount an attack on Port Deposit but reconsidered when a recently captured prisoner told them there was "a company of riflemen in the fort, each of whom could put a bullet in a man's eye at a distance of 100 yards." Admiral Cockburn then sailed back into the bay and continued eastward to the estuary of the Northeast River. Here, the British raided Charlestown, which had been evacuated, and burned a nearby foundry of the Principio Company which was engaged in producing cannons. On May 5, the British ascended the Sassafrass River where they burned Fredericktown and Georgetown. Thereafter the British did not return to Cecil County, but the people were continually in dread of another attack for the remainder of 1813 and the first eight months of 1814. Their minds were finally eased in September 1814 when the British attack on Baltimore was repulsed at North Point and Ft. McHenry. Other American victories on Lake Erie and Lake Champlain quickly followed and led to the official end of the war in 1815.

Despite the close approach of the British during West Nottingham Academy's first year of renewed operation, there was no significant interruption in studies. Education at the academy was very much like it had been in colonial times. The same classical courses were offered, Greek, Latin, and natural science, that Rev. Samuel Finley had taught more than fifty years before. The studies prepared the students for college and careers in the ministry, medicine, law, and education. The makeup of the student body was determined in part by terms of the state's annual appropriation of $800* that carried the stipulation that one needy scholar should be admitted for each $100 the state supplied. From other students the academy collected an annual tuition of $20. The number of students was comparable to the number in colonial times; an 1816 roll book shows 21 students as compared to the 20 or so students reported by Benjamin Rush when he was there from 1754 to 1759. However, the majority of students in Rush's time roomed and boarded with Rev. Samuel Finley, whereas most of the students in 1816 were probably day students from the immediate area. After 1820 when the revived academy regained some of its earlier reputation outside Cecil County, more students began to come from neighboring states.

New features of the reestablished academy were the brick building that replaced the colonial log schoolhouse and the Board of Trustees that was required by the State of Maryland. The board chose the principal who was not necessarily the pastor of the church as Rev. Samuel Finley had been. The board's function of overseeing the academy's operation included a regular biannual public examination that consisted of an exhibit of student work and oral performances. The trustees attended and other members of the community were invited. Exhibits consisted of English compositions, Latin and Greek exercises, cyphering, and copybooks. After the exhibits were shown, "public speaking and exercises in elocution were presented by students judged to be sufficiently advanced."** The public examinations took place just prior to the three-week vacations that began at the end of March and September.

The academy was in session during the entire calendar year except for the two three-week vacations in the spring and fall and special holidays, such as Christmas, New Year, Easter, and the Fourth of July. Other holidays were allowed to the extent that the aggregate did not exceed 10 days. The Rules of Government issued in 1817 specified the hours of attendance during the year to take advantage of available daylight as follows:

---

* A few years later the state contribution was reduced to $500 because Elkton Academy also became qualified for state support and began to receive $300 of the annual allocation of $800 to Cecil County.
  ** Rules of Government of West Nottingham Academy, 1817.

Months	Hours of Attendance
1 November to 1 February	9 to noon, 2 to 4:30 p.m.
1 February to 1 May	8:30 to noon, 2 to 5 p.m.
1 May to 1 September	8 to noon, 2:30 to 6 p.m.

The reduced hours of attendance during winter also reduced the amount of firewood needed. The firewood was to be provided by the principal to the students at cost. The only concession to summer heat was to start one-half hour earlier in the morning and delay the beginning of the afternoon session by one-half hour. In 1820, the Board of Trustees advertised the price of tuition at $20 per year, the same amount specified three years before by the Rules of Government. The advertisement offered "boarding, washing, ironing and mending at $100 per year," perhaps in Rev. James Magraw's household, or the same services "sufficiently close to the Academy at the very low cost of $80."

In the matter of offenses and punishments, the principal had full responsibility. He should consult the trustees, however, in cases of:

> heinous and gross transgressions or of evil habits obstinately persisted in by any of the pupils, ... the principal shall submit the same to the consideration of the trustees, by whose sentence only can the punishment of expulsion be inflicted; and no pupil who has been so expelled, shall ever again be re-admitted ... without the consent of the trustees.

The method of punishment was not spelled out. The Rules of Government simply stipulated that infractions should be punished "in the most exemplary manner." There is no eyewitness account of the rod being used at West Nottingham. However, Samuel Gayley, later a principal at Nottingham, states in an informal history written in 1892 that Rev. James Magraw switched students quite heartily if he found the academy classes disorderly when he made a visit.

During the first eight years after the academy reopened, there were four different principals. They were supervised by the Board of Trustees which included James Magraw, who, as pastor of the nearby West Nottingham church, was able to keep an eye on the day-by-day operation of the academy. Magraw also had the responsibility of finding principals for the academy when that became necessary.

One of Magraw's efforts to hire a principal involved Isaac Bird, who had graduated from Yale with distinction in June of 1816. By the end of that summer, Bird was becoming anxious because he had not found a job; furthermore, he was "somewhat in debt to Yale" and wanted "to pay up all dues without embarrassing my father." When Bird learned of the opening at West Nottingham through his professor, the noted scientist Benjamin Silliman, the young graduate unconditionally accepted the job in a letter to Magraw.

Bird's letter put Magraw, Secretary of the academy's Board of Trustees, in a quandary because Magraw, greatly worried about finding a principal late in the summer, had asked a friend in Philadelphia to find a prospective principal and make him an offer. Consequently, Magraw's reply showed great interest in Bird but raised the possibility that the job was already taken. Magraw's letter also gave teaching qualifications for the principal of the academy, namely, "to teach the English language grammatically, elocution and composition in the Latin and Greek languages *(in those he must be well-versed),* and Euclid's Elements of Surveying, Navigation, and Geography." Magraw then gave the salary as $700 to $1,000 which included the annual donation from the State of Maryland of $500 plus tuitions from the students. Magraw commended the location at the head of the Chesapeake Bay saying," it was as healthy a neighborhood as any in the United States and near the great Port Road between Maine and Georgia and in the immediate neighborhood of the Bridge over the Susquehanna at the head of the tide water." Lastly, Magraw requested "your certificate of literary attainments and *good moral character*—which is indispensable—to be laid before the Board."

Apparently no principal was found in Philadelphia and Bird's references were satisfactory because his journal reports that he left home in Connecticut for West Nottingham on October 19, 1816. He traveled westward to the Hudson River where he embarked for New York City, taking his first ride on a steamer. In New York, Bird saw General Scott, Commodore Porter, and "the duellist Aaron Burr." Upon arrival at West Nottingham, the new principal described "the academy as a small affair, but well-endowed by the state and having about twenty students, who gave me less anticipation of trouble, than if they had been, as in some academies, three or four times that number." The academy was housed in a building in the middle of the countryside with no buildings in sight other than the stone church without steeple or bell and the dwelling and outhouses of Rev. James Magraw. The new principal lived and boarded "with Mr. Magraw at a reasonable rate." The young Yankee schoolmaster became further involved with Magraw because three of Magraw's sons were in his classroom. Bird concluded one journal entry about the school by saying that:

> My retirement was a pleasant one, and my students, tho Southerners, were easily managed. Nearly half of them, I believe, were fitting for college. Two or three of them were in Homer.

Another entry in Bird's journal describes the public examination of his students on April 15, 1817. The examination began at 11:30 a.m. with but a few trustees present. The first two or three students answered the questions put to them about the exhibits so well that there was little left for the others to say. Student performances, starting at 4 p.m., consisted of speeches and two plays. The stage adjoined a window for the performers to enter from the temporary dressing room that had been set up outside. In the afternoon the crowd overflowed the assembly room so that many had to listen at the windows. When the program was finished, Magraw highly commended Bird and the students and then dismissed school for the three-week spring vacation. Bird joined the trustees for dinner in the upper room of the academy where a "well-united cheerfulness was the order of the day."

A glimpse of student boarding life is given in a letter from Samuel Groome to his father, Dr. John Groome in Elkton, the year before Principal Bird arrived. Samuel tells his father the date for the coming public examination and performances. On behalf of his brother, John, also a West Nottingham student, Samuel requests a copy of the play that John will need to study for his part in the performances. Samuel himself needs money for candle blacking and to pay for the wood used at the boarding house as well as the "wood we burn at the academy." Samuel is down to a one-half cent note, but a dollar or two would last until examination day, a month hence. Samuel goes on to request "coats with side pockets and hats for himself and brother, John, from Philadelphia as we don't have close [sic] fit to go to meeting." Samuel wants to get a proper fit for his hat by getting one that fits another brother, James, "middling tight." Finally, father is to "tell mama to send us up some cakes and send me a lock-up for my trunk." John

Groome, the letter writer's brother at West Nottingham, became a three-term senator in the Maryland legislature and was barely defeated for governor in 1857.

The worries of a widow about her son Gabriel at West Nottingham are expressed in a letter of January 31, 1817, to Principal Bird from Mrs. Juliana B. Davis of Pequa, Pennsylvania. Mrs. Davis states that her son has "a complaint in one of his ears that is hurtful to his hearing which makes him appear indifferent when spoken to." Mrs. Davis has no "doubt but he will need reproof betimes as he never knew what it was to have a father to stand in awe of, yet I hope if he has not had an earthly father that he has a Father in heaven that will never forsake him." Mrs. Davis said that Gabriel had not been accustomed to being away from home much so she was worried about his following boarding house rules. However, she had felt much better when she was able "to get lodging for him in Mr. Magraw's family."

After the successful public examination of his students on April 15, Principal Isaac Bird used his spring vacation to take a trip to Washington and visit Mount Vernon. At Mount Vernon, he was "shocked" to see "the sepulcher of such a man as Washington so dilapidated" with brick falling out of the wall of the vault. Judge Bushrod Washington, a nephew of the first president, apparently was living at Mount Vernon at the time, but was out of town so a black servant showed Bird around. On his way back to the academy, Bird obtained passage in Baltimore on an empty schooner sailing to Port Deposit. The ship departed about 10 a.m., but had progressed only ten miles or so by 2 p.m. through lack of wind. Later in the afternoon a stiff gale blew out of the north and enabled the schooner to advance by tacking beyond North Point before dark. The ship anchored a few miles south of Havre de Grace before 10 p.m., having sailed upward of twenty miles in two hours. Bird arrived in Port Deposit* about noon the next day where a letter from "Samantha rejoiced me much." He covered the last five miles of his journey on foot, reaching the academy in two hours. Bird had been

---

* Bird was told that Port Deposit had a busy shipping trade with Baltimore that involved 40 to 50 vessels. He observed 30 of them one Sunday in early June when he rode down to Port Deposit from West Nottingham.

gone nine days and noted that he had covered 250 miles without mishap.

As Isaac Bird's year at West Nottingham was coming to an end, he was complimented on his teaching by a trustee and wrote that "Mr. Magraw expressed his wish for me to continue another year, but I was fully bent on commencing my preparation for the ministry." After a final public examination of students on October 9, 1817, "Mr. Magraw made some pertinent and affecting remarks relative to our separation." A few mornings later, Bird set out for Connecticut astride a Magraw horse and accompanied by one of Magraw's sons. They rode for two hours until within four miles of Elkton where Bird dismounted and Magraw's son turned the horses around. As young Magraw waved good-bye, he was barely able to hold the horses to a reasonable pace as they headed toward their stables and plenty of oats at West Nottingham. Bird then walked into Elkton where he ate with Dr. John Groome, a trustee and a parent of West Nottingham students. By October 22, Bird had reached home in Connecticut and on November 8 had arrived at Andover Seminary to begin his theological studies. After graduation from Andover, Bird served as a missionary in Beirut for 13 years and later founded a seminary in Hartford, Connecticut, which he directed for many years.

7

James Magraw as Principal, 1820–1835

ALTHOUGH ISAAC BIRD undoubtedly did a creditable job as principal for the 1816–17 academic year, the frequent changes of principals from 1812 to 1820 retarded the school's growth. No principal was there long enough to build on his own experience and establish a favorable reputation for attracting students. The first principal of the reopened school had been Reuben H. Davis, who remained three years. After leaving, he served as the first principal of Bel Air Academy in Harford County where he stayed for many years. Davis's successor at West Nottingham was William McCrimmen, a native of Ireland, who was a fine scholar but was said to be "deficient in government," presumably meaning he did not maintain sufficient discipline. McCrimmen returned to Ireland after one year. He was succeeded by Isaac Bird who also stayed but one year before entering Andover Seminary in 1817. Samuel Turney then came from Chester Academy, Chester, Pennsylvania, to serve as West Nottingham's principal for three years until 1820.

There is no direct evidence of a common thread that explains the frequent departures of West Nottingham principals, but it is easy to imagine that the personality of Rev. James Magraw might have had an overshadowing effect on some of them. Magraw's leading role in opening the academy, his position as secretary of the Board of Trustees, and the proximity of the manse to the school, taken all together, may have led to oversupervision of the principals. It must be noted, however, that Isaac Bird's journal of his West Nottingham sojourn indicates a serene life while living in Magraw's household and being under his general supervision at the academy. After the departure of Turney in

1820, the Board of Trustees chose a principal who was not likely to depart, Rev. James Magraw himself, who was serving his 16th year as pastor of the Lower West Nottingham Presbyterian Church. Magraw probably did not teach classes except as a substitute but selected the teachers and oversaw the operation of the school. The teachers who taught under Magraw's supervision at various times between 1820 and 1835 follow:

Andrew Dinsmore
James Gerry, M.D.
Andrew Dinsmore Livingston
James C. Magraw—First son of the principal and an alumnus
John C. Reynolds, M.D.
Rev. John Patton—Alumnus of West Nottingham Academy
Samuel M. Magraw—Third son of the principal, an alumnus, and a future principal
Robert Evans, Jr.

As principal, Magraw probably took basic responsibility for discipline. The experience of one boy who got in trouble with Magraw comes to us through a letter* written in 1941 from the boy's grandson to the headmaster of the academy. The boy was James Armour Buyers, a boarding student from Lancaster, Pennsylvania, who enrolled in 1822 at the age of 13. The loss of the boy's father at an early age may have accounted for James' liveliness, which at West Nottingham apparently led to many an hour of confinement in which James was required to memorize a psalm or chapter in the Bible before being released. In later years, James Buyers had a remarkable ability to quote the Bible at length, but there were no immediate benefits of better behavior at West Nottingham. One day at dinner with the Magraw family, with whom he boarded, James threw his portion of fish out the window, thinking it was spoiled. Magraw seriously considered expelling young Buyers but finally decided to give him another chance. The happy result was that Buyers remained at the academy for over four years and became

---

* James Buyers' experience at West Nottingham Academy was related by his grandson, Rev. William B. Buyers, minister of the Latta Memorial Presbyterian Church, Christiana, Pa., in a letter of June 3, 1941, to J. Paul Slaybaugh, headmaster of West Nottingham Academy.

a great favorite of Magraw who liked to take the boy as a companion when he made his rounds of the countryside by horse and buggy. The annual enrollment from 1819 to 1829 averaged 20 students, but rose to 50 in 1826. Projection of 1819-29 records to 1835 indicates that between 1819 and 1835 there were about 120 students who stayed at least two years. Of that number, at least 36 had professional careers, or almost one out of three. The following list* of these alumni shows 24 ministers, one minister-educator, five medical doctors, two educators, three lawyers, and two railroad managers.

Ministers**	Class	Location of Career
John P. Cowan	1824	Missouri
Thomas Cole	1821	St. Louis
Robert McCachren	1821	Newville, Pa.
Matthew Henderson	1824	Newark, N.J.
William B. McIlvaine	1824	Beaver, Pa.
John Patton, D.D.	1822	Philadelphia, Pa.
Nathan Grier White	1825	Connelsville, Pa.
Reuben Frame	1826	Morris, Ill.
Cyrus H. Jacobs	1826	
George A. Leakin	1832	Baltimore, Md.
Henry H. Hopkins	1828	Owensboro, Ky.
John Wilson Irwin	1826	
M. Dugan	1832	
Alexander K. Nelson	1832	Chambersburg, Pa.
Alexander G. Morrison	1823	Coatesville, Pa.
John Dickey	1823	Bloomfield, Pa.
Corneilius H. Mustard	1826	Blackwater, Del.
John Scott, D.D.	1824	
Robert McCrea White	1832	
Alexander Ewing	1826	
Samuel James Miller	1821	
Andrew Boyd Cross	1832	Baltimore, Md.
George Inglis	1824	
William Worral	1826	
James Ramsey	1832	

Lawyers		
John A. Inglis	1826	President of convention that took South Carolina out of Union at the beginning of the Civil War

* This list from Samuel Gayley's *History of West Nottingham Church*.
** Eight of the future ministers first professed faith in Christ and joined the Church while at West Nottingham.

| Henry S. Magraw | 1828 | District Attorney of Allegheney County, Treasurer of Pennsylvania 1857–1861 |
| N. B. Smithers | — | Member of U.S. House of Representatives from Delaware 1863–1865. |

Educators

Nathan Covington Brooks	1824	Headed Baltimore's first high school, President of Baltimore Wesleyan Female College, and principal of two academies
John Scott, D.D.	1824	President of Washington and Jefferson College
Samuel Martin Magraw	1825	Principal of West Nottingham Academy

Doctors of Medicine

Robert Evans	1828	
William B. Rowland	1826	Cecil County
Francis J. Steel	1832	Camden, N.J.
John Steel	1827	
J. Harvey Rowland	1830	

Railroads

| Robert Mitchell Magraw | 1826 | First President of the Western Maryland Railroad |
| James Cochran Magraw | 1820 | General Freight Agent of Northern Central Railroad of Maryland |

Additional information about some of these West Nottingham alumni follows. John A. Inglis was born in Baltimore but became well-known as a jurist in South Carolina. He presided over the South Carolina convention that adopted Articles of Secession on December 20, 1860, making South Carolina the first state to secede from the Union after Lincoln's election that fall. The West Nottingham Class of 1824 produced two prominent educators, John Scott, D.D., and Nathan Covington Brooks. Besides being an educator, Brooks wrote books of poetry and individual poems that appeared in national magazines prior to the Civil War. John Scott's training in theology was a stepping-stone to the presidency of Washington and Jefferson College. It is also of interest that four of the sons of James Magraw, the principal, had professional careers: Henry S. in law and politics, Robert M. and James C. in railroad management, and Samuel M. in education.

The absence of regular teaching duties left Rev. James Magraw free to carry out pastoral responsibilities at West Nottingham and elsewhere.* He continued for 10 years to devote one-third of his time to the Upper West Nottingham Church after its organization in 1810. Magraw and Rev. Robert Graham of the Rock Presbyterian Church worked together in organizing the first Presbyterian congregation in Charlestowne, which Magraw served part-time after 1820. Magraw's main work at the Lower West Nottingham Church prospered, the number of members increasing from 30 at his arrival in 1804 to hundreds at his death in 1835. He conducted several revivals at the church, one of which added 75 members and another 50. In the summer he rode five miles down to Port Deposit to preach to the raftsmen congregated there who had brought lumber down the Susquehanna and were waiting for cargo to be unloaded from Chesapeake Bay ships for transport upstream. At Port Deposit, Magraw was also active in laying the groundwork for the Port Deposit Presbyterian Church which was organized in 1838. In 1825 at the age of fifty, Magraw's successes were so evident that Dickinson College awarded him a Doctor of Divinity degree. Rev. William Finney of Churchville, Maryland, describes Magraw's pastoral style as follows:

> He was not a student—apart from the Bible, his book of divinity was the world as it is, and his favorite motto: "Inasmuch as ye have done it unto the least of these [fellow men], ye have done it to me, etc." He wrote no sermons, other than naked skeletons. His usual preparations for the pulpit were made in the twilight of the morning while all around him were asleep. His manner in the pulpit was earnest and impassioned almost to a fault, and admirably calculated to wake up the slumbering sinner... his constant and single aim was to bring sinners under the shadow of the cross.

Samuel Gayley in his history of the West Nottingham Church adds that Magraw's "appeals to the impenitent were remarkable for their pointedness, pungency and power. The terrors of the law were used by him with more than ordinary effect... to awaken the secure sinner." Gayley describes Magraw as:

---

* George Johnston, 19th Century historian of Cecil County, wrote in 1880 that Magraw was the most successful minister in the county's history except for Hugh Jones in the North Sassafrass parish.

a man of great readiness who was seldom ... taken by surprise. If disappointed in his expectation of a brother to preach for him, or if he were called upon unexpectedly, such were his resources and activity of his mind that he would preach with as much acceptance and power as though he had had time for premeditation. Indeed it is said that these impromptu efforts are often best.

Besides his religious and academic responsibilities, Magraw efficiently managed his own farm of 260 acres which bordered the church and academy grounds. This land is now owned by West Nottingham Academy and still yields good crops. Members of Magraw's congregation not only accepted his judgment in spiritual matters but called upon him to settle worldly differences between them from time to time.

As the 1835 fall term was about to begin, there seemed no reason to doubt that James Magraw, a healthy if somewhat corpulent 60-year old, would continue to direct the academy for a number of years. That prospect suddenly became doubtful early in October when the horse pulling Magraw's carriage down the manse lane took fright and bolted. Magraw was thrown to the ground with such violence that he suffered a severe brain concussion. The robust minister had almost recovered from that mishap when an attack of typhoid fever proved fatal on October 20. Magraw's death preceded that of Rev. Robert Graham, pastor of the neighboring Rock Presbyterian Church, by 15 days. A fall from a carriage about a year earlier had finally proven fatal for Graham, who had been giving one-third of his time to the Rock Church since 1804, and had been co-organizer with Magraw of the Charlestowne Presbyterian Church. Magraw said to a friend shortly before his death that "his only desire to live was that he might longer preach the gospel and that he had never felt it so important as he did now in the near view of eternity."

8

Continuity Under Samuel Magraw and Rev. George Burrowes, 1835–1850

THE UNEXPECTED death of Rev. James Magraw, West Nottingham's principal, did not affect its operation greatly because of the availability of his 26-year old son, Samuel, as a replacement. He was already teaching at the academy and had married Harriet Steele Maxwell of Lancaster, Pa., the previous year. The younger Magraw had provided funds to construct a new academy building after a recent storm had severely damaged the old one. The new building stood in the same grove of trees but about 100 yards to the west. It was described as a "very plain and modest building without any pretensions to architectural style." The same site is now occupied by an ornate brick building and is used as the student canteen.

Samuel Magraw served as principal for five years during which he hired at various times the following teachers: Rev. John D. Whitman, Lorenzo Coburn, Thomas M. Bacon, William Cameron, John Murray, and Henry Rawlings.

West Nottingham Academy advertised for students in the first issue of the Baltimore Sun on May 17, 1837. The apparent intent was to enroll more students for the summer session which had already been underway for 10 days. Room and board for the five-month session ending October 10 was $40 and annual tuition was $20, essentially the same rates charged in 1820. The advertisement suggested two ways to reach West Nottingham from Baltimore: Captain William Owen's twice-weekly steamboat service from Baltimore to Port Deposit, five miles south of the academy; or steamboat service to Frenchtown, two miles below Port Deposit on the Susquehanna, which connected with daily stages passing within two miles of the academy. Room and board could be obtained with the principal's family or with Mrs. Hogg and Miss McMinn, who had opened a new boarding house nearby. This is the building that is now called the Wiley House and is still used as a girls' dormitory. Nothing else is known of Samuel Magraw's five-year service, ending in 1840, except for Rev. Samuel Gayley's statement in his history of the West Nottingham Church* that "the academy retained its former high reputation under Samuel Magraw's management." Magraw later served for a time as principal of Bel Air Academy in Harford County.

To replace Samuel Magraw as principal, the academy's Board of Trustees appointed Rev. George Burrowes. Burrowes was the scholarly young pastor of the Lower West Nottingham Presbyterian Church who had come to West Nottingham in 1836 to replace Rev. James Magraw after his fatal accident. Burrowes was born in Trenton, N.J. in 1811, graduated from Princeton College in 1832, and commenced study at Princeton Theological Seminary in the fall of 1832. While a student at the seminary, Burrowes tutored for Princeton College. Unlike Samuel Finley and James Magraw, who took brides immediately after being accepted by the West Nottingham congregation, George Burrowes found his bride after coming to West Nottingham. She was Miss Amelia Shotwell of England, who became acquainted with Burrowes while visiting in Oxford, Pennsylvania.

The academy teaching staff consisted of Edwin Clapp, persons with the last names of Belcher and McGalliard, William J. Rolfe, and Miss Louise Shotwell. Miss Shotwell may have been a sister or relative of Mrs. Burrowes; of more importance, she appears to have been the first woman to teach at West Nottingham.

In 1844 Rev. George Burrowes secured permission of the church's presbytery to change the name of the church and academy to Kirkwood, probably to avoid confusion with the Upper West Nottingham Presbyterian Church which was across the Pennsylvania line. The Lower West Nottingham congregation was not at all satisfied with the new

---

* Gayley became pastor of the West Nottingham Church in 1856 and issued his history in 1864.

WILEY—Earliest record was May 17, 1837, when the first issue of the Baltimore Sun carried Miss McMinn's offer to room and board West Nottingham students at this house.

name but held their peace for seven years. In 1851, however, at the first meeting of the presbytery after Burrowes had left, the congregation requested and received permission to take back the old name for the church and academy.

Burrowes served as principal until 1850, except for a brief period of a year or less when the academy was directed by Levi Janvier, a graduate of the Princeton Theological Seminary, who served as a missionary in India for the final 20 years of his life. Except for that break in service, Burrowes was both pastor of the church and principal of the academy until 1850 when Presbyterian authorities asked him to transfer to Lafayette College to serve as professor of languages. There is no direct evidence of Burrowes' impact on West Nottingham Academy. Rev. Samuel Gayley, who became pastor of the West Nottingham Church six years after Burrowes' departure, states that the academy "enjoyed a high degree of public favor" under his direction.

The year after Burrowes left West Nottingham, he gave two addresses that expressed his convictions on education and on the threatening disunion between North and South. In an inaugural address at Lafayette College, Burrowes' thesis was that classical learning was needed to understand the development of the scriptures. He concluded that classical learning, science, and "pagan" culture must all be used in constructing a finished Christian education. Later in 1851, Burrowes delivered the Thanksgiving sermon at the First Presbyterian Church in Easton, Pennsylvania, in which he staunchly if implicitly supported the Compromise of 1850, passed by Congress to settle peacefully the growing differences between North and South:

> No one sect, no one society, no one state, constitutes our country. The assemblage of all these forms the nation; and hence the design of the government is to consult the interest, not of any one of these as dissevered from the others, but of the whole so far as that interest can be promoted by such compromises according to the Constitution as may benefit them thus in union. Far be it from us to be so influenced by selfishness and fanaticism, as to allow a wrong, or even an oppressive act to turn us against our country. In such a spirit there is more of the temper of Arnold than of those faithful with Washington. When our country may seem to err, we will stand by her with greater faithfulness, and use efforts the more strenuous for correcting by legal means the error,—bowing with submission to the supremacy of the laws, and making ours the principle, our country, our whole country, and nothing but our whole country.

In the closing years of Burrowes' regime at West Nottingham Academy, Cecil County news reports had shown the divisiveness and danger of slavery to the United States. On November 7, 1847, a Cecil County slaveowner managed to recover three slaves through a trial by jury in Mount Holly, New Jersey, despite a near riot. In describing the incident the *Cecil Whig* of November 13, 1847, reported that the slaves made a rush for the door upon hearing the adverse sentence. The 300 Negro spectators sprang to the assistance of the defendants and were immediately opposed by 50 whites also at the trial. Only the presence of court-ordered soldiers outside prevented an escape and probable violence. Instead, the Negroes who did not live in Mount Holly obeyed the Sheriff's order to leave town. The following spring on April 29,

1848, the *Cecil Whig* reported a statement in a Wilmington, Delaware newspaper that Cecil County slaves were "running away in droves." Eight had escaped from George Kidd of Cecil County, and five had escaped from two other owners. Kidd intended to free three of his slaves in a few days. Kidd was probably one of the original members of West Nottingham's Board of Trustees or it may have been his son, George Washington Kidd, who graduated from the academy in 1834.

On June 3, 1848, the *Cecil Democrat*, the other principal newspaper in Cecil County, reported judgments of $2500 and $3500 against two citizens of Cecil County who had been found guilty of harboring runaway slaves. The fines represented penalties of $500 per slave, or five slaves whom one citizen had assisted and seven slaves whom the other defendant had helped escape. The money went to the owners of the slaves. The *Cecil Democrat* quoted the "hopes of the *Delaware Gazette* that the severe punishments would remove the rails from the 'underground railway'." Chief Justice Taney and Justice Hall of the U.S. Supreme Court had rendered the judgments, sitting as a U.S. Circuit Court. The severity of the penalties emphasized Taney's concept that because slaves were property, their ownership should be rigorously protected. This concept would lead to Taney's famous Dred Scott decision of 1857, which ruled that the slave Dred Scott could not become free even though he had been taken to a free state by his master and had stayed for an extended period. That decision doomed a peaceful settlement of North-South differences because it essentially nullified the Missouri Compromise of 1820 and later accommodations by which Congress had declared some states and territories free and some slave.

In the same issue of the *Cecil Democrat* that reported the penalties imposed for aiding runaway slaves, the following "for sale" item appeared, "A Negro woman and three children, all slaves for life. The woman is a good servant and sold for no fault. Inquire of the editor."

9

An Interim of Frequent Leadership Changes, 1850–1862

BETWEEN 1820 and 1850, West Nottingham Academy had only three principals, the two Magraws and Rev. George Burrowes. The next twelve years were marked by six changes in leadership. After Burrowes left the Academy in 1850 to teach at Lafayette College, the Board of Trustees hired Edwin Clapp as principal. Clapp had come to West Nottingham as a teacher the year before after his graduation from Amherst. Clapp's close friend and classmate from Amherst, W. J. Rolfe, also taught at West Nottingham that year. Rolfe described the year the two young Yankee schoolmasters spent together at West Nottingham as follows:

> The school and the schoolhouse were then very small, but I had a pleasant time there with my friend Ned (Edwin Clapp), enjoying the hospitalities of the good people of the neighborhood. I used to ride on horseback twice a week or so to the post office at Port Deposit.... We boarded at a very comfortable house, kept by a widow near the Academy.... Rev. Burrowes was our nearest neighbor ... and one of our most intimate friends.

The next year, when Clapp was appointed principal at West Nottingham, Rolfe left to become principal at Day's Academy in Wrentham, Massachusetts. Dr. Rolfe later achieved considerable fame as a scholar and editor of English literature. Edwin Clapp stayed only one year as West Nottingham's principal. There is no direct evidence as to how the academy fared under his supervision. His subsequent service of 12 years as head of Milton Academy, Massachusetts, suggests that Clapp did a good job at West Nottingham. In any case, he seems to have been successful in love because during his sojourn at West Nottingham, he found his wife, Miss Isabella Rowland, who belonged to a well-known Cecil County family long associated with the academy.

The Board of Trustees found a replacement for Clapp by persuading the pastor of the West Nottingham Presbyterian Church, Rev. Archibald Alexander Hodge, to take the post, starting in 1852. After education at Princeton College and Princeton Theological Seminary, Hodge had served as a missionary in India for two years before coming to West Nottingham as pastor in 1851. During Hodge's three-year leadership of the academy, Rev. A. H. Sill, a future principal, served as assistant teacher. Rev. Samuel Gayley, who succeeded Hodge as pastor in 1856, states in his 1865 history of the church that the academy "enjoyed a high degree of prosperity" under Hodge's "efficient management." Gayley also praised Hodge's ministry, noting that the church added 52 members during his stay of four years.

President L. H. Evans and other members of the Academy's Board of Trustees who gathered at Rev. Hodge's shaded manse in early August of 1855 learned that he had been offered the pastorate of the Presbyterian Church in Fredericksburg, Virginia, to start that fall. With the unfailing courtesy that characterizes his history of the West Nottingham Church, Rev. Samuel Gayley does not allude to the shortness of Hodge's notice which left the Academy without a principal for the fall session beginning in less than two months. The board instructed its secretary to advertise for a new principal in the *Baltimore American, New York Observer,* Cecil county newspapers, and Presbyterian publications. At its next meeting on August 22, the Board elected George Duffield and E. F. M. Faehtz as joint principals. On March 15, 1856, however, Duffield and Faehtz resigned after little more than six months service. The Board of Trustees continued to search in vain for a permanent principal in the period of general uncertainty that preceded the Civil War. The following table summarizes information on the six

Service	Principal	Birthplace-Education	Post Nottingham
1850–51....	Edwin Clapp	Probably New England-Amherst 1849.	Principal, Milton Academy, Milton, Mass. for 12 years.
1852–55....	Archibald A. Hodge	Princeton, N.J.-Princeton B.A., 1841; Princeton Theological Seminary 1847.	Professor, Allegheny and Princeton Theological Seminaries.
1855–56....	George Duffield and E. F. M. Faehtz	Not Known.	Not Known.
1856–57....	Alfred Yeomans	North Adams, Mass.-Princeton College B.A., 1852.	Graduated Princeton Theological Seminary 1860; Pastor, Orange, N.J., 1868–1889.
1857–59....	William P. Andrews	Doylestown, Pa.-Lafayette College B.A., 1853.	Served 3 years 104th Pa. Artillery Reg't; Lawyer in U.S. Treasury.
1859–62....	Rev. Amos H. Sill	New York-Union College, N.Y. B.A., 1848; Princeton Theological Seminary, 1851; Pastor, Churchville, Md.	Died West Nottingham, Md. 1863.

principals of the academy during the twelve years of frequent leadership changes between 1850 and 1862.

John Carson (J.C.) Kidd provides a sampling of student life at West Nottingham Academy just before the Civil War. J.C. was a son of George Washington Kidd of the 1834 class and grandson of George Kidd, a member of the academy's first Board of Trustees. In 1856, during J.C.'s first spring at the academy, Rev. Samuel A. Gayley arrived as pastor of the church. J.C. recalled that before Gayley moved into the parsonage, the farmers of the congregation got together and plowed the field that was to be farmed by the new pastor. The academy students had a half holiday to "drop corn" as their contribution to the new pastor's spring farming.

J.C. Kidd's reminiscences come to us through letters he wrote between 1926 and 1932 to Paul Slaybaugh, then headmaster of the academy, and Esther Maxwell, alumni secretary. As Slaybaugh gently prodded J.C.'s memories of student life, he also revived J.C.'s enthusiasm for the academy. In 1927 J.C. would not attend commencement at West Nottingham because, as the oldest living alumnus, he would be "shaking hands with myself" and "feel like an old leaf." In 1931 at the age of 87, however, J.C. declared that "I do not know of any place—other than my home—where I would rather spend May 30 and 31 than with the alumni of West Nottingham." J.C. goes on to say that in his time, "the last days of the session were not surrounded by such a display of girls and boys and their friends." The only ones present at the end of the session other than the teacher "would be some of the Board [of Trustees] of whom only two ever had anything to say." They were Rev. John Squier, pastor of the Port Deposit Presbyterian Church and secretary of the Board of Trustees, and Dr. William Rowland, treasurer of the Board of Trustees and alumnus of West Nottingham Academy. The two would ask the class a question in Latin and then differ with each other as to the proper pronunciation of the answer. One case was whether Cicero should begin with a hard or soft C. J.C. Kidd recalled that "we boys had to laugh to ourselves because the trustees were diverted from examining the students."

J.C. Kidd recalled that on Monday mornings when school was in session, he set out on foot for West Nottingham from his grandfather's house near Port Deposit. He must have gotten an early start to cover the four or five miles to the academy in time for morning classes. The exercise was invigorating and the spring scenery a dream of beauty as he hiked out of the steep, wooded valley of the Susquehanna and viewed the open vistas of ploughed fields and patches of hazy green woodland that lay before him. After morning classes, J.C. joined Miss Betsey McMinn's boarders and did full justice to her noon meal. He roomed and boarded with her for the rest of the week before returning to Port Deposit at a faster pace on Friday afternoon in anticipation of the weekend with his maternal grandfather, John Carson.*

Miss McMinn had opened the boarding house in about 1837. Now called Wiley House, it was bought by the Academy in 1928 for an

---

* Probably a member of the Board of Trustees in 1852–53.

emergency dormitory after the 1927 fire. J.C. noted that the porch did not run around the end of the house when he boarded there as it did in 1928. Besides student boarders, Miss McMinn had two of the principals of J.C.'s period stay with her, Rev. Alfred Yeomans and William P. Andrews. A nearby tract of timber, owned by Miss McMinn, provided firewood for the house and pasture for her cow.

By the eve of the Civil War, J.C. Kidd's work at Nottingham had prepared him for college. He had planned to go to Lafayette but did not go because of the war. His family presumably made this decision because there is no indication that J.C. wished to enlist in the forces of either the North or South.

Available records indicate a variety of responses to the Civil War by the West Nottingham community and academy graduates. West Nottingham seemed to reflect the mixed feelings of Maryland as a whole. Like the other border slave states, Delaware, Kentucky, and Missouri, Maryland stayed in the Union. Many Marylanders did not wish to join the armed forces of either side, whereas others felt strongly enough to go into military service on one side or the other. Some experiences of West Nottingham adherents of the North and the South follow.

Southern adherents included Rev. John Squier, secretary of the academy's Board of Trustees. Squier resigned as pastor of the Port Deposit Presbyterian Church in 1861 after nine years of service to accept a call from the Springfield church in Carroll County. A major reason for his leaving was that he did not share the strong antislavery sentiments of his congregation.* After the war, Squier returned to Port Deposit. The most important leader that West Nottingham contributed to the South was John Inglis of the class of 1827. Inglis presided over the convention that took South Carolina out of the Union on December 24, 1860, the first state to secede after Lincoln's election on November 6. Two other Nottingham graduates were forced to resign their positions with the Northern Central Railroad of Maryland when the Civil War broke out because they would not take oaths of allegiance to the U.S. They were James Cochran Magraw and Robert Mitchell Magraw, who were sons

---

* The community of Port Deposit apparently had many Union sympathizers because volunteer Union forces were organized there.

of James Magraw, the academy's former principal. Julian Golibart of the Class of 1856 had apparently chosen sides before he left West Nottingham because he spoke on "The Right of Peaceful Secession" in a student program one evening during his final year at the academy. Soon after the war's outbreak, Julian enlisted with the Confederate forces and was never heard of again, according to his brother, Simon, who was a postwar West Nottingham student. William W. Virdin, a West Nottingham graduate of 1845, joined the Confederate Army as assistant surgeon in 1861 and by the end of the war had been promoted to full surgeon.

On the Union side, a classmate of Virdin at Nottingham, John M. Cooley, waited until 1863 before enlisting in the Third New Hampshire Regiment in which he served for the duration. A West Nottingham graduate of 1832, Rev. George A. Leakin, served as chaplain in the Union army from 1862 to 1865. West Nottingham's principal from 1857 to 1859, William P. Andrews, served with the 104th Pennsylvania Artillery Regiment for three years. George M. Christie was a West Nottingham student who joined the Union forces at the age of 17 soon after leaving the academy. He served in Company G of the Sixth Maryland Infantry Division, which was commanded by his father. At the end of the war, he was quartermaster sergeant of his regiment. Another West Nottingham alumnus, Nathaniel Smithers, got involved in the politics of the Civil War. In 1861, President Lincoln asked him to persuade Delaware to accept a scheme for freeing the state's slaves. Smithers, a Republican lawyer and later a Delaware congressman, prepared a measure for the state legislature whereby the federal government would compensate slaveowners with an average of $500 for the freedom of each of Delaware's 1,800 slaves, amounting to a total of $900,000. Unfortunately, the legislature soundly defeated the proposal, which, if approved, might have induced other states to free their slaves before the end of the war.

West Nottingham Academy itself continued to operate during the Civil War. The following table shows few graduates between 1858 and 1865, suggesting that enrollment was down. This situation probably resulted from the general restlessness associated with the approach and waging of the war, making it difficult to find a permanent principal and to enroll students.

West Nottingham Graduates

1856	14
1857	6
1858	1
1859	1
1860	2
1861	3
1862	2
1863	2
1864	8
1865	7
1866	24
1867	27

No Civil War battles took place in Cecil County although Union troops once encamped at Colora with skirmish lines that extended to Rising Sun. Sounds of artillery fired in the battle of Gettysburg reached Cecil County on July 3, 1863, the day of General Pickett's brave but futile charge, often described as the high tide of the Confederacy.

Contemporary accounts do not indicate the effect of the war on the daily life of the academy. Rev. Samuel A. Gayley, president of the academy's Board of Trustees, does not mention the war in his history of the West Nottingham Church* which he issued to his congregation on May 15, 1865, just five weeks after Lee's surrender at Appomattox. The absence of this topic may very well reflect split sympathies in Gayley's congregation in which feeling about the war likely still ran high. Lack of comment on the war is also consistent with Gayley's emphasis on the church and its leaders in his history. Yet, Joseph T. Richards, a student who graduated in the spring of 1865, also failed to mention the war in lengthy reminiscing about the school and his classmates. One can surmise that the effects of the mighty conflict were so obvious and pervasive they were taken for granted and thus not memorable.

---

* An appendix summarizes the history of West Nottingham Academy.

10

George Bechtel and Samuel Gayley, 1862–1887

SAMUEL A. GAYLEY was installed as pastor of the West Nottingham Presbyterian Church on June 18, 1856. Unlike some of his predecessors, Gayley did not step in as principal of the academy when its Board of Trustees could not find a permanent principal in the uncertain times preceding the Civil War. Gayley was a Scotch-Irish immigrant, born in County Tyrone, Ireland, on December 22, 1822, and educated in America at Lafayette College and Princeton Theological Seminary. After missionary work in Whitehaven, Pa., Gayley had served six years as pastor in Lock Haven, Pa., before coming to West Nottingham. While Gayley was busy attending to his large new congregation (probably split between members of northern and southern sentiments), the academy had to find three new principals between 1856 and 1859. The third one was Rev. Amos H. Sill, who resigned in 1862 because of ill health that led to his death in 1863. George K. Bechtel, who succeeded Sill in the fall of 1862, did not have the robust appearance that would have been reassuring after Sill's lack of good health. A slight 23-year-old native of New Brunswick, N.J., Bechtel had graduated from Princeton with second honors in 1860. Bechtel was described by Hermann Hagedorn in his biography of Robert S. Brookings, as being "frail" and one "who would have no chance against his . . . barbarians if there had not been something behind steady eyes to outmatch ingenuity and brawn." The new principal also "was relentlessly thorough" and gave of himself with a generosity which took no account of a body often ill and in pain." As Gayley observed the young Princetonian's teaching in the academy across the road from the church, two thoughts occurred to him. George Bechtel was a born teacher, and the congregation of his West Nottingham Church had the resources to support the expansion of West Nottingham Academy. Gayley was content just to imagine what could be done with these assets while the Civil War raged inconclusively through the 1862-1863 school year, George Bechtel's first at West Nottingham. The fortunes of war turned on July 4, 1863, however, when Union forces triumphed at Gettysburg and Vicksburg. Those victories and the raising of the Confederate siege of Chattanooga in November 1863 probably convinced Gayley that the war was winding down. Now president of the academy's Board of Trustees, Gayley persuaded them to call upon the West Nottingham community for $2,000 to finance an academy building program. If the appeal were successful, the new academy building would be a place to which parents in the neighborhood could send their sons with pride.

Apparently it was easy for the Presbyterians to share Gayley's dream, especially with George Bechtel as principal. Even the state's withdrawal of its annual subsidy of $500 to the academy in 1864 did not discourage the members of the West Nottingham Presbyterian Church who contributed all but $60 of the needed $2000 and hauled the building material to the building site. The minutes of the board meeting of September 10, 1864, show the following list of contributors. Because their contributions do not add up to $2000, the list is apparently incomplete. With the money in hand, the board resolved to build a new academy, "the house to be 45 x 25 feet, one room 14 feet to flat ceiling with 3 circular windows" on north and south with a "double door in west and circular transom over the door. The roof to be slate." It was designed to accommodate 80 to 90 students.

James Nickle	$25.00	Joseph Fryer	$10.00
Amos Ewing	25.00	Rob't A. Evans	25.00
Moses Nesbitt	25.00	Wm. Gillespie	10.00
Jas. McCoy	25.00	Robert L. Tosh	5.00
Geo. W. Poist	20.00	Dr. James Turner	15.00
Rev. S. A. Gayley	20.00	E. Lanns	5.00
Mrs. Lucy M. McCullough	25.00	Jesse Ramsay	20.00
Corbin Cooly	25.00	Theodore L. Marshall	10.00
J. M. Evans	25.00	Amos Clendenin	10.00
Dr. W. B. Rowland	50.00	Jacob Slicer	10.00
Samuel Tosh	10.00	Samuel Hason	10.00
J. H. Rowland	50.00	Wm. Little	10.00
R. M. Magraw	30.00	Josh (?) Hall	10.00

D. Clendenin	20.00	Dr. J. H. McCullough	10.00
J. H. Hindman	5.00	J. L. Nickel	25.00
Rob't H. Nesbitt	5.00	Geo. Gillespie	25.00
Eli Coulson	10.00	C. L. Abrahams	5.00
John Nickle	10.00	John T. McCullough	10.00
Jas. Gollibart	10.00	James Hogg	5.00
Nevin Orr	10.00	J. F. Vanarsdae	5.00
John Barnes	10.00	George Moore	10.00
J. W. Mount	25.00	Gus. Coulson	5.00
T. J. Gillespie	25.00	H. L. Magraw*	350.00
John Hammersmith	20.00	David Rea	15.00
F. L. Linton	5.00	Wm. J. Evans	25.00
M. A. McCullough	5.00	Jacob Krauss	5.00
Mrs. Brickley	5.00	James Linestom	5.00
Wm. W. Moore	25.00	Hugh Steel	25.00
R. N. Hindman	25.00	Louis Coulson	5.00
John Tosh	25.00	Steven Richards	10.00
Rob't Montgomery	25.00	L. H. Evans	10.00
Ambrose Ewing	20.00	John P. Evans	25.00
John L. Ewing	20.00	W. W. Wiley	3.00
James O. McCormick	25.00	Total	$1,388.00

* The middle initial probably should be "S" instead of "L" because there is no record of an H. L. Magraw; and H. S. Magraw, son of the long-time principal, James Magraw, had moved back to West Nottingham in 1863 after a successful political career.

Construction of the new building brought Samuel Gayley's grand design to completion just as the Civil War was ending. Gayley now had a fine building to house the school as well as an excellent principal to teach the students. Would the students enroll and graduate in numbers to justify the faith of Gayley and his congregation in the future of West Nottingham Academy? Their hopes soon became reality, as the following table shows:

Year	Graduates	Enrollment
1856	14	—
1857	6	—
1858	1	—
1859	1	—
1860	2	—
1861	3	—
1862	2	—
1863	2	—
1864	8	—
1865	7	—
1866	24	—
1867	27	—
1868	35	—

Year	Graduates	Enrollment
1869	48	—
1870	16	—
1871	—	—
1872	16	50
1873	7	82
1874	62	—
1875	—	—
1876	—	—
1877	—	—
1878	12	c. 60
1879	18	c. 60
1880	4	—
1881	8	37
1882	23	44
1883	5	—
1884	24	49
1885	28	48
1886	15	—
1887	13	—

While the new academy building was being constructed, students attended classes in Miss Betsey McMinn's boarding house. A new student that year was Robert S. Brookings, whose creative concepts of economic research and analysis would lead him to a career of outstanding public service. Brookings was born in Cecil County on January 22, 1850, the son of a physician descended from Huguenots. After Dr. Brookings died when Robert was two years of age, his mother took the children to Baltimore where she married Henry Reynolds, a Quaker. When Civil War broke out, the family moved to Perrymanville in Harford County, apparently to avoid the unrest in Baltimore associated with the war. In the absence of an adequate school nearer to home, Robert's stepfather and mother sent him to West Nottingham Academy in the fall of 1864. Robert was four months short of 15 years when he moved into one of the rooming and boarding houses near the academy. Robert adjusted to his new life with little difficulty. He liked his landlady and admired the principal of the academy, Mr. Bechtel. Within three months, Robert's stepfather was congratulating his stepson on the improvement in his letters. He urged Robert to excel: "Now is your time to be all you desire. A man of talent has seldom, if ever, a competitor." Home for Christmas vacation, Robert somewhat shocked his parents by the foul language he had picked up so his mother started writing more often to keep the home ties stronger. At West Nottingham

Robert found time to visit his Aunt Jane Jenness on weekends at her farm near Rising Sun. Like Benjamin Rush, a student at West Nottingham over 100 years before, Robert enjoyed hunting and roamed the countryside on horseback with gun in hand. He met a girl who so impressed him that he had her initials tattooed on his leg.

Despite these diversions, Robert became restless during his second spring at West Nottingham because of letters from his brother, Harry, who had gone to seek his fortune in St. Louis. Harry urged Robert to join him, having found his employer, Cupples and Marston, lumber wholesalers, willing to hire a second Brookings. Robert could not wait to go even though his secondary education was far from complete. His time at West Nottingham Academy would be the last academic training that he received. His mother reluctantly gave her consent, not revealing that she was seriously ill and probably would not see him again. She died when he was 17, not long after he had departed. In St. Louis Robert accumulated a large personal fortune. At the age of 46, he retired from business to devote the rest of his life to public service. This decision led to his development of the Washington University Medical School in St. Louis, chairmanship of President Wilson's Price Fixing Committee in World War I, and founding of the Brookings Institution in Washington, D.C.

Samuel Gayley's grand design for West Nottingham Academy threatened to fall apart toward the close of the 1866–67 session when Principal Bechtel announced that he would be leaving to help organize a Presbyterian school in Media, Pennsylvania. When that project failed, Bechtel became principal of Newark Academy in Newark, N.J. At West Nottingham, Samuel Gayley persuaded himself to do something he had carefully avoided since coming as pastor of the West Nottingham Church—he took over as principal of the academy.

After five years Gayley had succeeded so well that prospects for enrollment in the fall of 1872 reached an all-time high. Feeling that his large Presbyterian congregation and the enlarged student body would be too much for him, Gayley was relieved when George Bechtel agreed to return to West Nottingham.

With the prospect of good enrollment in 1872–73, Bechtel probably could look forward to increased income because the principal's compensation was based on the number of students. Moreover, in 1868 Maryland had restored its annual subsidy of $500, which traditionally provided the base for the principal's salary. Bechtel's work at Newark Academy had earned such glowing tributes for his teaching and scholarship that he included several of them in the West Nottingham Academy Catalog. Word of Bechtel's return and the good enrollment prospects encouraged the trustees to add two wings to the academy building and purchase a cupola, bell, and new school furniture at a cost of $2,000. The improvements were ready to accommodate the record enrollment of 82 in the year of Bechtel's return. The following year some new ideas accompanied the continuing high enrollment. In regard to discipline, the catalog of 1873–74 states that the objectives are to "recognize the individuality of the pupil; to appeal to his manliness and self-respect rather than his fear of punishment; and to aim to be always firm, never degrading." Testimony from a number of Bechtel's students indicates that the principal practiced this philosophy and was quite successful in maintaining good conduct in the classroom.

Another development that promoted greater student responsibility was the founding of the Irving Literary Society with the encouragement of Marvin J. Eckels, an assistant teacher. Fourteen members convened on September 22, 1873, elected pro tem officers, and appointed a committee to draft a constitution. The initiation fee was 25 cents. Three days later, members adopted a constitution, elected D. Richardson as president, decided to call each other brother, and planned a program for the next meeting to consist of an oration, an essay, and reading by three different students. In that school year and the following one, the society held a number of debates. Principal Bechtel judged at least one of the debates and a member, Brother Haines, judged another. The debate topics follow:

> Which has suffered the most, the Indian or the Negro?
> Which is a better place for a University, the city or country?
> Is the pen mightier than the sword?
> Is woman's mind inferior to that of man?
> Should woman have the privilege of voting?
> Which affords the most beauty, nature or art?

According to the minutes of one meeting, "the president strived hard to keep order but was compelled to fine Brothers Rodgers, Sill, White-

OLD ACADEMY (Now STUDENT CANTEEN)—The congregation of the West Nottingham Presbyterian Church financed and helped with the construction of the Old Academy in 1864 to provide classrooms for the school.

hill, Frank Evans, Rowland, Springer, and Coats (two fines). There is, however, a better prospect in the future as the rules are now more severe."

On March 5, 1875, the society decided to call its paper, started the year before, "The Literary Advance." President P. W. Mount appointed E. N. Vallandingham as chief editor and as assistant editors, Brothers Coates and Gayley. That was the beginning of a student publication that was still being issued from time to time in the middle of the next century. In 1878, the society received a letter from the famous poet, William Cullen Bryant, thanking the society for electing him an honorary member. Later, the poet sent the society a set of books. The value of the Irving Society to the students was noted by T. R. McDowell, who recalled in 1895 that "The Literary Society especially was helpful" as an addition to the thorough formal instruction.

In the November 21, 1863 issue of the *Cecil Democrat*, the academy advertised courses of instruction including "ordinary English branches, higher mathematics, and classics." The academy offered to prepare students "for any of the college classes or for the counting room." Twenty years later the catalog of 1883–84 echoed the purposes of the academy given in 1863 and more thoroughly described the course of instruction as follows:

The design of the Academy is to furnish a thorough English education, to prepare young men for Classical and Scientific Colleges, or to fit them for business.

In the English Course are embraced all the branches fundamental to a liberal English education. The instruction has for its object not only to store the mind with facts, but to develop attention and train the reasoning faculties. Thoroughness is sought after, not display; quality, not quantity. It is self-evident, that unless by constant drill elementary principles are mastered, proficiency in higher studies is impossible and all seeming progress illusory.

Special care is taken in the study of English Grammar to combine exercises in the construction and the analysis of sentences. Common errors are noted and corrected.

The course of Reading embraces selections from the best English authors; interesting facts in their lives, characters, and writings are pointed out, with a view not only to elocutionary training, but also to the cultivation of a correct literary taste.

The Mathematical course embraces High Arithmetic, Algebra, Geometry, Trigonometry, Surveying, and Analytical Geometry. Practice in the use of the compass and chain forms part of the instruction in Surveying.

The Natural Sciences, including Natural Philosophy, Chemistry, and Physiology, receive due attention. Inorganic Chemistry is illustrated by experiments, for which the necessary apparatus is owned by the Academy. Physiology is illustrated by the skeleton and a full set of charts.

The Classical course embraces the Latin and Greek Grammars, Prose Composition, Classical Geography, Greek and Roman History, Mythology, with such authors as are necessary to gain admission into our leading colleges. The Ancient Languages are taught with special reference to the knowledge of our own tongue, and as preparatory to the study of Comparative Philology. When desired, pupils may be prepared for the Sophomore and Junior Classes.

The department of Modern Languages embraces French and German.

Particular attention is paid in all departments to Elocution and Composition.
Lectures are delivered during the school year by distinguished gentlemen.

Another part of the catalog states that the Bible forms the basis of religious instruction. Sectarianism is rigorously excluded. Pupils are required to attend divine worship on the Sabbath with the principal unless their parents request otherwise. T. R. McDowell remembered full Sundays of worship and study. He recalled that the boys went to church in the mornings "and the pews fitted so well that some of the boys rested." Sunday evening, they all met in the academy for Bible study. In addition to worship and Bible study, McDowell and the other boys benefited from the "moral and intelligent" population of the surrounding countryside and the absence of "drinking saloons or haunts of vice in the vicinity", according to the catalog.

The religious instruction described by the 1883-1884 catalog and recalled by McDowell resembled the religious training provided 125 years before by Rev. Samuel Finley. Finley had taught most of the courses described by the 1883-84 catalog. Of particular interest was the offer of the 1863 advertisement and 1883-84 catalog to prepare the student in the classical course for entrance in the sophomore and junior classes in college. This capability matched that of Samuel Finley who in 1749 sent Benjamin Rush and two classmates to Princeton for entrance as juniors.

The 1873-74 catalog declared that "delicate youth from the cities became healthy and robust in the mild and invigorating atmosphere of West Nottingham." This claim was reminiscent of the remarks of Benjamin Rush, a student in the 1740s from Philadelphia, who had remembered the lack of serious illness and the unusually good health enjoyed by the students during his five-year stay, a period when mortality for all ages was much higher than now.

The practice of holding public examinations, begun in 1812, continued under Bechtel. The catalogs of 1873-74 and 1883-84 state that "Examinations will be held at the close of each session." Those "at the end of the year" were to be held in "the presence of the trustees and others." Actual conduct of the examinations throughout Bechtel's regime is indicated by a letter in January 1887 from the principal to Adam R. Magraw,* secretary of the Board of Trustees, that schedules the exams and invites the trustees to attend.

Unlike the school calendar of the early 19th Century that provided for continuous schooling except for two three-week breaks in the spring and fall, Principal Bechtel's school calendar provided for substantial summer vacations. The 1873-74 and 1883-84 catalogs both show two semesters of about five months each that begin in early September and early February. The 1883-84 calendar follows:

Fall session began .... September 8
Christmas vacation .... December 24 to January 3
Examinations .... January 28 to 31
Spring session began .... February 2
Examinations .... June 15 to June 18
Commencement .... June 18

The school advertisement in the *Cecil Democrat* on November 21, 1863, gave the tuition for boarding students as $70 per five-month session. The tuition for day students ranged from $6 to $10 for the same period. The 1873-74 and 1883-84 catalogs show that charges per session of five months had risen as follows:

Boarding Students

English Department	$100.00
Scientific Department	110.00
Classical Department	110.00
Fuel and Lights	2.00

Day Scholars

English	16.00
Scientific	25.00
Classical	25.00
Fuel and Incidentials	1.50

---

* Grandson of James Magraw, who reopened the academy in 1812, and son of Henry S. Magraw.

Extras

German and French, each
Books supplied at city prices......................... 15.00

Terms of Payment

One-half in advance; the balance at the middle of the session.
No pupil taken for less than one-half session.
To those boarding from Monday morning to Friday night, a deduction of $18.00 from above rates.

When George Bechtel returned for his second tour of duty, his salary of $450 plus the tuition fees earned by the school was probably satisfactory because there were 50 students the first year and 82 the next. Such levels of enrollment were necessary for the principal because under the terms of the annual state subsidy of $500, the academy had to take five tuition-free students and hire an assistant teacher if the enrollment exceeded 30. Bechtel wanted the help but complained when there was not enough income to hire a competent assistant. The income apparently dropped whenever decreased enrollment reduced receipts from tuition. Assistant teachers often stayed only a year, but their teaching at West Nottingham provided some with stepping stones to posts of greater responsibility. Mervin J. Eckels later graduated from Western Theological Seminary, Allegheny, Pennsylvania, served as pastor at Salisbury, Maryland, and sometime before 1905 received a D.D. degree. James A. Stewart later became principal of a private school in Pennsylvania. Another assistant, Dan Purinton, was president of the University of West Virginia in 1909. The following table shows the assistant teachers between 1862 and 1887:

Principal	Assistant*
1862–1867 George K. Bechtel...........	Thomas B. Gillespie
	Brinton Jackson
	Gardner Clinton Deaver
1867–1872 Rev. Samuel A. Gayley......	James A. Stewart
	Dr. D. H. Richardson (1872–1877)
	Dan Purinton (1876–1877)
	Mervin J. Eckels (1877–1879)
	— Vallandingham (1875)

1872–1887 George K. Bechtel	Oliver F. Norton, B. L. (1884–1885)
	Edward A. Guernsey, A. B. (1883–1884)
	C. C. Tindal (1885–1886)
	— Marshall
	D. I. Green (1886–1887)
	James W. Barnes (1882–1885)
	Greenway

* Years of service may not be completely accurate.

At least one of Bechtel's students had a hard time settling down. Sidney Hall was a boarding student from Perryman, Harford County, between 1873 and 1875. In that time, he ran away from school twice, once taking a train from Perryville to home and another time spending a week rafting down the Susquehanna with loggers. In a letter of 1938 to Paul Slaybaugh, then headmaster, Sidney Hall admitted he was to blame for not getting along well with the principal. Perhaps the principal's influence eventually made itself felt, however, because Hall was a vice-president of the United States Fidelity and Guaranty Co. in Baltimore when he recounted his experiences at West Nottingham.

In contrast to the restlessness of Sidney Hall, the studious efforts of Albert McNamee of Principio, Cecil County, caused Bechtel to write Albert's father that his son's report card was "of a most gratifying character." Bechtel could "cheerfully commend him for his fidelity and success as a student and hope his future life may realize the promise of his student days at Nottingham." Bechtel concluded by expressing his readiness to serve as a reference.

A series of letters to Henry W. Archer, the father of one of Bechtel's boarding students, shows that teaching in the classroom was only part of the principal's responsibilities. After the boy's first month at West Nottingham, Bechtel felt obliged to write the father, Henry W. Archer, in Bel Air, Harford County, on October 1, 1877, that "James has a big job before him to prepare thoroughly for Princeton in one year." Instead, the principal suggested more time so James' "entrance . . . could be more creditable and his progress there more satisfactory." The following spring Bechtel strongly recommended another year at Nottingham for James. Bechtel also sent the elder Archer a bill for the current session and a school catalog to hand to the father of a prospective student in Bel Air. On another occasion, Bechtel sent Henry Archer a few catalogs for distribution to friends "if you can recommend us." By the end of James' second year, Bechtel informed the elder

Archer that James' final report card "was as usual quite satisfactory to us" and that James was ready for Princeton. The same letter informed the father that James was sick with a cold and it would be better to come and take him home where he would receive more attention. Thus, we see the principal serving as school nurse, guidance counselor, bill collector, and recruiter. Bechtel apparently wrote all the letters needed to manage the academy in his neat and legible longhand.

While the principal directed his attention to getting James Archer ready for Princeton, James had other things on his mind. In a letter to his father, James reported attending a small cattle show at Mr. Magraw's place and going hunting with a gun and dog lent by Mr. Stump. James planned to come home on the train that got to Edgewood, nearest railroad station to Bel Air, "at 12 o'clock as that is the only one that leaves Colora and connects with the train at Perryville." To make the trip, James needed the entire fare "for I have had to buy so many things that I am about broke." While on the subject of money, James proposed, "How would it do for you or mother to meet me at Edgewood and then we could go down to Balto and get my close [sic]."

Peter Tome, a classmate of James Archer, recalled in a conversation with Headmaster Paul Slaybaugh in 1938 that of Archer's ten classmates, two joined Archer at Princeton, two went to Dickinson, two, including Tome, went to Lafayette, and one went to St. Johns. Three did not go to college.

Students came to West Nottingham mainly from Maryland in Bechtel's period. The top enrollment of 82 in 1872–73 included 68 boys from Maryland, eight from Pennsylvania, four from Delaware and one apiece from New Jersey and Missouri. Ten years later, 41 boys came from Maryland and nine from Pennsylvania.

The ratio of boarding students to day students is not known, but information provided by Peter Tome, a student from 1877 to 1879 indirectly indicates a preponderance of boarding students. Tome stated that in his student days, the following four rooming houses served the academy:

In Charge	House (Current Name)	Capacity
Mrs. Amos Sill*	Tyson-Sill	25
Miss Margaret Porter	Wiley	25

Miss Carrie Weir, sister of Mrs. Sill	—	10
Mrs. Little	—	4
Total		64

* Widow of Rev. Amos Sill, principal 1859-62.

Even if the rooming houses were only two-thirds filled, boarding students would make up a large share of the student body in the following years of high enrollment:

Year	Enrollment
1871-72	50
1872-73	82
1877-78	c.60
1878-79	c.60

The academy and the boarding houses worked together closely. A letter to Mrs. Sill from the principal on July 26, 1873 included a check for $150 which paid off the boarding account of the session just ended and added a small advance for the next session. Bechtel enclosed a statement that showed the amount paid on each student. It appears that the academy collected fees for the boarding houses, but it is not evident how much control George Bechtel could exert over the boarding operation. One wonders if the principal had enough time and energy for such supervision even if the boarding house ladies were willing to accept it. Nevertheless, the catalogs of 1873-74, 1883-84, and 1884-85 stated that boarding houses were presided over by ladies of experience who were supervised by the principal. Furthermore, the latter two catalogs state that "these houses leave nothing to be desired in quality and quantity of food and in general provision for the moral and physical well-being of pupils." Something must have gone wrong in the boarding house situation by the end of Bechtel's regime, however, because in his letter of resignation, the principal gave as his first reason for leaving the defective boarding houses which were adversely affecting enrollment.

Eight years after the peak enrollment of 82 in 1873, enrollment declined to 37 in 1881, with an associated strain on the principal's salary and his capability for hiring an adequate assistant. Bechtel reported to the Board of Trustees on June 22, 1882, that he had great difficulty in "attracting the right sort of man" for an assistant teacher. "Meager as the amount [was that was] available for the assistant," Bechtel stated that he himself was "left with little more than the compensation of a district school teacher whose duties are less laborious and responsibilities less weighty than those required by my position." The principal went on to say that "unendowed academies are being pushed to the wall." Despite competition from high schools in cities, however, Bechtel did not believe they could do what West Nottingham Academy could. In the summer of 1882, Bechtel was gratified to report that enrollment had increased in the just-completed school year to 44 from 37 the previous year. The principal reported "the deportment and progress of the pupils to have been in the main satisfactory."

George Bechtel's teaching ability was undiminished after his return to West Nottingham, but his physical ability probably declined during his final years at the academy. Some of Bechtel's former students told Paul Slaybaugh, the academy's headmaster from 1924 to 1949, that they always thought of Bechtel as an old man "because of his chronic illness, his beard and his manner of dress." Yet, he was only 49 at the time of resignation. His students recalled, as reported by Slaybaugh, that:

> Many mornings he was so crippled up with rheumatism that he couldn't walk from his home to the school room—a distance of 60 yards. Several of the boys would carry him down. They had the greatest admiration for his scholarship, deepest respect for him as a man, and highest regard for him as a teacher [so] that they didn't annoy him very much, or give him much cause for employing extreme methods of conduct control. One of his students [Dr. J. M. H. Rowland], Dean of the Medical School of the University of Maryland for 27 years, has reiterated on numerous occasions that Mr. Bechtel was the greatest teacher he has known.

At different times Bechtel made known to the trustees his concern about a variety of issues: the fact that the academy was "very much demoralized by the prevalence of measles" at the close of the 1881–82 session; the unsatisfactory condition of the outhouses which "were open to tramps as well as school;" loss by storms of "grand old trees" which diminished the beauty of the ground around the academy; and lack of stables, which cost enrollment of some day students. In his last year Bechtel recommended that stables be built for a half-dozen horses. The trustees responded with plans that resulted in construction of stables for 20 horses that benefited future students but not Bechtel's.

When George Bechtel offered his resignation to the Board of Trustees on February 28, 1887, he had served as principal in two periods for a total of 20 years, longer than any of his predecessors. Bechtel's achievement seems even more remarkable in view of the frailness of his health, which at times limited his personal mobility. No other principal in the history of the academy has served even for a limited period without being physically mobile. In that respect Bechtel's service reminds one of the presidency of Franklin D. Roosevelt, who served longer than any president but could not move across a room without help.

The tone of Bechtel's letter of resignation probably reflects loss of physical vigor. He began by listing the following shortcomings of the academy:

(1) Boarding accommodations were defective so that enrollment was suffering. (It is not known in what way the private boarding houses near the school incurred Bechtel's criticism.)

(2) The decrease in enrollment had led to a loss of income which in turn did not provide enough money for a "competent assistant for carrying on the work of the school."

(3) Without a competent assistant, Bechtel stated that the personal strain on instruction and discipline were "greater than I should countinue to bear."

In conclusion, Bechtel stated:

I have devoted the efforts of the best years of my life to the work here . . . my aim has been to maintain and if possible increase the reputation of West Nottingham for thorough scholarship. I trust I have not been wholly unsuccessful in securing these results. Under present conditions, however, I do not think it wise to continue the struggle against what appears to me hopeless odds.

The Board of Trustees "reluctantly" accepted Bechtel's resignation because he had "insisted" and passed a series of resolutions that are paraphrased as follows:

(1) We cannot allow this relationship of 15 years* with Mr. Bechtel to close without expressing our esteem for him and our satisfaction with the ability and success with which he has conducted this institution.

(2) We bear testimony to his gentlemanly and Christian deportment, thereby gaining the esteem and respect of the community to his scholarly attainments, his thoroughness as a teacher, his tact in government, and his fidelity and zeal in the discharge of his duties.

(3) Our best wishes go with him for his future success in his chosen profession, and we most cordially recommend him to any party or parties seeking an experienced scholarly, thorough, successful and faithful instructor.

After his resignation, George Bechtel survived only three years, dying at the age of 52. His own claim of some success at the academy was very modest. He was highly successful in achieving his objective of academic excellence; and a number of his students attained distinguished positions in medicine, politics, and business, as the following table shows.

---

* The second of Bechtel's two periods of service.

Selected West Nottingham Students, 1862–1887

	Last Nottingham Year	Other Education	Career
Harry D. Barnes	1886		Medicine
E. Ambrose Bechtel	1883	Johns Hopkins A.B.	Dean, College of Arts and Sciences, Tulane University
George A. Bram	1885		Medicine
Robert S. Brookings	1866	None	Public Servant. Economist. Philanthropist. Founder of Brookings Institution, Washington, D.C.
Howard Bryant	1878		President, Baltimore City Council
J. T. Brown	1862		Medicine
George H. Buck	c. 1870–1875		Business. Wholesale lumber, Port Deposit
George A. Cameron	1882		Medicine
Harry E. Clemson	—		Medicine, Cecil County
Mary L. Clendenin	1901	Baltimore Womans College A.B.	Educator. Teacher at West Nottingham Academy
James Polk Cooley	c. 1881		Farmer. State Senator, South Dakota
A. A. Crothers	1875		Medicine
Austin L. Crothers	—		Governor of Maryland
Charles C. Crothers	c. 1866		Lawyer. State Senator, Elkton, Cecil County
R. R. Crothers	1881		Medicine
Henry C. Deaver	1875		Surgeon
John B. Deaver		Pennsylvania 1877, Pennsylvania Medical School 1878	Surgeon and Professor, Pennsylvania University; President, American College of Surgeons
Henry K. Denlinger	1884		Minister
W. A. Eckels	1879		Medicine
William Steel Evans	1864		Prosecuting Attorney, Cecil County
Joseph Lane Finley	1880		Medicine
John M. T. Finney, Jr.	—		Medicine

Selected West Nottingham Students, 1862–1887 (Cont.)

	Last Nottingham Year	Other Education	Career
James Gayley	1872	Lafayette 1876	Metallurgist. Managing Director, Carnegie Steel; Vice President, U.S. Steel Corporation
Oliver C. Gayley	—	—	Civil Engineer. First Vice President of Pressed Steel Car Co., Pittsburgh
William C. Gayley	1874		Medicine
Edward A. Gillespie	1881		Businessman. Nottingham, Penn.
Frank Gillespie	1884		Medicine
Sidney Hall	1875		Banker. Vice President, U.S. Fidelity & Guaranty Co., Baltimore
James J. Hanna	1883		Businessman. West Nottingham Board of Trustees
A. Lewis Hyde	1874		Minister
Wesley M. Hyde	1870	Lafayette 1873	Minister, Pennsylvania, Ohio, Maryland
John H. Jenness	1879		Medicine
Cecil Kirk	1887		Clerk of Court, Cecil County, elected 1909
Joseph Lort	1864		Medicine
Hiram R. McCullough	1870		Vice President, Chicago and Northwestern Railroad
Benjamin F. Mackall	1870		Pharmacist. As lay reader founded two Episcopal Churches in Fargo, N.D., and Moorhead, Minn.
William Hollingsworth Mackall	1874		Banker. Mayor of Elkton
S. P. Nickle	1882		Medicine
Charles B. Osborne	1874	Lafayette 1879	Farmer, Businessman. West Nottingham Board of Trustees
Alpheus Lee Porter	1885		Medicine
D. M. Regan	1887		Medicine
C. S. Reynolds	1878		Medicine
Harry F. Richards	—		Banker. Vice-President, Integrity Trust, Philadelphia

Selected West Nottingham Students, 1862–1887 (Cont.)

	Last Nottingham Year	Other Education	Career
James N. Richards	1866	Michigan Univ.	Medicine. Fallsington, Pa.
Joseph T. Richards	1864		Chief Engineer for Maintenance, Pennsylvania Railroad
Lewis H. Richards	1867		Lawyer. Media, Pa.
D. H. Richardson	1869		Medicine
J. M. H. Rowland	1886		Obstetrician. Dean, University of Maryland Medical School
Henry Rumer, D. D.	1869	Lafayette 1873 Princeton Theological Seminary 1876	Pastor of White Clay Creek Presbyterian Church, Vice-President of West Nottingham Board of Trustees
Frank Sheppard	1878		Life Insurance. Trustee and supporter of West Nottingham Academy.
Gordon G. Sill	1876		Pharmacist. Rising Sun, Maryland
John B. Slicer	1881		Medicine
William B. Steele	1875	Lafayette 1879	Business. Port Deposit, Maryland. Appointed Trustee of academy in 1891 and served until late 1930s. Probably longest service in academy history.
Arthur H. Stump	1875	St. John's	Judge of Supreme Bench, Baltimore
George Stump	1870		Medicine
Kurtz Taylor	1882		Cecil County Treasurer, elected 1909
Peter E. Tome	1879		Lawyer. City Comptroller, Baltimore
William T. Warburton	1870	Delaware College 1871	Banker. Lawyer. Founded Second National Bank, Elkton, Cecil County
Rowland Watts	1882	Washington College	Educator. Associate Superintendent of Baltimore Public Schools; Dean of Men, Western Maryland College. Medicine
Webster White	1877		Educator. Principal of Maryland and Pennsylvania public schools, state legislator

11

John Conner, 1887–1902

THE RESIGNATION of George K. Bechtel on February 28, 1887, left the Board of Trustees the task of finding a worthy successor to one of West Nottingham Academy's greatest leaders. Samuel A. Gayley, whose staunch leadership of the academy as president of the board dated back to the Civil War, decided that his alma mater, Lafayette College, might be a good place to look for a replacement. At Lafayette's commencement, Gayley asked the clerk of the faculty to recommend a prospect among the graduates. The clerk promptly recommended John G. Conner, a Phi Beta Kappa senior who had delivered the Latin Salutatory at commencement. Unconcerned when he learned that Conner's teaching experience was limited to five months when attending the Bloomsburg State Normal School, Bloomsburg, Pennsylvania, Gayley invited the young graduate to visit West Nottingham the following week. Conner recalled that he was very hospitably entertained by Dr. and Mrs. Gayley. After looking over the school, the community, and its people, Conner "promised to undertake the work."

When school opened in September of 1887, the young Lafayette graduate sported a new beard "in order to disguise my youth somewhat." Conner reported the tactic successful because "some parents who brought sons to school in September talked to me as if I had been through the Civil War." The new principal also had to deal with members of the local community who were upset with boarding students who had damaged property and had generally been an annoyance. To rectify this situation, Connor combined several approaches. The first was to keep the boys busy with sports after classes ended in the afternoon; Conner organized teams that played other schools, insisting on participation by all. Furthermore, the principal required retirement of the boys to their rooms for study at 6:30 p.m. and forbade visits to neighboring towns without consent of the principal. Conner claimed he was successful "in working off the surplus energy that every healthy boy had" because all complaints of student misbehavior in the community ceased after he came to West Nottingham.

Principal John G. Connor had as first assistant, his brother W. S. Conner, whom John described as "the most efficient" teacher at the academy. The presence of his brother at West Nottingham may have allowed John to accomplish at West Nottingham some of the study that was required for the Master of Arts degree which he received from Lafayette in 1890.* The two brothers roomed and boarded with Mrs. Sill along with 8 or 10 of the boarding students. The brothers separated in 1889 when John married Carrie Helen Sciple of Easton, Pennsylvania; and W. S. moved to California, where he taught for many years.

Principal Conner had about 40 students for the start of his first year at West Nottingham. More students reported later in the fall after farm work had been completed. Conner later stated that annual enrollment varied during his administration from 40 to 70 or 75. The following incomplete data from school records shows different categories of students, including the first girls in the history of the academy.

	Graduates		Non-Graduates (Final Year)		Total	Total
	Boys	Girls	Boys	Girls	Girls	Enrollment
1887–88.........	13	0	—	0	0	c.40
1888–89.........	6	0	10	0	0	—
1889–90.........	2	0	11	0	0	—
1890–91.........	5	0	7	0	0	45
1891–92.........	8	0	14	0	0	—
1892–93.........	4	0	28	0	0	—
1893–94.........	1	0	—	0	0	—
1894–95.........	3	0	—	0	0	—
1895–96.........	2	1	15	4	—	32
1896–97.........	3	1	10	5	14	52
1897–98.........	3	1	13	1	—	—
1898–99.........	2	2	7	3	—	—
1899–1900......	1	1	16	3	—	—
1900–01.........	4	4	4	2	12	42
1901–02.........	2	0	8	1	—	—

* J. G. Conner received an honorary degree of Doctor of Humane Letters from Lafayette, his alma mater, in 1947.

Attendance of girls came about, as Conner recalled, because "from time to time" parents in the neighborhood had asked the academy to admit their daughters. Conner and the Board of Trustees were receptive to having the girls because there was no proper secondary school in the community and the girls' parents felt they could not afford to send their daughters to boarding schools. Some of the first girls had been students of a school for girls that George Bechtel, the former West Nottingham principal, conducted in his home until his death in 1890. When Mrs. Bechtel discontinued the school, the trustees decided to admit the girls to the academy. The first girl to graduate was Cora M. Wiley of Ventnor, N.J., a member of the 1896 Class. Another early girl student, Rebecca Gillespie, later was murdered in the Boxer Rebellion in China with her husband, John R. Peale. Another girl, Frances R. Dicky, married her former principal, John G. Conner, in 1923 after the death of Conner's first wife in 1920. Conner's view about the girls at West Nottingham follows:

> They must live together as men and women and should do so early. Both the boys and girls became a little more careful about dress and conduct. They made a real contribution to the school in many ways and my greatest reward for the work I did for the school was to have one of them for my wife and boon companion, and helper in every good work.

Conner employed several women on his teaching staff, including his first wife, Carrie. These were the first female teachers at West Nottingham since the 1840s when the academy had its only previous female teacher, Miss Louise Shotwell. A list of Conner's teachers follows:

1887–1889	W. S. Conner
1889–1890	— England
1889–1896	S. Taylor Wilson
1895–1896	Mrs. J. G. Conner (Carrie Sciple)
1896–1902	Mary F. Gillespie
1896–1897	Horace C. Gillespie, Beaulah Worth Paschall
1899–1900	William C. Wancope, Horace C. Gillespie
	Margaret Vick
	J. Burton Wiley
1900–1901	Thomas P. Scott

During most of Conner's 15 years, the boarding students lived in two houses that were supervised by the principal and conducted by

Mrs. Amos Sill* and Miss Margaret Porter. When John Conner arrived, 8 or 10 boarding students lived in Mrs. Sill's house. If Miss Porter took care of 25, her capacity in the late 1870s, the total number of boarders would be in the 30–35 range. The reduction in boarding capacity from 64 in four rooming houses in the late 1870's to about 35 in two houses after 1887 may relate to Principal Bechtel's complaints about "boarding house deficiencies" in his 1887 letter of resignation. A possibility is that the Board of Trustees disqualified two of the rooming houses to resolve the "deficiencies" before Conner arrived. Conner was never critical of the Sill and Porter houses. The board's decision to build a 20-horse stable in early 1887 makes sense as a move to keep enrollment up with more day students in face of loss of boarding house capacity. Likewise, the admission of girls for the first time in 1895 increased the number of day students. The capacity for boarding students was increased slightly in 1897 with the completion of a handsome Victorian home for the principal, which could also accommodate a few boarding students.

Boarding students could reach West Nottingham on a now-abandoned branch of the Pennsylvania Railroad that ran southeastward through Colora** and followed a steep ravine down to the Susquehanna River en route from Philadelphia to Baltimore. Three trains arrived daily from Baltimore and two from Philadelphia. A carriage from the academy met arriving students. Conner reported that students from the surrounding countryside "rode or drove [from as far as] four or five miles to school and back every day" and stated that Robert H. Kay and a brother "did not miss a day in a year even when the roads were so drifted with snow that they had to . . . take to the fields."

The 1896–97 catalog announced that the new house being built for the principal would have a bathroom and be steamheated. The principal was to "take a few students into his family" for an additional $12.50 per quarter above the standard charge of $50 for room and board and tuition. The higher rate for living in the principal's home presumably reflected the indoor bathroom facilities. The standard overall $50 charge

---

* Widow of the Civil War principal.
** The community at the rail stop had come to be called Colora because Lloyd Balderston had named his farm Colus Ora, Latin for Breezy Ridge, when he moved to the area in 1842. Local usage had transformed the Latin into Colora.

per quarter for boarding students in the 1896–97 school year was the same as given in the 1873–74 and 1883–84 catalogs except that a science curriculum cost $5 per quarter more in the earlier catalogs. Room and board could be paid by doing chores. Franklin P. Williams of the Class of 1897 recalled "how I earned my board and keep by manicuring the cow, making the garden, and keeping the wood box filled for Mrs. Sill."

The 1896–97 catalog describes the academy's courses of instruction as follows:

Three courses of study lead to graduation—the Classical, the Scientific, and the English. These courses of study have been prescribed to fit students for our best colleges and scientific schools, but the training which is necessary for successfully meeting the demands of college life, ought to be no less useful to students in the university of the world.

It is advised that students pursue one of the prescribed courses, as it has been found that better results are secured in this manner than by desultory selection by the student himself. Few students have the experience or ability to choose such subjects as will develop them most. A diploma will be awarded to those students who successfully complete a course.

CLASSICAL COURSE

1st Year

First Term	*Second Term*
Latin Lessons	Latin Lessons
Arithmetic	Arithmetic
English Grammar	English Grammar
Geography	Geography
Autobiography of Benj. Franklin	Physiology

2nd Year

Latin Readings (Eutropius, Nepos, Caesar, etc.)	Latin Readings
English Lessons (Rhetoric)	English Lessons
Algebra	Algebra
Greek	Greek
History, United States	Physical Geography

3rd Year

Cicero
Anabasis
Algebra
English Literature
Civil Government

Cicero and Virgil
Anabasis and Homer
Geometry
American Literature
General History

4th Year

Virgil
Homer
Geometry
French or German
Political Economy

Latin, Special College requirements
Greek, Special College requirements
Geometry
French or German

Drawing, Declamations, Compositions, and Debates throughout the classical course.

SCIENTIFIC COURSE

The Scientific Course is the same as the Classical Course except that the Natural Sciences are substituted for Greek.

ENGLISH COURSE

1st Year

First Term

Latin Lessons
Arithmetic
English Grammar
Geography
Autobiography of Benj. Franklin

Second Term

Latin Lessons
Arithmetic
English Grammar
Geography
Physiology

2nd Year

English Lessons (Rhetoric)
History, United States
Algebra
Physics
Civil Government

English Lessons
Physical Geography
Algebra
Geometry
Book-keeping

3rd Year

English Literature	American Literature
Algebra	Chemistry
Geometry	Geometry
Political Economy	General History
French or German	French or German

Drawing, Declamations, Compositions, and Debates throughout the English course.

Satisfactory completion of any of the foregoing three- or four-year courses indicates diligence and achievement by students and teachers. West Nottingham graduates entered Princeton, Lafayette, Lehigh, Johns Hopkins, Pennsylvania, Maryland, Washington College and Western Maryland College. Conner recalled that "no student failed to be admitted if he had our certificate and none failed after admission. Some West Nottingham students failed who entered without our certification," Conner said. All three courses prepared students for college; Conner later claimed that preparation for college was the best preparation for students going directly into business. In support of this contention, Conner cited his post-West Nottingham experience as a business manager when he found that the honor graduates of high schools did better in business jobs than business college graduates. Conner felt that "the important thing is that a student learn to do well whatever he does."

The 1896–97 catalog stated that "we ought to have students before the age of 12 before their habits have become so fixed that they are not easily changed." This statement implies that the academy planned to graduate students at the age of 15 or that the academy provided pre-high school classes for the young students. In regard to parents, the catalog stated that the academy would report to them every four weeks on attendance, deportment, and class work. Parents, it said, should examine the report cards thoroughly and they were admonished:

> If you wish your children to be interested, you must be interested yourself. Do not criticize the teacher; you destroy his power for doing good. If you do not agree with him as to the policy pursued, go to him not the child.

John Conner had entered college with little or no training in public speaking and did not want West Nottingham boys and girls to have the same handicap. The Irving Literary Society helped meet this need by giving members assignments to tell a story, to introduce an important speaker, or to make an impromptu speech before Conner came to West Nottingham. Conner encouraged public speaking with an annual debating contest each June in which the winner won a gold medal of $10 value. The Board of Trustees chose the judge for the contest which involved at least four but no more than six debaters. The winner in 1895 was John A. Nesbitt, an outstanding scholar and athlete who would eventually serve as President of the Board of Trustees. The academy continued its traditional requirements that boarding students attend church on Sunday and that all students attend non-sectarian Bible classes, each with his own Bible in hand. Conner believed that "the Christian religion is the only foundation for character" and stated that most students who stayed long enough to graduate were "consistent church members." Conner was very conscious of the interdependence of the West Nottingham Church and the academy which had worked together for so many years. Conner further stated that "most of the prominent men in the community had been educated at the academy, and they made an intelligent church."

John G. Conner organized the first athletic teams at West Nottingham that played other schools. Yale and Harvard had played their first football game in 1886 and Conner fielded a West Nottingham football team soon after he arrived in 1887. West Nottingham adopted maroon and white as school colors and called its teams the Rams. The football and baseball teams used the south end of the academy's stables for a dressing room.

Conner not only organized the first Ram teams, but played on the football teams himself. His account follows:

> An athletic association was formed to have charge of baseball, football, and basketball. There was no fund for athletics, and the association had to finance itself, the players buying their own uniforms. Football was an entirely new sport, no one in the community had ever seen a game, so we had to start from scratch. I enjoyed the game, and played with the boys every day from the beginning of school in September to the Christ-

mas holidays. After that time, we played basketball in the grove in front of the Old Academy building until after the middle of March, when baseball began. In the first game of football with Tome Institute I had my nose broken. One football team defeated Delaware College. They got even with us, by refusing to pay the five-dollar guarantee when we went over to Newark for a game of baseball; said they would send it, but up to date I have never heard of it being paid.

The reason for the generally good teams Nottingham turned out, was our policy to have every boy play, unless physically unfit. Sometimes the older boys were inclined to reject the younger ones, but yielded on my insistence. I wish to say for the boys that we played together always in harmony and no attempt was ever made when back in the school room to take advantage of this familiarity.

We played a baseball game with Lincoln University.* We were never treated more courteously anywhere. They gave us lunch, and a square deal on the diamond. Of course they won, but by a small margin. When a long left field foul was made the umpire threw out to me in the pitcher's box, a ball that felt like a bundle of hay. Thinking the black boy could not hit it out of the diamond, I pitched him a nice easy underhand ball. He hit it to the sky, but the center fielder had plenty of time to let it fall into his mitt.

The West Grove High School team was defeated on our grounds. When we went up there for a return game, they had some big Irishmen from the nearby marble quarry. They knew no football, only rough house. I came out of the game with both eyes in mourning, and a lump on top of my head like an egg where one of them slugged me as I was rising from scrimmage. That ended relations with West Grove.

Generally speaking, the best athletes were the best students. I could mention any number, but I might omit some who should be named. But I must name John A. Nesbitt, a student of the highest type. Tho small of stature, [he was a] good football and baseball player, [and a] fine influence in school or on the field.

The Ram football team of 1895 was the terror of every school within 50 miles that had taken up the sport. The strength of the team, com-

---

* This school, located in Pennsylvania, was founded by Presbyterians in 1854 to educate Negroes.

posed of 10 students and the principal, did not depend on the size of the players; only three were as heavy as 175 pounds. The team's pride, toughness, and speed made it formidable. Helmets and shoulder pads were not yet in use, but long hair was thought to provide protection of a sort. Tightly-laced but unpadded canvas jackets braced collar bones and ribs. The players donned quilty-padded knickers, wrapped towels around their legs and covered them with knee-length stockings.

Dave Hanna, a day student from Rising Sun, recalled that the big game of 1895 was against the Washington College varsity at Chestertown, Maryland. The morning of the game, Dave arose at 4 a.m., put on his uniform, ate breakfast, and by 5 a.m. had saddled the family's best horse for the ride to Port Deposit. An hour later, Dave and his teammates boarded the early steamboat for Betterton, which lay across Chesapeake Bay. At Betterton, they climbed on a horse-drawn bus that got them to Chestertown at 12:30 p.m., in time for the game at 1 p.m. Hanna couldn't recall details of the contest, but remembered that West Nottingham edged Washington College by one point. On Tuesday, November 5, 1895, "Old West Nottingham" toppled Oxford 32-0, the fourth straight win over that team. The West Nottingham *Literary Advance* reported that a "number of Jacob Tome students were out to see the game," apparently scouting. "On the second down, H. Gillespie, seizing the ball, rounded the end and scored the first touchdown to the consternation of the awestricken opponent." West Nottingham's points came from three touchdowns by Childs, two by Gillespie, and one by R. Nesbitt; Lawson Tosh kicked four goals out of six.

In early 1902 Conner suddenly had the opportunity to replace his uncle as president of the Conner Millwork Company in Trenton, N.J. After serving as principal for 15 years, his only job since graduating from Lafayette, Conner welcomed the opportunity to manage a business. He did not forget West Nottingham, however, but supported it with generous contributions for the rest of his life. In addition, Conner conscientiously served as a member of the Board of Trustees for many years; he was an honorary member when he died in 1961 at the age of 94.

During his term of office, Principal John C. Conner had wrought important changes in the academy's life without apparent opposition, namely, admission of girls, regular employment of female teachers, and the beginning of varsity athletics. The changes probably came so easily because of Conner's ability to get along with everyone, including his football players, his brother, and the Board of Trustees.*

Conner attended the board's twice-yearly meetings. When the president of the board, Jacob Tome, became quite deaf in his later years, he would have the principal "sit at his right hand to repeat what [Tome] did not hear; he could hear what [Conner] said perfectly." Conner described all of the members as "very estimable men, foremost citizens of the county who faithfully attended board meetings."

Although Conner obviously had had a comfortable relationship with the board members, he remarked many years later on the academy's failure throughout its history to attract large contributions. Conner declared that "lack of vision seems to have characterized the management of West Nottingham. They were always satisfied with what they had." Conner included himself among those who had not obtained significant contributions. He believed that "I might have secured an endownment from Mr. Tome ... if it had not been for my youth and inexperience."

Although John Conner did not build an endowment for West Nottingham Academy, he ably upheld its tradition of educating students who would become worthy citizens and leaders. The number of achievers was large, especially in proportion to the relatively small number of students whom Conner graduated. The careers of some former Conner students follow.

Careers of West Nottingham Students, 1888–1902

	Last West Nottingham Year	Career
Chester R. Atkinson	1902	Mining Engineer
John Leonard Baer	1898	Anthropoligist at Smithsonian. Died in 1924 during Darien Expedition in Panama.
Arthur G. Barett	1891	Medicine
Henry S. Breckinridge	1900	Assistant Secretary of War in President Wilson's cabinet, Lt-Col US Army, World War I

* See Appendix A for list of trustees in Conner's term.

Howard Brown	1893	Medicine
Frances Dickey	1901	Teacher
Horace C. Gillespie	1892	Headmaster, West Hottingham Academy, 1908–1911
A. M. Hanna	1888	Banker
William G. Jack	1899	Medicine. Bank President
Walter T. Johnson	1894	Lawyer
Robert H. Kay	1902	Superintendent of Coal Mines for Thropp Co. in Saxton, Pa.
Walter B. Kirk	1888	Medicine, Graduated from Maryland Univ. Medical School, Baltimore.
Russell H. McCullough	1892	Medicine
John H. Magraw	1892	Lawyer
John Alison Nesbitt	1897	Chaplain in France, World War I. President of Board of Trustees, West Nottingham Academy, 1928–1937. Pastor, Catonsville Presbyterian Church
James L. Nesbitt	1901	Lawyer
Charles Rea	1889	Medicine
G. Hampton Richards	1900	Medicine. Volunteer with British and Doctor with U.S. Rainbow Division in World War I.
Harry F. Richards	1893	Banker. Treasurer of Federal Trust Company, Philadelphia
Earnest S. Rowland	1892	Medicine
Thomas B. Shannon	1891	Minister
Cecil C. Squier	1889	Lawyer
Roger J. Whiteford	1902	Lawyer. Named General Counsel of FHA by President Roosevelt in 1935
J. B. Wiley	1889	Educator. Teacher, West Nottingham Academy; Principal, Red Bank, N.J. High School; Superintendent of Schools, Morristown, N.J.
Franklin P. Williams	1897	Naval Officer
S. Taylor Wilson	1889	Businessman. President, Trippett & Wood Co. (Manufacturer of Iron Bridges & Standpipes)

12

Eleven Principals, 1902–1924

BETWEEN 1902 and 1924 eleven generally capable and conscientious principals served West Nottingham Academy well, overcoming to some extent the shortness of their terms. The following tables give the principals, their staffs, and enrollments for this period.

Enrollment Data, 1902–1924

	Graduates Boys	Graduates Girls	Non-Graduates in Final Year Boys	Non-Graduates in Final Year Girls	Total Girls	Total Enrollment
1902–03	5	0	4	1	—	—
1903–04	0	1	8	3	—	—
1904–05	2	4	4	0	—	c. 20
1905–06	3	2	6	2	14	33
1906–07	5	4	15	2	15	41
1907–08	1	2	5	2	—	—
1908–09	0	0	5	6	—	—
1909–10	0	0	13	2	—	*
1910–11	8	3	7	2	11	43
1911–12	1	1	11	4	—	—
1923–13	7	2	8	2	—	—
1913–14	0	0	5	1	—	—
1914–15	0	1	6	3	—	—
1915–16	3	1	4	5	—	—
1916–17	1	3	6	9	17	30
1917–18	0	1	8	3	—	35
1918–19	0	2	5	3	16	38
1919–20	0	0	7	3	17	37
1920–21	1	2	5	4	—	—
1921–22	3	3	4	5	—	—
1922–23	2	4	9	11	—	—
1923–24	4	11	4	5	16	25

* The total is not known, but the tennis club had 25 members.

Principals and Teachers, 1902–1924

Service	Principal	Service	Teachers
1902–1908	Clifton C. Walker Hamilton A.B., M.A.; 1899, 1900		Mary McCachran, Assistant; Metzger College A.B. Mary F. Gillespie, Music Mary L. Fryer, Assistant
1908–1911	Horace C. Gillespie, West Nottingham 1892, Johns Hopkins A.B. 1902	1909–1910	Hubertis M. Cummings, Latin, Greek, French, English; Princeton A.B., A.M.
		1908	Marie Ebeling, Piano
		1909–1910	Mary L. Clendenin, German History, English, Women's College, Baltimore
		1909–1913	Rev. Samuel Polk,* Bible, Football Coach (Pastor, West Nottingham Presbyterian Church); Princeton B.D.
		1909–1913	Mrs. Samuel Polk Drawing; Maryland Institute of Art
			Robert M. Woodbury, Greek, German, History; Clark A.B.
			Flora E. Farmer, Latin, English, French, Music; Illinois A.M.
1911–1913	William F. H. Wentzel Science, Penn State M.S.	1911–1912	Emma Forster, Language Bryn Mawr
		1911–1912	Jessica R. Terry, Piano and Organ; Leefson-Hille Conservatory of Music
		1912–1913	Elizabeth D. Schultz, Language
		1909–1913	Rev. Samuel Polk,* Bible, Football Coach
		1909–1913	Mrs. Samuel Polk, Drawing
		1910–1913	Albert L. Lawsing, Agriculture
1913–1914	George B. Pfeiffer		
1914–1915	Rev. F. Harl Huffman* A.B., A.M.		Carl G. Eliason George B. Pfeiffer

ELEVEN PRINCIPALS, 1902-1924

1915-1916	Walter L. Graefe A.B.	1915-1916	George F. Marsh, B.S.A.
		1915-1919	Mary E. Kennedy
1916-1917	Rev. F. Harl Huffman* A.B., A.M.	1915-1917	Walter L. Graefe, A.B.
		1915-1919	Mary E. Kennedy
		1910-1913 1916-1917	Albert L. Lawsing, Penn. State A.B., Agriculture, Sciences, Mathematics
		1916-1917	Carl Rowe
1917-1919	Joseph F. Leuthner	1915-1919	Mary E. Kennedy
			Rev. F. Harl Huffman, Bible
			Mrs. J. F. Leuthner
			Elizabeth Yingst
			Rev. A. B. Hallock,* Bible
1919-1920	T. H. Grim A.M.	1916-1917	Carl Rowe
		1919-1920	Miss Faukie Kline
1920-1922	Frederick A. Torrey A.M. Princeton, Language & Mathematics		Anna P. Torrey, Trenton State Normal A.B., History, English, Drawing, & Domestic Science
			Mary E. Weaver, Sasquehanna U. A.B., Science & Latin
			Ruth Benson, L.W.H. National Training School, Eighth Grade
			Rev. Thomas P. McKee* Wooster A.B., Bible
1922-1923	Dean E. Shull		Mrs. Dean E. Shull
			Mrs. Eleanor J. Moore, Eighth Grade
			Thomas W. Smith, Dickinson A.B., Assistant Teacher
			Mrs. Fannie Rosenfeld
			Rev. Thomas P. McKee, Bible
1923-1924	William K. Cummings B.S., M.A.		E. W. Chamberlain
			Mrs. E. W. Chamberlain
			Rev. Thomas P. McKee* Wooster A.B.

* Pastor of West Nottingham Presbyterian Church

The first principal, Clifton C. Walker, served the longest, succeeding J. G. Conner in 1902 and staying until the end of the 1907–1908 school year. Walker's sister, Eunice, attended West Nottingham for three years while her brother was principal. She recalled happenings both "hilarious and otherwise." Eunice remembered that her brother and two members of the Board of Trustees, J. J. Hanna and William Fryer, traveled to Baltimore to visit "former students and solicit funds, but it was at that time uphill work." The Irving Literary Society met on a Friday afternoon each month. Its members provided each other with a program of "music, debates, recitations, and declarations." The academy conducted a speaking contest each year in which four girls and four boys were chosen for the final competition.

Principal Walker's period of service was marked by the purchase of the Magraw stone mansion and farm of 260 acres, which were adjacent to the academy. The Board of Trustees planned to use the large mansion to provide student rooming and boarding. There were few, if any, boarding students, however, until Paul Slaybaugh came as headmaster in 1924. The academy lost the handsome residence for its principals in the summer of 1908 after Walker had completed his third and final year and departed for New York State. The Victorian home, built just 11 years before, burned to the ground after being struck by lightning.

Horace C. Gillespie succeeded Walker as principal in the fall of 1908. He had been an academy student from 1887 to 1893 and had taught at West Nottingham in 1897 and 1899. At this time, the Irving Society, unlike in earlier years, included all the students. One of the society's main projects was to print and publish the *Literary Advance* which hitherto had been handwritten. The *Advance* reported on student and alumni news and also published stories, poems, and essays written by students. The following appreciation of spring at West Nottingham appeared in the April 1910 issue.

SPRING IN WEST NOTTINGHAM

Some may imagine that spring is very much alike in all parts of the world—or rather in all places in the same latitude. It is evident that such persons have never spent a spring in West Nottingham.

With spring fever, usually comes a desire to go off somewhere. But around West Nottingham all is "somewhere," anywhere. The great trees, where the gay squirrels chatter and sport over the leafy branches, invite one to linger on the benches below, or to wander dreamily beneath their shade to pick the clusters of bluettes and deep-eyed violets that dot the grass. Or, if fancy chooses, one may search through the woods dodging under snowy dogwood boughs to find the shy spring beauty, the hepatica, the bloodroot or dainty anemone, or down in the marsh, the yellow marigolds. But the prize of all the wildflowers grows among the cedars and mosses, the darling of the hillside—the pink arbutus.

George C. Garrett was the editor of the publication as of December 1908 and continued as editor until his graduation in 1911. Six boys and two girls worked with Garrett as assistant editors in December 1908, and by June of 1910 there were 13 editors, including five girls.

While Gillespie was principal, the Board of Trustees decided to use the adjacent Magraw farm as a means of adding an agriculture course to the curriculum. Gillespie had the task of explaining the board's plan at a meeting of the Cecil County Farmers Club in the Spring of 1910. By way of introduction, he reminded his audience of the competition faced by the academy from the well-financed private Tome School in Port Deposit and the numerous public high schools. The agricultural education would help meet this competition and also serve the surrounding agricultural community. Gillespie explained that the new course would help boys who wished to practice agriculture in Cecil County but who were not interested in college. Furthermore, the farm could serve as a local experiment station to help solve Cecil County problems. In conclusion, Principal Gillespie sought the support of the Farmers Club to obtain an increase in the state's regular support of the academy from $500 to $3,000 to finance the agricultural course the following year. The Board of Trustees also presented their case directly to the appropriate committee of the Maryland Commission on Education. The board's lobbying efforts for financing the course were apparently successful because Albert Lawsing, a Penn State graduate, began to teach a course in agriculture at the academy in September 1910. The board provided him with a laboratory and paid him a monthly salary. Lawsing conducted the program for three years, skipped two years, and then was back on the academy staff for the 1916–17 session. Since then, the academy has not revived this effort.

During Gillespie's years, West Nottingham athletic teams won some victories and suffered a few lopsided defeats. In the fall of 1908, the football team played six games and was beaten six times, the last being a 53–0 shellacking by Havre de Grace High School on Thanksgiving Day. The *Literary Advance* reported that "during the last half the field was practically covered by the crowd; a circle about 10 yards across was left for the players." In commenting on the disastrous season, the *Advance* stated, "There is a tendency in the schools of the surrounding towns to play boys on the team who are not bona fide students." Undaunted by the losses of the 1908 team, the 1909 gridders started the next season "with plenty of energy and enthusiasm." Although the second team was too weak to provide realistic opposition in practice, the first team had mastered a number of plays for the first game. The team's record for the season follows:

West Nottingham		Opponents
27	Kennett Square	11
6	Tome School (Olympians)	16
23	Elkton High School	0
17	Elkton High School	0
10	Oxford High School	12
12	Oxford High School	0
0	Tome School (Pythians)	35
95		74

The West Nottingham baseball team of 1909 defeated Calvert High School twice and Oxford and East Nottingham High Schools; it lost to Avondale, Tome, and East Nottingham in a return game. The Tome loss came after a spur-of-the-moment invitation to West Nottingham on the morning of the day the game was to be played. The Rams, loath to ignore a challenge, could hardly wait until the end of afternoon classes before setting out by horse and buggy for Port Deposit. By 4:30 p.m., the teams were ready to play in weather that the *Advance* described as "outrageously cold with a high wind blowing" even though it was late in May. Tome ignored the weather, swamping West Nottingham 16 to 1. The following spring so many boys wanted to play baseball that West Nottingham fielded two teams. The second team scored two victories in its only games, but the first team could win but two out of nine games. Besides two varsity teams, all of the academy was divided into the Maroons and Whites who played a best three out of five series. The Maroons won the academy championship in four games.

Principal Gillespie was paid under an arrangement whereby he received the annual $500 appropriation from the state and then added to his salary with student payments for tuition. The principal was responsible for providing board for the students and so had to break even in that enterprise as well as collect tuition from the students. By December 3, 1910, the principal had to ask the board to advance him $500 because the state appropriation had not yet come through. The trustees complied and, sensing Gillespie's difficulties, appointed a committee on February 3, 1911 to see about relieving the principal of boarding the students and paying him a regular salary. The board was too late; it received Gillespie's resignation on March 10. Gillespie's financial difficulties were not over, however; on April 7, he informed the Board that his indebtedness from school operations at the end of the year would be about $1,000. The board refused to assume the debts in return for a personal note of indebtedness from the principal. But by June 30 the board did accept Gillespie's notes of indebtedness for remaining obligations. While Gillespie was beset by financial problems, he managed to graduate eleven students in his final year, the highest number between 1888 and 1924.

Despite Gillespie's experience with the board, which might have led to bitter memories, he wrote fondly of the academy in sending greetings on the occasion of West Nottingham's bicentennial celebration in 1946. Gillespie stated that "through all the long years of almost heartbreaking effort made by principal after principal there has remained unbroken and abiding belief [by teachers and students] . . . that there can be no true education that does not give first place to the development of moral character, coupled with the influence of religion."

In the spring of 1911 the task of finding a replacement for Principal Horace Gillespie was taken up by Albert Lawsing, the instructor in agriculture. Lawsing thought that one of his former classmates at Penn State, William F. H. Wentzel, might be interested. He visited Wentzel at California, Pa., where Wentzel was probably associated with the State Teachers College. Wentzel recalled years later how much the West Nottingham catalog had impressed him because of "the beautiful setting of the Magraw building and the remarkably attractive rural environment." Wentzel suffered a letdown when he visited West Nottingham "and cast my eyes upon the three exceedingly modest classrooms which constituted the academy." Nevertheless, Wentzel accepted the board's telegraphed offer of $1,200 per year on June 8, 1911. Much later in his life, Wentzel described his two-year sojourn at West Nottingham as follows:

> Our small group of boys became enthusiastic for athletic prowess, and with a team that required a substantial majority of the boys to make a minimum squad, went forth with the type of ambition that brought creditable success. For the steering of this program, strange to say, we depended on Reverend [Samuel] Polk, our beloved minister in the local [West Nottingham Presbyterian] church, to function on the faculty of the Academy, as athletic coach, teacher of Bible, and cultural and spiritual advisor. To broaden the scope of opportunity in the school, Mrs. Polk, the pastor's wife, provided teaching in art.
> Professor Lawsing assumed the task of custodian of buildings and property along with a liberal and varied scope of teaching in agriculture and the mastery of the science of crop production. A special teacher in languages, a full schedule for the Principal in history and mathematics, and scientific subjects by our master of agriculture served basically to carry on the much overloaded teaching program.
> After two years effort, long on energetic and devoted service and short on essential patience, the humble headmaster accepted an attractive call from the State Teachers College, California, Pennsylvania, and surrendered the reins of noble West Nottingham to more worthy hands.

On February 10, 1913, in Principal Wentzel's last year of service, the Board of Trustees received an offer by the Presbytery and Synod of Baltimore to establish a college at West Nottingham if the board turned over the academy and farm to the Synod of Baltimore free of all debts. The Presbyterian Board of Colleges in New York would provide an endowment of $150,000 for the project. Looking with favor on the proposition, the board appointed James J. Hanna as chairman of the committee to raise the money to pay off the $7,000 mortgage on the farm. Hanna was a West Nottingham graduate of 1883 who had been a member of the board at least since 1906. Hanna handled the problem of the $7,000 mortgage by taking it over himself. Subsequently, a number of contributors from the West Nottingham neighborhood and alumni elsewhere apparently paid Hanna all or a substantial portion of the money he had needed to buy the mortgage. Another condition required by the Synod of Baltimore was that the synod would select future members of the academy's Board of Trustees. Accordingly, board meetings of July 6 and November 26, 1915, implemented the desired changes in membership by the following actions:

(1) On July 6, the board accepted resignations from the following members:

     Charles K. Abrahams
     Howard Bryant
     H. T. Porter
     William F. Warburton
     Dr. J. M. Rowland

On December 27, the Board accepted additional resignations from:

     Robert F. Cameron
     W. B. Steel
     Rev. F. H. Huffman
     Charles S. Pyle

(2) On December 27, 1915, the board elected the following new members who had been nominated by the Baltimore Synod. Four were to serve terms of four years; and five, terms of six years:

Rev. Paul R. Hickok	Washington, D.C.
Charles B. Osborne	Aberdeen, Md.
Rev. Henry Rumer, D.D.	Darlington, Md.
Rev. William Crawford	Wilmington, Del.
Frank Sheppard	Wilmington, Del.
John McKinzie	Baltimore, Md.
Judge Stanton J. Peele	Chevy Chase, Md.
Rev. John Palmer, D.D.	Washington, D.C.
John B. Larner	—
Rev. F. H. Huffman*	Pastor, West Nottingham Presbyterian Church

(3) To provide continuity and satisfy a requirement of the academy's new charter that three board members be from Cecil County, the board

---

* Huffman's term may not have been stipulated, but he served at least until 1926.

retained the following old members whose terms were to expire on January 10, 1918:

> James J. Hanna
> William F. Fryer
> S. J. Wiley

(4) The nine new members, three old members and Rev. F. H. Huffman (elected after resigning from the old board) brought the number of trustees to 13, the number stipulated by the new charter, which was adopted by the board on November 26, 1915.

Although the Synod of Baltimore did take over jurisdiction of the academy, the plan to establish a college with a $150,000 endowment did not get past the idea stage. The financial support from the General Board of Education of the Presbyterian Church USA did not exceed $1,900 in any one year until Paul Slaybaugh arrived in the fall of 1924. Then the board began to contribute $5,500 annually.

While the board was in the midst of its membership changes, it continued past practices for finding a principal. William Wentzel's successor as principal, George B. Pheiffer, chose to serve only for the 1913–14 school year. Belatedly learning of Pheiffer's plans, the trustees tried the time-honored procedure of electing the pastor of the West Nottingham Presbyterian Church to be principal of the academy. In this case, the pastor, F. Harl Huffman, had not been warned even though he was a member of the board. Huffman's fellow board members, sensing his surprise, decided to give him a little time to make up his mind. They discussed a few other matters in a desultory way, apparently hoping that Huffman would decide before the end of the meeting. In the end the board got its principal, as evidenced at a board meeting the following week in which Huffman proposed to prepare and have printed 300 school catalogs and made a motion to advertise the academy in the *Philadelphia Inquirer,* the *Baltimore Sun, Midland Journal* (Rising Sun, Md.), *Oxford Press* (Oxford, Pa.) and *Cecil Democrat.* George Pheiffer, no longer the principal, accepted the board's offer to stay on to teach mathematics, science, and Bible. Huffman served as principal for one year, skipped a year, and then served again in the 1916–17 session. Thereafter, he taught the academy Bible classes for a year or two and continued as an active member of the Board of Trustees until June

1926. No other principal served more than two years until Paul Slaybaugh became headmaster in 1924.

Besides the shortness of terms of its principals and limited financial support from the Presbyterians, the academy had to adjust to the conditions that arose after United States entered World War I. The United States declared war on Germany on April 6, 1917. On May 3 the academy's Board of Trustees decided to close school a month early because of the great demand for labor on farms from where most of the students came. The academic program had already been weakened by the departure of two teachers for war work. On June 7, the board granted a request from Rev. John Nesbitt, a member from Catonsville, Md., that a Catonsville troop of Boy Scouts be allowed to use the dormitories for a month beginning on June 25. The Boy Scouts planned to work on the farms in the community "owing to the serious need for food in the great world crisis." The boys would bring their own cots and cooking utensils and would pay for anything broken. The board decided upon a charge of $12 for each boy for the month.

Usually sound of judgment on educational issues, the Board of Trustees was carried away by the excitement that arose during the last great German offensives on the Western Front in the spring of 1918. The minutes of the board's meeting of June 24, 1918, follow:

> Being impressed by the fact that we are in the midst of war and that German propaganda is being disseminated throughout the country, Mr. Hanna moved that the teaching of the German language be discontinued and that German be stricken from the curriculum. He also recommended that French or Italian be required in its stead. This resolution was passed and the recommendation adopted.
>
> It was then resolved that each day there be the singing of the Star Spangled Banner, and that a flag be placed in the school rooms and the children taught the customary salute of the flag. This resolution was adopted."

Later in 1918, the influenza epidemic, which claimed 20 million lives worldwide, struck relatively close to West Nottingham when Philadelphia suffered the worst 24-hour loss of life in its history, 289 flu deaths on October 6. The academy closed for a time. A presumption that there was no West Nottingham loss of life is supported by the absence of any reference to victims at the meeting of the trustees on February 10, 1919, in which they recommended to the principal that "the daily and weekly amount of work be increased so as to make up as much as possible of the time lost during the influenza [epidemic]."

The academy's enrollment stayed in the 35–40 range during the two war years (1917–19), but the only graduates were three girls. The postwar years showed a steady increase of graduates from none in 1920 to 15 in 1924, the most since 1886 when George Bechtel was principal. However, the academy had become a day school for the surrounding countryside in contrast to the many 18th and 19th Century students who came from other parts of Maryland and other states. Another change was the presence of a large proportion of girls in the student body. After the admission of a few girls as day students in 1895, their number had gradually increased until they were a majority in the 1923–24 session. That year, 11 of the 15 graduates were girls.

The acquisition of the large Magraw home in 1906 to accommodate boarding students was not followed by a concerted effort to recruit them; consequently, few came. By 1923–24, there were none. Part of the trouble probably lay in the board's practice of putting the responsibility of managing the rooming and boarding facilities on the principal even to the extent of having him take personal financial responsibility. Principal Gillespie had gotten behind in collecting fees from the students for room and board to the extent of $2,000 before he left after two years. This type of arrangement with the principals may have reduced their effectiveness as teachers and supervisors of teachers and led to their early departure. Nevertheless, the individual efforts of principals and teachers kept the academy in operation. In the absence of any endowment or long-range plans, the future looked typically unpromising in the spring of 1924 when the trustees undertook the too frequent task of finding a new principal.

13

Growth as Boarding School under Paul Slaybaugh, 1924–1949

THE HISTORY of West Nottingham Academy in the second quarter of the 20th Century starts at Mercersburg Academy in Mercersburg, Pennsylvania, in the spring of 1924. Mercersburg had a handsome set of buildings on a large campus and a reputation that had induced President Calvin Coolidge to send his two sons there. The headmaster was William Mann Irvine who confidently and capably managed the academy. One of Irvine's instructors in math was 28-year-old J. Paul Slaybaugh who lived in and supervised the dormitory with the rowdiest boys. Slaybaugh had been restless for several weeks since he had learned of an opening for the job of headmaster at West Nottingham Academy in Maryland. He already knew something of the school— that it was small and served a rural neighborhood in Cecil County. One of his Dickinson College classmates had briefly taught there. Slaybaugh wasn't dwelling on its present status, however, but was dreaming of what West Nottingham Academy could be—a prosperous boarding school for boys like Mercersburg, directed by Headmaster J. Paul Slaybaugh. Perhaps his dream for West Nottingham's future also was affected by some awareness of its proud past—filled with achievements of its 18th and 19th Century Presbyterian teachers and alumni of Scotch-Irish descent, Slaybaugh's own ancestry on his mother's side. Slaybaugh's restlessness became so evident that William Irvine, the brusque headmaster at Mercersburg, asked "What are you thinking about, Paul?" Slaybaugh immediately informed his supervisor of the West Nottingham opening and of the attraction this challenge held for him. Irvine replied, "I know that school. I took two football players from there in 1914. It is rundown and it will take a lot of effort to put it on its feet." He offered his math instructor a substantial raise; but then, sensing Slaybaugh's determination, Irvine gave his blessing, adding, "I'll even help you after you get there if I can."

Encouraged by his supervisor's attitude, Slaybaugh set out in his Chevrolet to visit West Nottingham. Upon arrival, he was met by James J. Hanna, a member of the Board of Trustees who lived near the academy. It was late so Hanna took the prospective headmaster to a tiny store across the road from the graveyard of the West Nottingham Church. The proprietor agreed to put Slaybaugh up for the night in the unheated bedroom on the second floor. It was a raw, wet night in March. Recalling the discomfort of that night years later, Slaybaugh wondered at his own persistence the next morning in pursuing the position at West Nottingham. Undaunted, though, Slaybaugh inspected the school. He found a student body of 25, 16 girls and 9 boys.

A century before in the 1820s, there had been no girls and around 20 boys, of whom a few lived in private boarding houses in the neighborhood. In 1924 there were no boarding students although some of the girls stayed overnight in the old Magraw House when the weather was too severe to reach home by foot. Much of the campus was a wilderness of brush and briars that had grown up since the purchase of the old Magraw mansion and farm in 1906. The only other academy building was the ornate brick structure built during the last year of the Civil War, where academy classes had been held ever since.

As Paul Slaybaugh thought the situation over on his drive back to Mercersburg, he concluded that he would need help if he were to take charge of West Nottingham Academy. He visited without delay a dear friend of college days, Gertrude Lynch. They had become acquainted when she was a student at Wilson College, a Presbyterian school for women, and Paul was a student at Dickinson College. Gertrude patiently heard Paul's account of the job's drawbacks, but also sensed his dreams for the future. She accepted Paul's offer of a partnership for life that would start at West Nottingham Academy. In a meeting of April 14, 1924, in Baltimore, the West Nottingham Board of Trustees hired Slaybaugh as headmaster for the coming year at a salary of $2,500 plus a two-room apartment in Magraw House.

The new headmaster arrived at West Nottingham on July 4, 1924, and immediately attacked the briar patch with hoe and mattock, the beginning of a new campus. In the evenings Slaybaugh wrote a new catalog and painted the rooms in Magraw House where he and Gertrude would live. He slept in Magraw and took his meals with Mrs. Keene, a widow in her eighties who lived close by. Near the end of the summer the new headmaster traveled westward to St. Clairsville, Ohio, to marry Gertrude and bring her back to West Nottingham. As they approached the old bridge across the Susquehanna some miles upstream from the present location of Conowingo Dam, Paul pointed out the darkness enveloping the hills that loomed ahead on the Cecil County side of the river. He told her that they would travel through darkness for the remainder of the journey, which lay through thinly settled country that in the mid-1920s did not yet have electrical service. Gertrude did not mind the dark countryside nor the rough accommodations she found when they reached West Nottingham. In early October, her parents paid the young couple a visit. As they were leaving, Gertrude's father said to her, "Come on back home with us. Certainly Paul can find a better job than this." Gertrude firmly declined. In a few years Gertrude's father revised his judgment, partly because he shared Paul's interest in educating boys.

During his first summer at West Nottingham, Slaybaugh had mailed out 134 catalogs and traveled 1400 miles to visit prospective students, but he had failed to recruit any boarders. Prospects for a Mercersburg-type boarding school looked hopeless as the fall semester started with an enrollment of 17 day students, fewer than the year before. When William Irvine, Slaybaugh's former supervisor at Mercersburg, wanted to help by transferring one of his boarding students to West Nottingham at the beginning of the second semester, Slaybaugh felt that the boy would be too lonely as the only boarding student but hated not to take him. While mulling the situation over, Slaybaugh suddenly thought of his brother James, who was still at home in Mt. Alto, Pennsylvania, and a sophomore in the township high school. Slaybaugh thought that West Nottingham might stimulate his brother's lagging interest in school. In turn, James would provide companionship for

George Baynum,* the boy whom Irvine was transferring from Mercersburg. Irvine apparently was correct in believing that George would benefit from the smaller West Nottingham student body because he attended for three years.

The addition of two boarding students and enrollment of one more day student during the year brought the total enrollment to 20 at the end of Slaybaugh's first year. The following September, Slaybaugh's recruiting paid off with the enrollment of 16 boys as boarding students to join an enlarged group of 27 day students. At the time of Slaybaugh's arrival, the academy operated under the Baltimore Synod of the Presbyterian Church of America. In 1915 the Board of Trustees had transferred jurisdiction of the academy to the Baltimore Synod in hopes of putting the school on a sounder financial basis. To look after its new responsibility, the synod appointed nine new members of the Board of Trustees to join four who remained from the old board.

One of the most active trustees in Slaybaugh's time was James J. Hanna, who had twin sons attending the academy. Hanna had shown Slaybaugh around on his first visit to the campus in the spring of 1924. The following fall, soon after Slaybaugh and his bride had settled down for their first semester, Hanna took a notion that Slaybaugh should be fired. He wasn't able to gain support from his fellow board members, however, so nothing came of it. Hanna's opinion of the new headmaster soon changed when he noticed that his sons, Gress and Jim, were bringing books home from the academy to do homework. Hanna must have continued to approve of the headmaster because after Slaybaugh had been at West Nottingham for twelve years, Hanna, still a member of the board, wrote of the pleasure in his long service as trustee and of the problems that had been solved "one by one" with the guidance of Jesus. Hanna's Scotch ancestry showed itself when he requested a fair market price or a little more for the boxes of strawberries that he personally delivered to the academy's kitchen from his nearby garden. Hanna, the representative of a large drug company, forgot his Scotch tendencies on numerous occasions, however, and gave generous financial support to the school.

---

* Forty-five years later, shortly after Baynum's death on January 16, 1969, his wife made a generous gift to the academy in memory of her husband.

Another active trustee was John A. Nesbitt, a West Nottingham graduate of 1897 who had been a board member since 1920. The board elected Nesbitt president in 1928, and he served in that office until shortly before his death in the spring of 1937. John G. Conner, a fellow board member and Nesbitt's headmaster at the academy, praised Nesbitt for his leadership, writing him on February 2, 1937, that "it has been chiefly because you were at the head of it that I have done what I have been able" to provide financial support. Nesbitt made a habit of visiting the campus at least once a week, usually on a Monday, as a change of pace from his duties on Sunday as pastor of the Catonsville, Maryland, Presbyterian Church. After making the rounds of the academy and eating a satisfying dinner with the headmaster and boys, Nesbitt would retire to Gayley, the headmaster's residence, light a good cigar, and have a long social visit with Paul Slaybaugh before going to bed.

The academy had no endowment and its only income besides tuition consisted of rent from the adjacent 260-acre farm, about $5,500 annually from the Presbyterian General Board of Education, and $500 annually from the State of Maryland for scholarships to needy students. The ever-recurring topic at the meetings of the Board of Trustees during Slaybaugh's period was the need for money and efforts to raise it. A steady succession of loans had to be obtained from the Rising Sun and Port Deposit banks. Besides Hanna, other trustees were continually lending or donating money. The board also sponsored various fund-raising drives.

Slaybaugh himself turned out to be an effective money raiser. He approached fund-raising with a certain gusto. He enjoyed the challenge and liked to meet important leaders of the day such as alumnus Robert S. Brookings, founder of the Brookings Institution, and Samuel Robinson, president of Standard Stores, a large national grocery chain. Robinson, a staunch Presbyterian, informed Slaybaugh one day that his contribution to West Nottingham Academy would be contingent on the number of students who learned the Short Catechism of the Presbyterian Church. As the Headmaster mulled over the details of the offer on his drive back to the academy, he became somewhat disheartened as he realized that under Robinson's terms the best possible performance of his students in learning the catechism would net only

$500. But the next day's mail brought a check for $1700 signed by Samuel Robinson with no strings attached.

On the other hand, early efforts to obtain a substantial contribution from Robert S. Brookings failed. First the Board of Trustees elected Brookings to its membership but were unable to get him to attend meetings. Then in the wake of the devastating fire of December 1927, Slaybaugh wrote Brookings a long letter that described the seriousness of the situation and the pressing need for funds, but to no avail. Characteristically undeterred, Slaybaugh eventually established a relationship with Brookings that resulted in helpful contributions even though Brookings was having difficulty in raising funds for his own Brookings Institution.

A fortuitous fund-raising effort developed one afternoon in Philadelphia after Slaybaugh had finished his business in the city earlier than expected. All day he had been thinking that the time was ripe to seek a contribution from Samuel A. Gayley, the wealthy vice-president of the academy's Board of Trustees who was named for his grandfather, long-time president of the board in the 19th Century. Although Slaybaugh had a little time, his good sense told him it was too late in the afternoon for talking about money. He couldn't put the idea out of his mind, however, and found himself driving up East Spruce Street to the entrance of the handsome Gayley home. Slaybaugh spent a "lovely hour" visiting with Samuel Gayley and his sister. The visit ended with a contribution of $1,000, a large amount for that period, which had resulted from a happy conjunction of dedicated asking and giving.

As Paul Slaybaugh and Gertrude drove away from the campus for Christmas vacation on December 17, 1927, they could look back on their first three years with satisfaction and to the future with hope. Their optimism was solidly based on an increase in enrollment from 20 to 57 and an increase in boarding students from zero to 30 since their arrival. Just three days later, a long distance call shattered the Slaybaughs' vacation with word that fire had completely destroyed Magraw House, the principal building of the academy, which housed the boys' dormitory, laboratories, and school library. Slaybaugh returned to the academy immediately and wrote the boarding students to report what had happened and make clear that there was no financial obligation if any did not wish to return and put up with makeshift accommodations for the rest of the school year. A few weeks later, Slaybaugh found to his delight that "every boy is returning" and that more than half the boys had written offering "to return immediately ... if there was anything they could do."

Because all the boys were coming back, "some quick thinking and planning had to be done" by the headmaster to find places for them to live. The first move was to make a long distance telephone call to George Orris Bechtel who owned a house adjacent to the academy property where his father had lived when headmaster. Bechtel and his wife used the house in the summer but were glad to let Slaybaugh and his wife use a couple of rooms in the emergency. The Slaybaughs' move to the Bechtel home left Gayley available for about 15 boys. An arrangement with Burton Wiley and his wife provided space for another 15 boys. The Wileys were alumni who also owned a summer home near the academy. Some of the boys had to sleep on outside screened porches during the winter but did not complain a lot, according to Slaybaugh. In looking back years later, Slaybaugh commented that the willingness of everyone to adjust exemplified "the soul that had been West Nottingham's," which had "kept it alive" over the centuries.

The first response of the trustees to the fire was to authorize the headmaster to hire a math teacher and secretary to give Slaybaugh time to solicit building funds. By April 14, 1928, Slaybaugh had raised $1700, but firm plans had not been adopted to cope with the loss of Magraw House. At the board meeting on that date, the representative of the Board of Education of the Presbyterian Synod of Baltimore proposed four alternate courses of action:

(1) Close the Academy and pay as much as possible to creditors.
(2) Rebuild Magraw House for $37,500.
(3) Rent a new cottage in the neighborhood to serve as a dormitory and conduct classes in the old academy building as before and also use the chapel of neighboring West Nottingham Church as a classroom.
(4) Sell the property, including the 260-acre farm, and move to the Washington suburbs as a country day school, possibly combined with boarding students. Hope for more aid from Washington alumni.

After a discussion of these alternatives, the board passed a motion by Dr. G. H. Richards of Port Deposit to proceed with the plan to rent a cottage and continue the school. This decision did not seem like progress to Headmaster Slaybaugh who had already raised $1700 toward a new Magraw House and had long been committed to a bigger and better academy. He told the board that he would resign unless it undertook the rebuilding of Magraw House. By next morning, Slaybaugh had reconsidered and said he was willing to work with the board.

Slaybaugh's strong opposition to the board's decision may well have affected its thinking. At its next meeting on May 1, the board moved to build the permanent masonry basement of the new Magraw House with money that was already available and to continue construction as money was received. John G. Conner, the board member who was once a dynamic headmaster of the academy himself, pledged $5,000 for the next stage in the construction. If construction did not actually go forward, Conner would reduce his contribution to $1,000.

Despite the positive action taken in the May 1 meeting, the board's determination was again challenged at its meeting of May 26. One of the board members not attending, Paul Freeman, sent a letter that forcefully recommended closing the school and disposing of its property in view of the magnitude of the academy's debt. James J. Hanna, long a strong supporter of the academy by word and deed, vigorously objected. He outlined a series of moves that would persuade the National Bank of Rising Sun to grant further credit to the school and was authorized by the board to act accordingly.

Other crucial support for the new building came from Presbyterians, mainly from their National Board of Christian Education. The board started by making its normal annual $5,000 pledge before construction started. Eventually, Presbyterians contributed $15,000 to construction costs. In 1929, Headmaster Slaybaugh reported that "through the last six years . . . the Church has put $44,000 into the school . . . and the finest thing about it all is, we believe they are not yet through." Funding for construction of the new Magraw House was often on a week by week basis. If there were insufficient funds on Monday to continue, John G. Conner always made up the difference. Construction proceeded with very little delay through 1928 and 1929 with just enough money always seeming to be available to keep going. Finally, on February 28, 1930, two years and two months after the fire, "one great day dawned in the history of West Nottingham Academy," as phrased by the student newspaper, the *Literary Advance*. That day the boys moved from their scattered sleeping quarters into the handsome and spacious new Magraw House. After a 6:30 a.m. breakfast, the boys moved their personal possessions and then brought the "Grand Concert" piano from the Old Academy to the new club room. At 2:30 p.m. all were ready for a soup, fish, and turkey dinner in the new dining room. The new $50,000 stone structure stood on the same site as the old Magraw House, which had netted $7,700 in fire insurance. The basement included a kitchen, boiler room, shower room, and dining hall, which had large windows on three of its walls. The other inside wall provided an entrance of double doors and the opposite end had a single outside door to the campus. The first floor consisted of three classrooms, two offices, and a large club room with a fireplace for the boys living on the second and third floors. The second and third floors each had eleven rooms for students, one room for an instructor, and a bathroom and shower. Each student room had space for two boys so the new Magraw could accommodate 44 boys and the two instructors as compared to the old Magraw's capacity of 18 boys and four instructors.

It had been difficult for the headmaster to keep up enrollment in the two years following the fire. Although academy students had loyally finished out the school year in which the fire had occurred, the lack of accommodations reduced enrollment to 32 for the next year. By the spring of 1930 after the new dormitory had opened, enrollment reached 49, close to the pre-fire level. Thus, Headmaster Slaybaugh with the loyal help of the Board of Trustees and especially John G. Conner had overcome the greatest threat yet to developing a solid boarding school for boys at West Nottingham.

As though the fire were not a great enough test of West Nottingham's ability to survive, the Great Depression began to reach into all sectors of the national economy after the crash of the stock market in 1929. The drastic reduction in economic activity stalled the growth in academy enrollment until the fall of 1933. One benefit may have been that the scarcity of teaching jobs helped keep the academy teachers from switching to other schools for higher pay. At a meeting on October 22, 1932, the Board of Trustees cut all academy salaries and passed a motion "expressing appreciation of the cuts in salary accepted by Mr. Slaybaugh and other teachers." At that time 15 million Americans were out of work; and, like the West Nottingham faculty, millions more took cuts in wages and salaries because of the severely deflated currency.

Retrospectively, the fire and Great Depression seemed to have had stimulating effects on the life of the school and its headmaster. In 1930 the academy obtained accreditation when it became a charter member of the Association of Colleges and Secondary Schools of the Middle States and Maryland. The graduating class of 1931 published West Nottingham's first annual, *Pegé*, which is the Greek word for source. John A. Nesbitt, Jr., son of the President of the Board of Trustees, had the idea and served as the first editor. The seniors have published *Pegé* each year up to the present. The first issue and every *Pegé* since have been attractive and are good records of academy life. On April 29, 1928, in the first spring after the fire, Paul and Gertrude Slaybaugh gained a new member of their family with the birth of Eleanor Jane. In 1931, Slaybaugh began graduate studies at the University of Pennsylvania, which led to an M.A. in education in 1933.

In 1933, the academy conducted a summer program, the first since before the Civil War. The eight-week session, running from mid-July to early September, combined the features of an organized academic program and a summer camp. The purpose was to enable high school students to complete work needed for promotion to the next class and to enable seniors to complete one or two courses that might be necessary for college entrance in September. The schedule called for all classes in the forenoon, sports and special projects in the afternoon, and a study period of one and one-half hours in the evening. The 1933 enrollment was only five and three years later only nine, but the headmaster reported to the alumni in the spring of 1941 that 40 boys had attended in 1940. Cost of the program at that time, including instruction, was $16 per week plus a registration fee of $5 for those who had previously attended and $25 for newcomers. Slaybaugh noted that each year some boys new to West Nottingham liked the summer session so well that they enrolled in the fall. While giving the academy some favorable publicity and a few new students, the summer program usually came close to breaking even financially. The following tabulation gives information on enrollment up to 1949.

GROWTH UNDER SLAYBAUGH, 1924-1949 125

Magraw House—Construction of the present Magraw dormitory was completed in 1930, replacing the original Magraw home at this site which was destroyed by fire in 1927.

Enrollment at West Nottingham Summer Session

1933	5
1934	—
1935	—
1936	9
1937	17
1938	20
1939	24
1940	40
1941	42
1942	27
1943	40
1944	56
1945	55
1946	56
1947	31

In the fall of 1933, the academy's enrollment resumed its upward climb despite the slow improvement of national economic conditions.

Table I
Boarding and Day Students, Faculty
1923–1948

Academic Year	Boarding Students (Boys)	Day Students Boys	Day Students Girls	Academy Enrollment	Faculty & Professional Staff
1923–24	—	9	16	25	—
1924–25	2	8	10	20	5
1925–26	16	14	13	43	6
1926–27	18	20	16	54	8
1927–28	30	13	14	57	8
1928–29	18	8	6	32	6
1929–30	25	12	12	49	7
1930–31	29	11	9	49	8
1931–32	28	12	6	46	11
1932–33	30	10	6	46	12
1933–34	27	21	4	52	9
1934–35	39	16	—	55	10
1935–36	42	19	—	61	10
1936–37	35	13	—	48	10
1937–38	50	17	—	67	13
1938–39	72	18	—	90	15
1939–40	60	14	—	74	15
1940–41	69	10	1	80	18
1941–42	93	17	1	111	22
1942–43	67	10	1	78	21
1943–44	73	10	1	84	19
1944–45	86	8	1	95	—
1945–46	103	6	—	109	—
1946–47	111	6	—	117*	—
1947–48	90	8	—	98*	—
1948–49	95	10	—	105*	—

* Includes World War II veterans, numbering 19 in 1946–47, 11 in 1947–48, and 13 in 1948–49. The following year there were 5.

Table I shows that for Slaybaugh's 25 years from 1924 to 1949, the boarding students generally accounted for the increase in the total student body. The number of day students actually declined from a 15–30 range between 1924 and 1933 to a 10–15 range after 1933. The reduction in day students after 1933 resulted from the ending of attendance by girls, Slaybaugh's goal since coming to West Nottingham. World War II caused enrollment to fall in 1942–1943 and 1943–1944 from an all time high of 111 in 1941. In 1944–1945, however, enrollment

Table II
Student Geographic Distribution
1924–1948

Year	Md.	Penn.	Del.	N.J.	D.C.	Va.	N.Y.	Ohio	Conn.	Other	Total
1924–25	18	1	1	—	—	—	—	—	—	—	20
1925–26	31	8	2	1	1	—	—	—	—	—	43
1926–27	41	8	2	1	1	—	—	—	—	—	54
1927–28	36	11	—	5	1	1	1	2	—	—	57
1928–29	24	4	1	2	—	—	—	1	—	—	32
1929–30	42	8	1	1	—	—	—	—	—	—	52
1930–31	39	6	—	2	—	—	1	—	—	1	49
1931–32	31	5	2	2	1	—	3	1	—	1	46
1932–33	31	5	1	2	—	—	2	2	1	2	46
1933–34	35	5	—	4	—	1	2	3	1	1	52
1934–35	37	7	1	4	1	2	—	2	—	1	55
1935–36	41	11	4	1	—	2	—	1	—	1	61
1936–37	35	8	3	—	—	2	—	—	—	—	48
1937–38	37	12	1	7	3	2	—	2	1	2	67
1938–39	45	15	5	9	5	2	—	3	2	4	90
1939–40	33	16	2	6	4	1	—	5	1	6	74
1940–41	35	13	6	11	6	3	4	—	—	2	80
1941–42	52	20	13	9	6	2	5	—	—	4	111
1942–43	34	11	7	9	4	4	4	—	—	5	78
1943–44	43	12	3	3	15	4	3	—	—	1	84
1944–45	47	13	3	5	16	4	2	2	—	3	95
1945–46	43	19	3	8	10	5	9	1	2	9	109
1946–47	37	17	10	7	6	3	14	1	1	21	117
1947–48	28	19	8	9	4	1	11	2	1	15	98
1948–49	33	14	15	8	4	4	9	2	—	16	105

again reached about 100 and stayed there during Slaybaugh's last five years.

As the number of boarding students increased, the geographic distribution gradually widened as shown in Table II. This experience was roughly that of Rev. James Magraw whose success in making the academy widely and favorably known in the 1820's drew students from neighboring states. Slaybaugh's students came mainly from Maryland and Pennsylvania until the 1930s, but the number outside those two states had gradually increased by the late 1930s to one-third of the total. For some years in the 1940s, more than one-half the student body came from outside Maryland and Pennsylvania.

In keeping with its strong Presbyterian ties, the proportion of Presbyterian students at West Nottingham varied roughly between one-

Table III
Student Religious Affiliations, 1924–1947

Academic Year	Presbyterian	Methodist	Other Protestant	Catholic	Jewish	None & Other	Enrollment
1924–25	10	3	1	—	—	6	20
1925–26	18	15	5	1	—	4	43
1926–27	17	20	8	1	—	8	54
1927–28	17	19	10	3	—	8	57
1928–29	13	12	3	—	—	4	32
1929–30	33	8	7	—	—	4	52
1930–31	27	8	9	1	—	4	49
1931–32	28	6	7	1	—	4	46
1932–33	22	12	5	2	—	5	46
1933–34	21	16	6	3	—	6	52
1934–35	26	12	10	—	—	7	55
1935–36	27	11	14	—	—	9	61
1936–37	34	9	5	—	—	—	48
1937–38	34	17	10	6	—	—	67
1938–39	39	25	17	8	1	—	90
1939–40	31	15	13	11	3	1	74
1940–41	28	19	21	7	5	—	80
1941–42	43	21	27	8	4	8	111
1942–43	35	17	22	3	—	1	78
1943–44	29	14	30	3	4	4	84
1944–45	40	16	25	4	7	3	95
1945–46	34	19	34	10	8	4	109
1946–47	33	14	35	17	10	5	114
1947–48	22	12	25	16	12	11	98

fourth and one-half of its student body from 1924 to 1949. Table III also shows that the academy maintained its colonial tradition of welcoming non-Presbyterians, enrolling many other Protestants and after 1940 a number of Catholics and Jews.

The Bible course that the headmaster taught was generalized enough to accommodate the religious beliefs of most of the students. On one occasion, Slaybaugh consulted with the Catholic parish priest in Port Deposit about the course content, anticipating that three new Catholic boys might raise some questions, possibly related to a desire for less homework. A few days later, the priest had a telephone call from three young West Nottingham students and was able to satisfy them that Slaybaugh's Bible course was consistent with Catholic beliefs.

The distribution of West Nottingham students among grade levels appears in Table IV. After 1931, when more complete records are

Table IV
Student Distribution by Grade Level*
1924–1948

Academic Year	9	Grades 10	11	12	Total	Grades 7 & 8	Other**	Academy Total
1924–25	—	—	—	2	—	—	—	20
1925–26	—	—	—	5	—	—	—	43
1926–27	—	—	—	3	—	—	—	54
1927–28	—	—	—	14	—	—	—	57
1928–29	—	—	—	6	—	—	—	32
1929–30	—	—	—	9	—	—	—	52
1930–31	—	—	—	11	—	—	—	49
1931–32	—	—	—	13	—	—	—	46
1932–33	9	3	16	16	44	2	—	46
1933–34	3	9	15	18	45	6	1	52
1934–35	11	10	10	17	48	7	—	55
1935–36	5	9	22	13	49	8	4	61
1936–37	8	8	11	18	42	3	—	48
1937–38	13	11	19	18	61	6	—	67
1938–39	13	11	28	25	77	12	1	90
1939–40	11	13	19	26	69	5	—	74
1940–41	12	14	22	19	67	10	3	80
1941–42	14	19	23	38	94	12	5	111
1942–43	8	14	20	21	63	8	7	78
1943–44	11	14	12	19	56	16	12	84
1944–45	20	15	13	18	66	16	13	95
1945–46	21	14	23	23	81	18	10	109
1946–47	30	17	21	35	103	13	1	117
1947–48	10	17	22	33	82	15	1	98
1948–49	18	13	17	40	88	11	6	105

*From 1925 to 1932, the number of graduates are given in the 12th grade column; otherwise the breakdown among classes is not known before 1932.

**The bulk of students in this column are boys in the 4th, 5th, and 6th grades during the 1940's. In addition the column includes a handful of post-graduate and special students.

available, the number of students in the 11th grade is close to the number of 12th grade students the following year. This correlation indicates that most graduating students spent at least their last two years at West Nottingham. Until 1941–42 the number of sophomores was only about 50 percent of the number of juniors in the following year. In 1941–42 and thereafter, however, the number of sophomores usually was at least 75 percent and often a larger proportion of the next year's junior class. This relationship indicated that over half of

West Nottingham's graduates had begun to attend for three years or more.

All boys below the ninth grade were members of the junior school and had their own dormitory and teachers. There were probably few seventh and eighth graders before 1932 and only a handful each year until 1938 when the number reached 12. Thereafter until 1949, the number of seventh and eighth graders usually exceeded 10 each year and averaged 13. Starting in 1940, the academy took 5 to 10 sixth, fifth, and fourth graders per year, who are included under the "Other" column of Table IV.

As enrollment increased, the number of faculty and professional staff increased proportionately as shown in Table I. Consequently, the ratio of students to faculty and staff stayed roughly constant, starting at 5 in 1924, rising to 6 in 1930, and leveling off at about 4.5 in 1940 and 1944.

Although the destruction of the old Magraw House by fire in 1927 had hurt enrollment of boarding students in 1928, opening of the new Magraw House in 1930 with far superior facilities may have had a stabilizing effect on the length of time that faculty and staff members stayed at West Nottingham, as shown by Table V. Everitt, Tosh, Edwards, Durigg, and Kirk each stayed between 3 and 5 years. Hibsham, the pastor of the West Nottingham Presbyterian Church, taught history at the academy for four years. Stetson stayed one year and then came back in 1938 and stayed until 1942 when he joined the War Department. Gress Hanna, son of the board member, came in 1933 and stayed at West Nottingham until he left for service in World War II. Loss of Hanna and Stetson plus the additional losses to war service of Douglas, Lindaman, Powell, Thomas, Holstein, Bishop, Finch, Boyd, Honore, and Kutz were termed a "terrible blow" by the headmaster in 1944 as he sought to adequately fill the vacancies in the midst of World War II.

Besides a larger faculty and staff, the increasing enrollment steadily led to a larger number of college entrances, as shown by Table VI. Table VII gives the number of former West Nottingham students actually in college as of 1933, 1941, and 1949 as well as some of the institutions being attended.

The construction of the new Magraw House was the beginning of

GROWTH UNDER SLAYBAUGH, 1924-1949 131

Table V
FACULTY AND PROFESSIONAL STAFF—1924-1949*

Service	Name	Field/Position	Education
1924-25	Ward W. Stewart	Latin, History, French, English	
1924-25	Russell Moore	English, Science, History, Athletics, Piano	
1924-49	Gertrude Slaybaugh	Dramatics	Wilson College A.B.
1924-49	Paul Slaybaugh	Mathematics, Bible/ Headmaster	Dickinson A.B. Pennsylvania M.A.
1924-29	Rev. Thomas P. Mc Kee**	Bible	Wooster A.B.
1925-28	Stanton C. Phelps	Latin, French	Harvard
1925-28	Merrill Reed	Science	
1926-28	George R. Dulebohn	History	
1926-28	Douglas M. Smith	English, Mathematics	
1929-33	Albert H. Hibsham**	History	Heidelberg A.B., A.M., PhD
1929-34	Donald Everitt	English	Princeton A.B.
1929-32	John L. Tosh	Physical Education	
1930-34	William W. Kirk	French, Latin	Delaware B.A. University of Paris
1930-31	George E. Stetson	Science, Mathematics, Latin	Bowdoin A.B. Harvard M.A.
1938-42		Assistant Headmaster/ Mathematics, Latin	
1930-42	Fred Reburn	Commercial/Business Manager	Pierce School of Business Administration
1931-34	Frank B. Durigg	Science, Latin Science, Shop	Washington & Jefferson A.B., A.M.
1933-41	Gress Hanna	History, Mathematics/ Director of Athletics	Lafayette A.B. Columbia M.A.
1932-37	Charles L. Edwards	Music	New England Conservatory of Music
1934-36	George O. Ackroyd	English	Moravian College A.B., A.M.
1934-36	Cecil K. Vaughan	History, Physical Education	Colgate A.B.
1936-42	Francis C. Lindaman	French, German, Spanish/Registrar	Gettysburg College A.B., M.A.
1937-39	William Fowler Buck Jr.	French, Latin	Oberlin College B.S.
1937-39	Herman H. Slaybaugh	Junior School	Shippensburg College B.S.
1937-41 1945-49 1949-52 1952-54	Richard W. Holstein	Science, Organ, Piano/ Registrar, Acting Headmaster, Science	Lebanon Valley College B.S.
1937-44	Russell Faber	Physical Education, Coach/Director of Physical Education	New York B.S.

Table V (Continued)

Service	Name	Field/Position	Education
1938–40	Benjamin W. Early	English	Virginia B.A., M.A.
1938–42	William S. Douglas	Mathematics/Registrar	Franklin & Marshall A.B.
1938–42 1946–52	York Honore	Art, Mech. Drawing, Shop	Highland Park College, Mich.
1939–42	Herbert Finch	Modern History/Librarian	Franklin & Marshall A.B.
1940–44	Robert K. Bishop	Latin, French/Assistant Headmaster	Princeton A.B., M.A., PhD
1940–42	Powell S. Thomas	English	Gettysburg A.B., Penn. A.M.
1941–42	Leslie R. Boyd***	English/Assistant for Public Relations	Haverford A.B.
1941–43	George A. Mattson	Reading	Bucknell A.B., Penn. A.M.
1941–44	Carey Thomas	English, French	Haverford A.B.
1941–43	Loy Kutz	Music	Lebanon Valley, Peabody
1939–41	Robert K. Robison	Junior School	Millersville State B.A.
1943–45	George R. Stubbs	Mathematics	Trinity A.B. NYU B.A.
1943–45	Francis J. Donahue	English	
1943–45	Charles B. Remaley	Junior School/Basketball Coach	Allegheney B.S.
1943–45	Helen L. Remaley	Junior School	Loch Haven Lafayette A.B.
1945–47	William F. Hemphill	English	
1946–47	Gus W. Van Beek	Bible/Chaplain	Tulsa U. B.A. McCormick Seminary B.D.
1945–47	Arthur E. Desimone	Junior School	Tusculum B.A.
1945–49	David E. Proctor	Latin and French	Harvard A.B. Boston U. M. Ed.
1946 Present	C. Herbert Foutz	Mathematics/Dean of Faculty	Gettysburg A.B.
1946–69	Charles F. Bauer	Latin, German, Spanish	Franklin & Marshall A.B., Penn. U. PhD
1944–45 1946–47	Maurice S. Nichols	History	New Hampshire A.B.
1948–52	James L. Buchanan	Director of Athletics/Coach of Football, Basketball and Track	Delaware U. B.S.
1947–52	Robert B. Miller	Junior School, History, Bible	Waynesburg College B.S. Ed.
1949–52	R. R. Schellenberger	English, Dramatics	Princeton A. B.

*Includes those who served more than one year in that period except for two 1924–25 members.
**Pastor of West Nottingham Presbyterian Church
***Started March 1941.

Table VI
College Entrances 1925–1949

Year	WNA Graduates	College Entrances
1924–25	2	2
1925–26	5	4
1926–27	3	2
1927–28	14	8
1928–29	6	6
1929–30	9	5
1930–31	11	8
1931–32	5	2
1932–33	16	12
1933–34	17	13
1934–35	18	12
1935–36	14	12
1936–37	15	12
1937–38	20	16
1938–39	24	20
1939–40	26	22
1940–41	15	10
1941–42	30	17
1942–43	21	14
1943–44	15	9
1944–45	13	5
1945–46	20	13
1946–47	—	—
1947–48	31	29
1948–49	41	—

a number of important physical additions and improvements that took place in the years after the fire. The immediate lack of dormitory space caused by the fire prompted the trustees to purchase the Porter-Wiley Cottage in the spring of 1927 for $5,000. This building, now called Wiley House, had served West Nottingham students since the 1830s as a private boarding house. After purchase by the academy, it served as a temporary dormitory for the boys forced out of old Magraw until the new Magraw was occupied in February of 1930. In 1936, Wiley was remodeled to provide offices on the first floor for the headmaster and business manager and apartments on the second floor for staff and faculty. Slaybaugh had come to sense a disadvantage in having his office in the new Magraw House. He felt that it would be better to show the handsome and large Magraw building to prospective students and parents in the course of a campus tour that started from his office

Table VII
College Attendance as of 1933, 1941, and 1949

School	1933	1941	1949
Maryland	1	11	—
Washington College	2	5	—
Delaware	2	5	—
Lafayette	2	4	—
University of Miami	0	3	—
Dickinson	1	2	—
Dickinson, Williamsport	0	2	—
Franklin and Marshall	2	2	—
Washington and Jefferson	1	2	—
Princeton	2	1	—
Princeton Theological Seminary	2	0	—
Johns Hopkins	0	2	—
Lehigh	0	2	—
Hampden-Sydney	0	2	—
West Chester State Teachers, West Chester, Pa.	0	2	—
Others	9	24	—
Total	24	69	118

in Wiley rather than to start the tour in Magraw and have no other building to show of comparable size and appearance.

In 1930, James J. Hanna provided a permanent residence for the headmaster by selling Gayley Hall and its fifty acres of land adjacent to the campus to the school for $7,000. Hanna had purchased the property from the West Nottingham Church at public auction for that amount in 1920. He had planned to sell the property to the academy at cost, but the board did not act at that time. The property had been the manse for the pastor of the West Nottingham Church for more than a century. It was named for Rev. Samuel A. Gayley, who lived there for 37 years, long serving as president of the academy's Board of Trustees and also serving as principal of the academy for five years.

A summary of information about the buildings acquired during the Slaybaugh period follows:

GROWTH UNDER SLAYBAUGH, 1924–1949

Building	Use	History	Cost
Gayley Hall	Headmaster's residence.	Manse for pastor of West Nottingham church from about 1830 to 1920. Bought from church by J. J. Hanna and sold to Academy at cost in 1930.	$7,000 for building and 50 acres
Magraw House	Boys' dormitory, dining room, classrooms.	Replaced Magraw Stone Mansion acquired in 1906.	$50,000
Porter-Wiley Cottage	Dormitory, after 1936 offices for headmaster and business manager, apartments for faculty.	Private boarding house for academy students since 1830s. Academy purchased in spring of 1928 after Old Magraw House burned. Doubled in size 1946–47.	$5,000
Field House	Gymnasium, basketball court.	Converted from barn between 1935 and 1945.	$5,000
Hill Top Cottage	Boys' dormiatory, faculty residence	Built in 1939 from remnants of building donated by West Nottingham church.	$4,000
Tyson-Sill	Quarters for two married and one single staff member. Dormitory for junior school boys.	Purchased 1944. Built 1856 for wife of Rev. Amos Sill who was principal of academy 1858–62.	$6,000
Bechtel Cottage	Two apartments for staff	Donated by G. O. Bechtel 1941. Built and occupied by his father, G. K. Bechtel, principal 1862–67 and 1872–87.	$15 per month for life of G. O. Bechtel or wife
Log Cabin	Library 1952–1961, faculty residence after 1961.	Built as representation of Samuel Finley's colonial school house from logs of old house bought 1947. Completed with student labor 1952.	

When the headmaster stood on the porch of the new Magraw House in the early 1930s, he could view the spacious rolling grounds of the campus extending toward the West Nottingham Church. The land sloped gently from Magraw to a small draw a couple hundred feet away. One day, Slaybaugh realized that the draw and adjacent low ground could become a lake that would add to the beauty of the campus. The problem at the depth of the Great Depression was to find money. Slaybaugh found the solution in the federal Works Progress Administration (WPA) which had been established by the administration of Franklin D. Roosevelt to provide work for millions of unemployed Americans. By commencement in 1935, Slaybaugh's vision had become a 180-by 100-foot shimmering lake in the middle of the campus. Since then, lakeside plantings have become overhanging trees, reflecting an ever-changing record of the seasons. Extra dirt not needed in building the dam was used to improve the modest golf course that Slaybaugh had established on the campus a few years before.

The curriculum of the academy in effect when the new dormitory opened in 1930 provided three types of preparation that led to graduation after four years—classical, scientific, and general, as shown in the following tabulations, with each course unit equal to one year of study. Graduation also required non-credit study of the Bible. For the years 1928–1931, twelve ministers of the Baltimore Synod gave an annual series of lectures that constituted the required Bible course.

Types of College Preparation, 1930

CLASSICAL	course years	SCIENTIFIC	course years
Greek.	2	Modern Language.	3
or French	3	Science	3
Latin	4	Mathematics	1
Elective. . . . . .2½ or 3½		Elective. 2½	
Required (Note). 5½		Required (Note) 5½	
Total	15	Total 15	

GENERAL
course years
A Foreign Language. 3
History 1
Science 1
Elective. 4½
Required (Note) 5½
Total .15

Note—Required for all graduates:

	course years
English	3
Elementary Algebra	1
Intermediate Algebra	½
Plane Geometry	1
Total	5½

The curricula in the 1934 and 1936 catalogs had the same requirements for graduation as the 1929–31 catalog except for three changes:

(1) Greek was no longer offered in the classical program and three years of any other modern foreign language could be used as well as French.

(2) In the general program, the requirement for a modern language was reduced from three to two years.

(3) The Bible requirement had changed to consist of two noncredit courses, the Old Testament and the New Testament, which alternated from year to year.

In contrast to the curricula of 1929–31, 1934, and 1936, the curriculum in the 1941–42 catalog (Table VIII) provides separate requirements for non-college students and does not distinguish between classical, scientific, and general types of college preparation. The requirements for college preparatory students were tightened to increase requirements for English from three to four course years, to specify Chemistry or Physics for the science requirement, and make Bible a credit course. As in 1934 and 1936, the Bible requirement for all students consisted of two courses, the Old Testament and the New Testament, which alternated from year to year. However, the 1941–42 catalog specifies three hours of class meetings each week and grants one-half credit for each Bible course.

The English course requirements given in Table VIII include public speaking performances for each of the four years. Ninth and tenth graders had to recite from memory a poem or prose selection of 600 words before a school assembly of the Irving Literary Society. Eleventh graders had to compose a speech of 1000 to 1500 words and deliver it before a committee of the faculty. The subject, outline, and composition must have had prior approval. For graduation, twelfth graders had to write a speech of 1500 to 2000 words and deliver it at a school assembly.

Table VIII
Requirements for Graduation (course years)

Year Course	1929–31	1934–36	1941–42 College Preparatory	Non-College
English	3	3	4	3
Algebra	1	2	2	2[b]
Plane Geometry	1	1	1	
One Foreign Language	3	2	2	1
History	1	1	1	1[c]
Science	1	1	1[d]	1[e]
Elective	4	5	4	7
Bible	a	a	1	1
Physical	—	—	f	f
Cultural	—	—	g	g
Total	15	15	16	16

[a] No credit given.
[b] May use 1 yr. of General Mathematics to meet part of requirement for 2 Algebra courses.
[c] Economic Geography may be substituted for a History course.
[d] Must be Chemistry or Physics.
[e] Agriculture or Physical Geography may be used.
[f] For each year, four periods a week of athletics or work during both terms.
[g] For each year, four periods a week for one term of Music, Art, Publications, Debating, or Activity Club.

Any boy could satisfy his public speaking requirement for the year by participating in the annual midwinter debate in which two academy teams formally debated a public issue. The winning side was determined by visiting judges. In addition to required public speaking, the boys were free to enter speech contests that were conducted at commencement each year. The 11th and 12th graders competed in one flight, the 9th and 10th in another, and the 7th and 8th in still another flight.

The requirements for physical activity given in Table VIII could be satisfied by participation in football, basketball, baseball, track, hockey, golf, tennis, or work. The headmaster used the manual labor of the students in planting trees, preparing the field-house for basketball, and building the campus lake. The towering evergreens that now separate the campus from the academy's farm are the result of student work.

The requirements for cultural activity listed in Table VIII could be satisfied by membership or work in one of the following organizations or offices:

Orchestra
Glee Club
Nottingham News
Pegé
President or Secretary of Student Senate
Irving Literary Society
Athletic Association
Chairman of Social Committee
Debating Team
Art (one period a week)
Hobby Shop
Airplane, Kodak, or Nature Club

Among the listed cultural activities, two were publications, *Pegé* and *Nottingham News*. *Pegé* is the academy's annual, which the seniors started to publish in 1931. The *Nottingham News* first came out in March 1939 to handle academy news when the *Literary Advance* discontinued its news coverage to resume its much earlier role as a literary publication.

Paul Slaybaugh, a strong believer in the value of an athletic program, had to start from scratch because he had only 20 students the first year, 11 of whom were girls. The next year, however, Slaybaugh fielded his first football team. A predecessor, Headmaster J. G. Conner, had himself sometimes played in football games against other schools in the 1880s and 1890s. Slaybaugh did not go that far to fill out his starting eleven but did use faculty members in the early seasons. The record shows that West Nottingham teams performed well in football and other sports, but Slaybaugh never granted athletic scholarships and turned down prospects who sought reduction of school charges on the basis of athletic skill alone.

The person most responsible for making Slaybaugh's plans for a spirited football team come true was H. Gress Hanna, a West Nottingham student when Slaybaugh arrived in 1924 and son of James J. Hanna. Gress had played on Slaybaugh's earliest teams at West Nottingham before graduating in 1927. After an A.B. degree from Lafayette in 1931, Hanna coached the Milford (Delaware) High School team to a 5-2 record in the fall of 1931. After earning an M.A. at Columbia University, Hanna returned to West Nottingham in the fall of 1933 to coach football. During the summer he had attended a coaching school, which had Harry Stuhldreher, one of Notre Dame's famed Four Horsemen, on its teaching staff. The high-powered counsel may have helped because Hanna coached his first West Nottingham team to an unbeaten season in 1933. In their eight games the West Nottingham gridders outscored their opponents 91 to 0, but did have to settle for four scoreless tie games.

In 1937, Russell Faber became instructor of physical education and assisted Hanna with the football team. After 1937 Faber took over as head coach while Hanna shifted to assistant coach. Between 1937 and 1940, Faber and Hanna produced a four year West Nottingham football record of 22 wins, 2 ties, and 2 losses. The 1939 team was unbeaten and untied—the most successful season in West Nottingham's history. Here are the scores:

West Nottingham Academy	Opponents	Opponents
30	Boy's Latin School	0
45	Newark (Del.) H.S.	0
20	Delaware Univ. J.V.	6
60	St. James School	0
15	Valley Forge Military Academy	0
45	Wildwood (N.J.) H.C.	0
39	Stony Brook School	0
26	DuPont YMCA	0
Total 280	Total	6

Notable among West Nottingham's 1939 victories was the 45-0 trouncing of the Newark, Delaware, High School Yellow Jackets, a team that West Nottingham had never defeated. The humbling of Valley Forge Military Academy was preceded by a pep talk by Assistant Coach Hanna who reminded the West Nottingham players that the magnificent Valley Forge buildings they could see around them and its enrollment of 500 students did not matter once the game had started.

The outstanding player on the 1939 football team was Richard "Duke" Alexander from Laurel Springs, N.J., the greatest athlete in the history of the academy. Playing end on the 1939 team, Duke scored

83 points for an all-time academy record for individual scoring. Duke Alexander's exploits in track seem even more spectacular. In a meet against Towson, Duke was responsible for 25 points in West Nottingham's 39-24 triumph, winning the 100- and 200-yard dashes, the high and broad jumps, and the shot put. In a Southern Conference open meet at Chapel Hill, N.C., where he competed against collegians, Duke won the high jump with a record-breaking leap of six feet four inches. After graduation from West Nottingham in the Class of 1940, Duke Alexander entered the University of Maryland. As a freshman, he won 19 of the 23 intercollegiate track events he entered, earning 103 points out of a possible 115. As a sophomore end on the University of Maryland football team, he was selected all-Maryland by the Associated Press. Duke was never to reach his full capability as an athlete, however. He enlisted in the Marine Corps in early 1942 and in October of that year was killed in action against the Japanese during the invasion of Guadalcanal.

14

World War II and Bicentennial

ON DECEMBER 7, 1941, Japanese aircraft destroyed most of the American battleships in the Pacific in an attack on Pearl Harbor. Five days later Germany declared war on the U.S., thus fully engaging America in World War II. The impact of Pearl Harbor on West Nottingham Academy was relatively as disorganizing as it was on the United States, according to Headmaster Slaybaugh's report of January 1944 to the alumni. Slaybaugh explained that the fine faculty that had been assembled since 1930 had exactly the qualifications which made the armed services desire them. Consequently, 12 of the pre-Pearl Harbor faculty had left to join the war effort.

Slaybaugh recalled that in September 1941, three months before Pearl Harbor, the academy's enrollment had reached an all-time high of 93 boarding students and 18 day students "because of the school's program, friends, and effective public relations work by Gress Hanna, Russell Faber, and Leslie Boyd." After Pearl Harbor, "the organization began to disintegrate immediately" as George Stetson, Powell Thomas, and Gress Hanna left for service. Because of their public relations and recruiting ability, the loss of Hanna to the Navy and, a few months later, Leslie R. Boyd to the Red Cross hurt the academy's enrollment of boarding boys for the coming year. Consequently, enrollment dropped to 70* in September of 1942 even though the academy "had enough prospects during the summer to fill the school." Although 15 boys left during the 1942–43 year, most to the Army or Navy, Slaybaugh reported to the alumni that all 15 had been replaced. Slaybaugh concluded his alumni report of April 1943 with an answer to skeptics who questioned the future of independent schools:

---

* Other academy records show an enrollment of 78 for 1942–43.

Some people here and there are raising questions about the security of independent schools and colleges. The skeptics are always with us. There are more of them in times like these. Some independent schools and colleges have closed during the last few years. That is always happening, too. But any independent school which is meeting a need and which has something to offer boys will withstand the shock. During two hundred years West Nottingham Academy has weathered many severe storms but she stands today stronger than ever and with her face to the winds. West Nottingham Academy is a secondary school with a soul and a spirit, a purpose and a mission; a board of trustees, an administration, and a faculty—some of whom are temporarily in the service of their country— all with a will to continue her existence. Her security depends on her hundreds of friends and a thousand alumni. I have confidence that they will not let her down.

The first spring after the U.S. entered the war, Slaybaugh received the honorary degree of Doctor of Laws from Waynesburg College, Waynesburg, Pennsylvania. Waynesburg's President, Paul R. Stewart, conferred the degree at the commencement exercises of 1942 in which Slaybaugh gave the baccalaureate address to the graduating seniors.

The loss of unmarried staff and faculty members to the armed services led West Nottingham to hire married men with families who were more likely to be exempt from military service. Living quarters had to be found for the new employees in school facilities and elsewhere in Cecil County, where housing accommodations were already strained by the new workers needed for munitions production in Elkton and the huge Bainbridge Naval Training Station. Bainbridge, which was located on the hills above Port Deposit, four miles south of the academy, served as the Navy's training camp for all East Coast enlisted recruits. The total number of Navy staff and trainees there reached 40,000 at one time. Later in the war, Bainbridge also cared for large numbers of wounded servicemen.

In September of 1942, one of the many thousands of refugees who had fled to America in mortal fear of Hitler's regime found his way to a teaching post at West Nottingham Academy. Richard K. Goetz had been drama and art critic for *Der Wiener Tag*, a liberal newspaper published in Vienna until German troops marched into Austria in March of 1938. At West Nottingham, Goetz bolstered the academy's depleted

J. Paul Slaybaugh—Headmaster, 1924–1949.

staff as a teacher of Latin and History. He was "quite enthusiastic about his work" and soon "gave evidence of being a good teacher." After only two months, however, ill health caused him to undergo a physical examination in New York. He was never able to return and died on February 2, 1943. Mrs. Slaybaugh took over the Latin class that Mr. Goetz had been conducting and taught it for the remainder of the year.

In the fall of 1943, temporary inability to fill faculty vacancies forced the headmaster to carry the heaviest teaching load of his life in mathematics for a few weeks. Once he taught the junior school (pre-ninth graders), a Modern History class, and supervised a Latin class, all in the same day. When the kitchen help dwindled to one person, Mrs. Slaybaugh and the students pitched in until more help could be found. Because of food shortages, different vegetables sometimes were served at different tables. In 1945 Slaybaugh reported:

> We have the best chef we have ever had ... but it is a terrible tough job trying to find food to put up 10,000 meals a month as we had to do last Winter.... We planted a right good size garden and we had 600 nice young chickens until a terrible storm drowned about 50 of them. Some will soon be big enough to fry.

By January 1944, Slaybaugh informed the alumni that "there is much encouraging evidence that gradually we are bringing order out of chaos." He also found a number of the new staff promising and praised the academic efforts of the new group of boys even though "they haven't done very well in football." The headmaster referred to the young 1943 team which averaged only 145 pounds per man and lost all six games on its schedule. In a July 1945 report on the "home front" to West Nottingham men in service, Slaybaugh noted that Mrs. Slaybaugh and his daughter, Eleanor Jane, had neglected upkeep of their campus residence to do much of the work in the business office in the past year after the business manager left. A new business manager was expected by July 15. Eleanor Jane was working for the summer at the hospital school at the nearby Bainbridge Naval Training Station where the work was more interesting and paid more "than working for Pop." Slaybaugh's daughter was going to college at Skidmore in Saratoga Springs, N.Y., in the fall.

The headmaster became officially involved in the defense effort in

1942 when Governor H. R. O'Connor commissioned him as a captain in the militia of Maryland. The governor asked Slaybaugh to organize one of four companies of "minute men" in Cecil County who were to replace the National Guard troops who had been called to active duty. Upon Captain Slaybaugh's request, Robert L. Harding of the West Nottingham Class of 1932 was commissioned 1st lieutenant. A short recruiting period resulted in the enlistment of about 140 men who were organized into nine squads. By the spring of 1943, the men had completed preliminary training and were practicing maneuvers for guarding the high tension lines from Conowingo Dam and the highways in Cecil County.

While the headmaster kept the academy in operation amid the uncertainties of wartime, about 300 out of the 1000 living West Nottingham alumni were engaged in the war against Germany and Japan. They are listed in Appendix B. Because of the steady increase in academy enrollment in the late 1930s, an unusually large proportion of alumni were eligible for military service. Some of the younger alumni who weren't eligible to serve tried to get in military service by concealing their physical defects or tried to join organizations that operated in combat zones, such as the Red Cross and American Field Service. One West Nottingham boy from Elkton, Thomas L. Evans, who was able to conceal his defective hearing from Army recruiters, eventually found himself facing German troops with hearing that was becoming progressively worse in the constant din of battle. He took it upon himself to go to a hospital for treatment. Losing track of Evans, his superior officer reported him missing in action. The War Department promptly informed Evans' parents of the bad news. Ten days later his parents received a letter from their son saying he was well. Evans was captured later in Luxembourg during the Battle of the Bulge, the final German effort to turn back American forces on the Western front. Hitler's death on May 1, 1945, and the capitulation of Germany led to Evans' release and return to the U.S. for leave, training, and promotion to corporal. Evans was a good prospect for transfer to the Pacific theater and invasion of Japan until the destruction of Hiroshima and Nagasaki by atomic bombs in early August brought about Japan's surrender. Evans then returned to civilian life and re-enrolled at West Nottingham in September 1946 for a year of study.

Unlike Thomas Evans, Barry Tome, a former West Nottingham student from Wilmington, Del., was rejected for Army duty, having been classified 4-F because of an asthmatic condition. Tome tried to enlist with the foreign service of the Red Cross but was rebuffed because he was too young. He then turned to the American Field Service in which he served as a front-line ambulance driver with the British Eighth army in North Africa, on the Anzio beachhead in Italy, and in Rome. Tome came home in the fall of 1944 after his first enlistment had expired, but he must have found life at home a little boring with most of his friends still in service because he was soon thinking of rejoining the American Field Service to work with French combat troops.

Another West Nottingham graduate, Marine Corporal James H. Lyon of Havre de Grace, was awarded a Bronze Star for his part in the capture of the island of Iwo Jima, a stepping-stone in the conquest of Japan. The citation read:

> For heroic and meritorious service in connection with operation against the enemy while serving as demolitions specialist in an engineer squad on Iwo Jima on 20 February 1945. Corporal Lyon was one of a group of five men directed to remove an enemy minefield after dark, located on one of the flanking beaches. Working with painstaking care, chiefly by touch, and under very heavy and sustained enemy mortar fire, he, with the other four, cleared the beach of over 70 mines in the face of intense bombardment through which he worked. His courage, conduct and devotion to duty throughout were in keeping with the highest traditions of the U.S. Naval Service.

A West Nottingham graduate of 1935, Major Edward N. Jenkins of Rising Sun, was one of four brothers who served in the U.S. Army. Major Jenkins' service as operations officer of his Signal Corps battalion during the invasions of New Ginea and the Philippines earned him the Legion of Merit.

Barton B. McAuley of Elkton followed two older brothers into service after graduating from West Nottingham in the spring of 1943. He was preparing to enter the Navy's V-5 program for training naval aviators but for some reason was diverted to the Navy's enlisted corps. Although Barton did not become a naval aviator, he served as a Navy fireman in the South Pacific. Barton's morale looks high in a July 1945 picture

Old friends—Anne Collins of Elkton and Barton McAuley, US Navy (West Nottingham Class of 1943), meet at Navy repair shop in South Pacific, July 1945.

taken at a Navy repair shop in the Admiralty Islands. His visitor was Anne Collins, a friend from Elkton who discovered Barton while serving as a member of one of the United Service Organization shows assembled to entertain overseas servicemen.

Undoubtedly the luckiest serviceman from West Nottingham in World War II was Peter J. Garretson of Wilmington, Delaware, who enlisted in the Navy out of West Nottingham Academy in June 1942. In early 1943 Garretson's ship was ploughing homeward in the Atlantic when struck by a torpedo at 4 a.m. The vessel survived the hit, which was 30 feet aft of midship; but the explosion threw Garretson 100 yards out into the Atlantic. Moreover, the torpedo's firing pin had pierced the muscles of his left shoulder and its fumes had seared his lungs. In the early morning confusion, Garretson wasn't missed so his ship continued on its westward course, leaving him bobbing alone on 16-foot waves in his "Mae West" life jacket. Wounded and cold, he could not believe he had a ghost of a chance. Losing track of time and only partially conscious, Garretson gradually became aware of voices. Then clearly he heard someone say, "What in the hell are you doing away out here?" Garretson barely managed, "Just swimming." Then he was pulled out of the water by sailors from an American destroyer. Against almost impossible odds, an alert lookout on the destroyer had spotted Garretson's limp form in the vastness of the Atlantic. After treatment at the naval hospital in Boston, Garretson was discharged because of his damaged lungs.

A tragic counterbalance to the adventure, achievement, and luck of West Nottingham alumni in the service of their nation was the toll of 16 lives lost—all men of promise who had no chance to live out their mature years and exercise their full capabilities.

World War II had the relatively minor impact on West Nottingham Academy of postponing the celebration of its bicentennial from 1944, the actual 200th year after the school's founding, to 1946, the first full year of peace after the war. Headmaster Slaybaugh managed and coordinated the arrangements for the celebration with particular enthusiasm because of his great interest in the history of the academy.* Ever since his arrival at West Nottingham in 1924, Slaybaugh had been

---

* Slaybaugh was elected President of the Cecil County Historical Society in 1940.

seeking historical information wherever available and especially from alumni, one of whom had attended before the Civil War. While building fresh loyalty and support among earlier alumni, the headmaster gathered and organized much historical data that would otherwise have been lost. Slaybaugh and the Board of Trustees decided to have the bicentennial celebration start on October 19, the Saturday of the academy's homecoming weekend when alumni traditionally gathered to watch the football game and see old friends. This time many younger alumni had plenty of war stories to tell. Those alumni who stayed for the full bicentennial program heard much about their fellow alumni of other generations.

The three-day-long program began outdoors on a crisp autumn day with the dedication of the Richard Alexander Athletic Field, honoring "Duke" Alexander, West Nottingham's greatest athlete and its first alumnus to be killed in World War II. With the vivid blue sky forming a background for the golden and scarlet foliage of hickory, beech, oak, and sumac, the dedication began with short addresses by Franklin Eby, president of the Alumni Association, and Robert Swain, president of the academy's Board of Trustees. Swain spoke of West Nottingham's pride in Duke Alexander and called upon future academy athletes to follow his example of sportsmanship and determination to excel. Clark Shaughnessy, Duke's football coach at the University of Maryland, then told of Alexander's track and football exploits during his two years at Maryland. After the dedication, the field was put into immediate use with the homecoming game between West Nottingham and Mercersburg Academy, which West Nottingham lost by 8 to 0.

On Sunday the bicentennial celebration continued with two worship services that emphasized the relationship of the academy with the Presbyterian Church. In the morning service Dr. Frederick W. Evans, Moderator of the Presbyterian Church, U.S.A., congratulated West Nottingham Academy on its long and useful history and emphasized the opportunities for greater service in the future by West Nottingham and Christians in general. Dr. Rex S. Clements, President of the national Presbyterian Board of Education delivered the evening sermon. He noted that West Nottingham was the only secondary school formally related to the national Presbyterian Church although there were 45 Presbyterian-related colleges. Dr. Clements congratulated West Nottingham on its bicentennial and commented on the longevity of schools and churches as follows:

> To live through two hundred years is an achievement of which you have every right to be proud. And yet, nothing lasts like the church and the school. What else is there in this community that was here when the Academy was founded? . . . [The church and school] represent those permanent, continuing interests in life that build and feed.

Dr. Clements then linked West Nottingham's past, present, and future with these words:

> We should be thinking tonight about the strong and true men who laid so well the foundations of this school. We should think too about what its history should mean to us today. And finally we should think about our tomorrows. We begin by realizing our relationship to those who have gone before. We are tied to them; this present is a bridge, with one end in the past and the other reaching out into the future. The work of those who built their lives into this school is not finished. Without us, they shall not be made perfect; their work will be completed only as we complete ours in their spirit.

The chairman of the Monday session of the bicentennial was Daniel M. Henry, a direct descendant of an early West Nottingham student, Governor John Henry of Maryland, who was also Maryland's first U.S. Senator. Noting that he was chosen as bicentennial chairman only because of his ancestry, Henry went on to introduce the first principal speaker of the day, Major General Norman T. Kirk, Surgeon General of the U.S. Army. The surgeon general recalled the lives of the great doctors of medicine who had attended West Nottingham Academy. The five he chose studied under Rev. Samuel Finley, the founder, and had prominent roles in early American medicine. They were: John Morgan and William Shippen, founders of America's first medical school (part of Pennsylvania University); John Archer, first to graduate from the Pennsylvania Medical School and a successful teacher himself; Benjamin Rush, who has been called the "Father of American Psychiatry" because he realized the need for treating the mentally ill; and James Tilton, a pioneer in preventive medicine, whose philosophy Kirk called a keystone to the Army's extensive immunization policy.

The second main speaker of the final bicentennial day was Glenn R. Morrow, dean of the College of the University of Pennsylvania. In paying tribute to West Nottingham's achievements, Dean Morrow spoke of the non-exclusiveness of education in the following words:

> Those of us whose lives are devoted to education and learning are engaged in an enterprise whose very nature is non-competitive. We are dealing with goods that increase in quality and in quantity the more they are shared with others. The achievements of your forebears are our heritage, as well as yours; and your qualities today add to the resources on which we must all rely for the realization of our finest purposes.

Dean Morrow then delved into some achievements of West Nottingham alumni in the field of education. He mentioned the pioneer efforts of colonial alumni in medical education and noted another kind of educational contribution made by Benjamin Rush, the Philadelphia physician. While Rush was still a medical student attending the University of Edinburgh, Princeton's trustees were trying to persuade the famous Scottish clergyman, Dr. John Witherspoon, to come to America and accept the presidency of Princeton. As a kind of last resort, the trustees sought the aid of Rush, a recent Princeton graduate. The young medical student, not a Presbyterian, must have shown an unusual degree of intelligence and charm in his call upon the distinguished clergyman because Witherspoon soon decided to accept Princeton's offer. After a voyage of 13 weeks in heavy seas, Witherspoon, his "brave, but heartsick" wife, and five children landed in Philadelphia on August 7, 1768. Another president of Princeton, Woodrow Wilson, observed 150 years later that Witherspoon "found upon landing that he had always been an American." Witherspoon became one of Princeton's greatest presidents and was the only clergyman to sign the Declaration of Independence. Dean Morrow then considered the career of Robert S. Brookings who received his only formal education at West Nottingham Academy soon after the end of the Civil War. After making a fortune in business, Brookings turned his attention to education and became President of the Board of Trustees of Washington University in St. Louis. Brookings rebuilt the university and developed its medical school to a high level of distinction. Brookings' experience as chairman of the Price-Fixing Committee of the War Industries Board in World War I led him to found Brookings Institution in Washington, D.C., which conducts economic research to provide data on which to base national policies.

Henry Breckinridge rounded out the final day of the bicentennial by speaking of West Nottingham's contribution to America's political life. Breckinridge had graduated from West Nottingham in 1903, became a lawyer, and had served as Assistant Secretary of War in President Woodrow Wilson's cabinet. He brought the bicentennial celebration to a high point near the end of his address when he turned from praise of famous alumni to pose the following challenge to the current West Nottingham teachers and students:

> What a quest for the teachers! To inspire, to lead these boys to the fulfillment of the best that may be in their bodies, minds and souls. What a glorious consummation of the teacher's life, if most of the young boys coming from West Nottingham bring to the world, honesty, industry, loyalty, common sense! If, in the infinite complexity of heredity, training, and opportunity, no genius appear, the greatness of the school need not be lessened. Good men leaven the lump of the nation. In the ministry, medicine, law, engineering, business, teaching, and manifold other activities of life, there is opportunity for public service. Each individual life, soundly lived, is a public service. Without widespread individual worth there can be no permanent national greatness. The individual is the root, the foundation.

After the bicentennial, West Nottingham Academy picked up where it had left off when disrupted by World War II. Enrollment rose to prewar levels, and Headmaster Slaybaugh rebuilt the teaching staff with war veterans who included one returning faculty member and five newcomers. The following list includes two later headmasters as well as the veterans hired by Slaybaugh.

At West Nottingham	Field / Position	War Service
1938–42 York Honore 1946–52	Art, Ceramics	1942–45: 82nd Airborne Div.
1946–Present C. Herbert Foutz	Mathematics / Dean of Faculty, Dean Emeritus	1942–45: U.S. Army Signal Corps, Africa, Europe

WORLD WAR II AND BICENTENNIAL 155

At West Nottingham	Field / Position	War Service
1945–49 David G. Proctor	Latin, French	1942–45: U.S. Army Counter Intelligence Corps, Europe
1946–69 Charles F. Bauer	Latin, German, Spanish	1942–46: Captain, U.S. Army
1947–52 Robert B. Miller	Junior School, History	1943–46: 26th Infantry Div., Europe
1948–52 James L. Buchanan	Director of Athletics, Coach	1942–45: U.S. Marine Corps
1952–61 Charles W. Blaker	Headmaster	1943–45: Flight Instructor, U.S. Army Air Corps
1958–61 Norman C. Farnlof 1961–72	Assistant Headmaster Headmaster	Captain, U.S. Marine Corps

West Nottingham also benefited by the attendance of students who were veterans of the war. The 1949 *Pegé* gave brief summaries of the war service and college plans of the 13 veterans. The *Pegé* of 1950 referred to the five veterans at West Nottingham as "leading personalities on campus, respected by ... their friends and looked up to by the younger students." The following tabulation gives the number of veterans and school enrollment for the years that most of the veterans attended:

	Veterans	School Enrollment
1946–47	19	117
1947–48	11	98
1948–49	13	105
1949–50	5	63

Although the veterans were serious students, they were not used to the restrictions normally imposed on boarding school students. Realizing that the veterans were older and more independent, Slaybaugh gave them more freedom.

Paul Slaybaugh was completing his 25th year as headmaster when the Board of Trustees offered him a contract on Februry 29, 1949, that he did not find acceptable. After staying longer than any of his predecessors, Slaybaugh may have felt he had done about all he wanted to do at the academy. Therefore, he was somewhat unbending when he met with the board for a final decision on May 26. The board's position vis-à-vis Slaybaugh was advanced mainly by Norman Anderson, who was not yet a board member although he would soon join at the board's meeting on October 28, 1949, and Sidney Venable, pastor of the West Nottingham Presbyterian Church. After considerable discussion, the trustees accepted Slaybaugh's resignation, granting him a year's leave of absence with monthly compensation at the rate of $4,200 per year plus use of the headmaster's house.

Slaybaugh did not need the use of the headmaster's residence. Within a few weeks after his resignation "and out of a clear sky," Slaybaugh received an offer from President William Gell of Westminster College in Fulton, Missouri, to come to Westminster as director of admissions. After two years at Westminster, Slaybaugh learned that the presidency of Wesley Junior College in Dover, Delaware, was vacant. Slaybaugh had not pursued an overture from Wesley for its presidency in 1943 because he wanted to stay at West Nottingham longer than anyone else and he didn't feel he was quite ready to be president of a college. Now, in 1951, Slaybaugh "felt ready to accept the challenge" and within two weeks was elected president. In the manner of his transformation of West Nottingham, Paul Slaybaugh was able to invigorate Wesley College, which he had found in a weakened condition. In ten years, Wesley was healthy and Slaybaugh was ready to retire from academic leadership.

15

Hard Times and Rescue by Charles Blaker, 1949-1961

AS PAUL SLAYBAUGH and his wife drove away from the West Nottingham campus for the last time on that hot, early summer day in 1949, there were expressed and unexpressed concerns among the onlookers that the school could not survive without its headmaster. For many of the faculty as well as the alumni of the past 25 graduating classes, Paul Slaybaugh and West Nottingham Academy were indistinguishable and inseparable. Franklin Eby, President of the Alumni Association and member of the Board of Trustees, walked out of the meeting of the board that accepted Slaybaugh's resignation. That same afternoon he resigned as president of the Alumni Association. After Slaybaugh left, it was reportedly difficult to raise money from the graduates of his era because many of them felt that their beloved headmaster had been treated unfairly. The first year after Slaybaugh's departure, the senior class dedicated their yearbook to him, describing the headmaster as "a friend, counselor, and diligent crusader."

After Slaybaugh's resignation, the Board of Trustees had the immediate problem of finding a replacement for him. The trustees* were probably surprised that they had not been able to come to terms with their longtime headmaster, and they may not have been willing or able to offer enough money to obtain a capable outsider. The net result was an offer of the job to the academy's registrar and teacher of science and music, Richard W. Holstein. Reluctant to give up his teaching duties, Holstein accepted the board's offer on the condition that he would serve as acting headmaster and for only one year. Holstein had

---

*Appendix A gives membership of board at its meeting of October 28, 1949.

graduated from Lebanon Valley College in 1933 and taught science and music at West Nottingham from 1937 to 1941. After working in a munitions plant in Elkton from 1941 to 1945, Holstein had returned to West Nottingham to teach and serve as registrar. Holstein began his stint as acting headmaster in September 1949. The following June a respectably large class of 34 graduated; but the number of the junior class fell to 6, and enrollment dropped to 63 as compared to 101 in 1948-49. The treasurer's report for Holstein's first year showed that the budget was barely balanced by keeping the salaries at the level established in July 1947 before postwar inflation became substantial. (The 1947 level provided $2,800 annually for the headmaster.) Furthermore, needed painting and building repairs were postponed.

Although Holstein's first year gave the Board of Trustees a year to find a willing and permanent headmaster, they successfully appealed to Holstein's loyalty to the academy in persuading him to serve a second year. To economize on faculty salaries, Holstein planned to carry the whole teaching load for science to avoid hiring a science teacher—a saving of $2,100 to $3,000. As Holstein began his second year in the fall of 1950, he had only 47 students despite intensive recruiting that he described to the Board of Trustees in October 1950 as follows:

> Since March I have made more personal visits to prospects, more phone calls and other contacts with prospective patrons and agencies than Dr. Slaybaugh and I together did in any one year.

The same month Holstein reported to the board that the academy had reached the "nadir" of its existence. In the following months nothing happened to improve the outlook. Later in the year, the Board of Trustees persuaded Holstein to stay as acting headmaster for still a third year while enrollment continued to slide to the levels shown in Table IX.

During the three discouraging years that followed Slaybaugh's departure, the school was fortunate in retaining three dedicated teachers. Holstein praised them because "they had been cooperating wholeheartedly in this crisis, offering to do extra duty [and] putting forth greater effort to give the students the best they can offer in classes and extracurricular activities." The teachers who served under Holstein were C. F. Bauer, C. H. Foutz, and K. R. Nilsson. The same teachers continued under the next headmaster, Charles W. Blaker, who also had

Charles W. Blaker. Headmaster, 1952-1961.

a high opinion of the teaching staff. Ted Wills, a student, considered Foutz and Nilsson to have been among the finest teachers he ever had, including Wills' instructors when he studied at Oxford as a Rhodes Scholar.

Another cohesive force was the athletic program, conducted by James L. Buchanan who came to West Nottingham as director of athletics in the fall of 1948. The following record of his teams during a period of seriously declining enrollment is outstanding:

	1948-49*	1949-50	1950-51	1951-52
	(W-L)	(W-L)	(W-L)	(W-L)
Football	5-3	3-3	4-2	5-1-1
Basketball	8-8	14-8	9-7	7-7

* The year before Holstein became acting headmaster.

Table IX
Enrollment at End of Spring Semesters
(1950–1961)

By Grade Level	Slaybaugh 1949	1950	Holstein 1951	1952	1953	1954	1955	1956	Blaker 1957	1958	1959	1960	1961
Graduates	41	34	14	14	9	9	17	18	27	14	40	35	31
Post Grads	0	0	2*	0	0	9	7	0	11	14	0	0	13
Juniors	16	6	8	5	9	—	11	20	13	23	15	25	26
Sophmores	14	7	6	11	6	—	15	4	20	18	21	22	21
Freshmen	17	6	8	8	11	—	7	7	14	15	12	14	16
Junior School	14	10	13	9	0	3	6	11	9	13	13	9	19
Totals	102	63	51	47	35	71**	63	60	94	97	101	105	126

* Status unknown.
** Probable enrollment at beginning of school year, September 1953.

During his third year Holstein was so adamant about stepping down that the Board of Trustees realized they had to find somebody else or close the school. The option of closing was discussed in an "adjourned" meeting of the board on April 25, 1952, in which the trustees considered a hiatus for a year or two before reopening. Rev. Sydney J. Venable, a board member and pastor of the West Nottingham Presbyterian Church, declared that if the academy closed, it would never reopen. Fortunately, Venable and others prevailed in their determination to keep the academy in operation. Venable's West Nottingham Church maintained its 200-year tradition of helping in times of need by contributing $945 in a fund-raising drive conducted on behalf of the academy in the Baltimore Synod in late 1951 and 1952. Contributions from 58 churches totaled $6,099 of which the largest givers were:

Western Presbyterian, Washington, D.C.	$1,000
West Nottingham Presbyterian, West Nottingham	945
First Presbyterian, Baltimore	710
Hanover Street Presbyterian, Wilmington	350

Heartened by the financial support provided by the Presbyterians, the trustees turned to the task of finding a new headmaster. They preferred a Presbyterian clergyman to encourage Presbyterian support. In what was one of the most fortunate moments in the history of the academy, the board persuaded a recent Presbyterian divinity graduate, Charles W. Blaker, to come to West Nottingham from the faculty of Washington and Jefferson College. It would have been difficult for Blaker to have found a more challenging task. His ability to instill confidence was shown almost immediately when the Baltimore Presbyterian Synod agreed to continue its support although it insisted upon receiving a projected budget that was in balance before the beginning of the new term. Nevertheless, Blaker submitted a projected imbalance "with apology and explanation, and with an unspoken prayer that the effect would not be destructive" when the synod considered support for the following year. Blaker need not have worried because the synod did not falter in its assistance.

The new headmaster, who came to West Nottingham at the age of 34, was born in Pittsburgh and had graduated from the University of Pittsburgh in 1937 with a B.S. in Electrical Engineering. He was a sales engineer with Westinghouse Electric until 1943 when he joined the Army Air Corps, serving as cadet and flight instructor. Not long after his discharge in 1945, Blaker turned away from engineering to seek a career in religion. He graduated from Pittsburgh Theological Seminary in May 1949 and was ordained by the United Presbyterian Church USA in July 1949. Subsequently, Blaker took a teaching position at Washington and Jefferson College, which he held until coming to West Nottingham Academy on July 1, 1952.

Blaker was a handsome man who had been active in dramatics in high school and college and had participated in the Pittsburgh Playhouse and Pittsburgh Opera Society. At West Nottingham, Blaker's dress and appearance reminded one student, Ted Wills, of a youthful forest ranger. Wills also states that:

> Blaker was a combination of traditionalist and innovator. He had a military man's commitment to the letter of the law and enforced it with no exceptions. There were about six expulsions in my time (two academic years), but he never acted arbitrarily or unpredictably. He regularly mixed with the students in informal settings and never exercised even a hint of favoritism. With students as with faculty he was willing to listen to responsible complaints and when the facts so warranted, correct them. In the winter of 1955 he replaced the head cook in response to a student petition while making it clear he would tolerate no personal abuse or harassment of the cook in the interim.

Immediately after his arrival Blaker set about reversing the three-year decline in enrollment, which had fallen to 47 that spring. After intensive efforts during the rest of the summer, Blaker found he had lost ground; only 34 boarding students and three day students started school in September, marking the fourth consecutive year of declining enrollment. Blaker's early recruiting experience resembled that of Paul Slaybaugh more than 25 years earlier when Slaybaugh became headmaster and sought to establish a boarding school. Despite vigorous recruiting, Slaybaugh did not get his first two boarding students until the second semester of his first year, but continuing recruiting efforts brought in 16 boarding students at the beginning of his second year. The cumulative effect of Blaker's recruiting likewise paid dividends in his second year, as shown in Table IX.

The September 1953 upturn in enrollment and general revival of the academy inspired the venerable John G. Conner, former headmaster and long a trustee and generous giver, to contribute $10,000 toward restoration of Gayley Hall, the headmaster's campus residence. Enrollment would have increased again in Blaker's third year if the academy had not begun to require a series of pre-enrollment exams that resulted in 10 applicants not being accepted. This requirement continued in the years that followed, but enough qualified students applied to increase the enrollment. Table X shows that more boarding students began to come from Washington, D.C., and its environs in the late 1950s. This region includes the Northern Virginia suburbs and Montgomery and Prince Georges Counties in Maryland. Also more foreign students began to come.

Prior to Blaker's arrival, the school's poor financial situation had caused the Board of Trustees to cut the faculty to six members and reduce the support staff. Blaker recalled that the teachers he found at West Nottingham were his "salvation." The faculty members for Blaker's first year, who are listed in Table XI, consisted of three who had helped acting headmaster Holstein keep the school together, two newcomers, and Holstein himself, who stayed on as a teacher.

The upturn in enrollment in September 1953 brought the hiring of David Morrix as supervisor of Magraw dormitory and Burdette "Bud" Buck as West Nottingham's first guidance counselor. Buck soon noticed that the students didn't have any place to gather on the campus for social activity. He mentioned this lack to the headmaster. As Blaker recalled, "Almost at the same time, he and I thought of the Old Academy building, unused and in disrepair, but ideally located in the center of the campus." Blaker remembered that:

> We borrowed a truck, scrounged some money from somewhere, and bought lumber, light fixtures ... Working with some student help, Bud and I rebuilt the interior of the Old Academy, fitting it with a stage, booths with padded seats, a snack bar. The Canteen, as it came to be called, was used for movies, dances, performances, and just plain relaxation ..."

West Nottingham celebrated the opening of the canteen with a dance before Christmas vacation in 1953. Herb Foutz, the academy's math-

Table X
Approximate Geographical Distribution of Students at Midyear, 1949-1958 (1955-56 missing)

School Year	Day	Boarding Md.	Pa.	Del.	Metro Wash., D.C.**	N.J.	Other US	Foreign Nationality	Boarding Total	Grand Total
1949-50*	13	4	5	2	5	3	2	1	22	35
1950-51*	4	—	2	1	—	1	2	4	10	14
1951-52*	6	—	2	2	—	—	2	3	9	15
1952-53	6	11	5	—	2	1	7	5	31	37
1953-54	28	8	14	1	4	2	9	6	44	72
1954-55	26	9	12	1	4	—	8	8	42	68
1956-57	36	15	19	2	8	5	6	7	62	98
1958-59	35	14	26	3	9	11	16	5	84	119

* Includes graduates only.
** Includes Northern Virginia suburbs plus Montgomery and Prince Georges Counties in Maryland.

Table XI
West Nottingham Faculty 1952–1960

a. As of September 1952–

Service		Field/Position	Education
1946–69	Charles F. Bauer	Latin, German, Bible	Franklin and Marshall A.B. Penn. Ph.D.
1937–41	Richard W. Holstein	Science/Director of Summer Camp Science, Music	Lebanon Valley College B.S.
1949–52 1952–54		Acting Headmaster Science	
1951–55	Karl R. Nilsson	Social Studies/Coach JV Basketball	Temple B.A.
1946–Now	C. Herbert Foutz	Mathematics	Gettsburg A.B. Penn State M.A.
1952–55	Hugh G. Ford	English	Dickinson A.B. Stanford M.A.
1952–55	Horace W. Ewing	Coach of Football & Baseball	Delaware B.S.

b. Faculty Additions (1953–60)–

1953–59	Burdette H. Buck	Guidance Counselor/Basketball Coach	Fairmont State A.B. Pittsburgh M.A.
1953–59	David H. Morrix	Religion/Dormitory Supervisor/Dramatics	N.Y. University B.S., M.A.
1954–55	Rev. Charles W. Eby	Junior School	A.B., B.D.
1954–55	Richard A. Gessner	Biology, Science	B.S.
1954–55	Ronald H. Aires	Language	B.A., M.A.
1954–55	Margaret Fry	Physics, Chemistry	B.S.

Table XI (Continued)

Service		Field/Position	Education
1955–56	K. L. Onderdonk	Social Studies	—
1955–56	Mrs. R. L. Onderdonk	English	—
1955–56	Mary L. Hackett	English	—
1955–56	Diran Alexanian	Languages	—
1956–58	Andrew A. Casale	Social Studies	Denver Univ. A.B., M.A.
1956–59	Kenneth Birmingham	Football, Baseball, Golf Coach	Fairmont State B.S.
1956–59	Mrs. Grace Birmingham	Girls Coach	Fairmont State B.S.
1957–72	Robert E. Badenhoop	English	Dickinson A.B.
1957–72	Carol W. Badenhoop	English	Wilson A.B. Union Seminary
1957–58	Niniv Y. Ibrahim	Drama	—
1957–59	David W. Pullen	Mathematics	Rutgers B.A.
1958–59	Arnold Ulbrich	—	Ursinus A.B.
1958–62	Norman C. Farnlof	Assistant Headmaster	Philadelphia Episcopalian Divinity School
1962–72		Headmaster	

1959–64	David T. Jones	Junior School	Wheaton College B.A.
1959–61 1965–Now	Richard L. Funk	English, Junior School Mathematics/Guidance Counselor	Lock Haven State B.S.
1959–61	Lewis F. Acker	Social Studies, Arithmetic	Allegheney College B.S. Pittsburgh U. A.B.
1959–62 1967–Now	James E. Spiro	Director of Athletics/Football, Basketball Coach Director of Admissions	Fairmont State College, B.A.
1959–60	Mary Wright	Girls' Athletics	Wesleyan Junior College, Dover, Del., Towson State A.B.
1960–62	Mary Wright Spiro	Girls' Athletics	
1967–81	Mary Wright Spiro	Librarian/Girls' Athletics	
1959–62	Charles X. Carlson	Art	
1959–67	John L. Gallagher	Biology, Chemistry, Science, Algebra/ Head of Science Department	Delware B.S., M.S.
1960–68 1968–72 1972–81	Kenneth Dietrich	History/Librarian Assistant Headmaster, Headmaster	Dickinson A.B. Pennsylvania M.A.
1960–64	Clarence Miller	Algebra, Physics	Lincoln Univ. B.S.

ematics teacher since 1946, and Bud Buck became the faculty advisors for the student club that operated the canteen. Club activities included selling snacks and soft drinks, sponsoring all school dances, and showing weekly movies with the help of Mr. Foutz. For the 1960–61 school year, the Canteen Club had 40 members, making it the largest club at West Nottingham. That year it sponsored Sadie Hawkins and Christmas parties, and the members treated themselves to skating and swimming parties and two banquets.

By early 1954, the teachers who had stayed with the academy in its time of trouble fully realized that the school's future looked better. They did not see any move to improve their salaries or security, however. Aware of their restlessness, Headmaster Blaker appointed a faculty committee to work out a statement of their needs on the basis of policies at other private schools and public schools. Blaker presented the proposal at the May 1954 meeting of the Board of Trustees. Norman Anderson, vice-president of the board, "cut it to shreds," leading to the departure of three experienced faculty members that summer as well as four others who had been at the academy for one year. Blaker later stated that he felt that faculty of equal caliber were not found for another five years. Ted Wills, then a student, comments that the drastic turnover in faculty at this time affected him more than any other event in his two years at West Nottingham, calling the loss of K. R. Nilsson "devastating" to the school and describing another departing teacher, Hugh G. Ford, as outstanding. Blaker continued to seek more money for the faculty. In a request to the board of February 24, 1955, Blaker described his ideal boarding school teacher as follows:

> The kind of person who can teach at a boarding school is a strange breed of human. He must be ... more interested in those he teaches than in what he teaches them ... such a teacher throws himself completely into the total program of a boarding school seeking to discover and deal with student problems both academic and personal, outside of class as well as in, careless of his own time if the giving of it means the strengthening of the student ... We have some like that on our faculty ... such people, however, are worth many times more than they are paid under our prevailing salary scale and once we find them, we must hold on to them with every resource at our command.

Annual Canteen Club Dinner. Philadelphia, Spring of 1958.
First Row—Mac Harter, Herb Foutz, Bud Buck, David Morrix; *Second Row*—Cathy Wood, Scotty Laughlin, Beth Hamdy, Richard Jenkins, Merton Lau; *Standing*—Dusty Miller, Whitney Williams, Sue Castle, Glen Gilchrist.

In the years that followed, the academy hired a number of new teachers and coaches because of greater enrollment and vacancies left by departures. Among the prospective faculty members considered by Headmaster Blaker was Richard Funk. In early 1959, Funk was a senior student at Lock Haven State College, Pennsylvania, looking for a teaching job. He decided to start his search at West Nottingham because it was less than forty miles from Coatesville, Pennsylvania, where he was spending spring vacation with his sister. Upon his arrival at the school, Funk was directed to Wiley, an old frame house where the headmaster's office was still located after its removal from Magraw House years before by Headmaster Slaybaugh. Funk went inside and found himself in an empty waiting room amid a number of pieces of wrought-iron lawn furniture. Although the room was empty, he felt that he was already being sized up when he noticed the stern faces of Samuel Finley, Benjamin Rush, and Richard Stockton staring at him from three large portraits hung on the mustard green wall. The only other decoration consisted of plastic green window shades. When a man in a long black coat and dark hat suddenly walked in, Funk sprang to his feet to greet Headmaster Blaker. Instead, it was the president of the Board of Trustees, Norman Anderson, who identified himself and corrected Funk's mispronunciation of "Blaker." Next came Norman Farnlof, the assistant headmaster, whom Funk also mistook for the headmaster. The third person to enter wore a plaid jacket and hunting cap. He walked over to Funk, introduced himself as Blaker and gave the young job seeker the impression that he was the most important person Blaker had met in some time. Blaker's entrance seemed to be the signal for the entrance of four or five soberly dressed men, and young Funk began to wonder why he was getting so much attention. All assembled in the headmaster's office in which the central piece of furniture was a door that had been converted into a table with iron brackets and served as the headmaster's desk. Funk took a seat near the door, and turning to close it, he almost fell out of his chair. One of the interviewers whispered to Funk, "This is my first time too." The formidable number and appearance of the interviewers did not result in a particularly grueling interview, as Funk remembers. Afterwards, he and his sister drove up to Magraw House through a sea of mud. Feeling lucky not to have gotten stuck, they cut short their tour of the campus and returned to Coatesville. Somewhat to his surprise, Funk received notice of his acceptance by mail a few weeks later, the beginning of a long association with the academy, which he now serves as assistant headmaster.

Funk found out later that the gentleman, who informed him that it was his first time, was Arthur Stevenson, who had just begun his service on the Board of Trustees as a member of the faculty committee. Other members of the interviewing panel also were members of the faculty committee. Its interview of prospective teachers was part of the effort of Norman Anderson, then president of the board, to keep close control over the faculty.

The interviewing duties of the board's faculty committee apparently did not continue the following year because Kenneth Dietrich applied for a teaching position the following January in the same office with the same furniture but minus the panel of interviewers. At the time of his visit, Dietrich was working in a department store but was anxious to get a job that would make better use of his A.B. from Dickinson and M.A. from Pennsylvania. Dietrich found his way to the right building at West Nottingham, but there was no way to tell which door opened into the headmaster's office. On a hunch, Dietrich cautiously pushed open a door that did not quite fit its frame. Immediately, a nattily dressed headmaster rose to greet the young applicant in a rich and mellow voice. Headmaster Blaker never stopped talking as he held the young job hunter spellbound for forty minutes. When the interview, which was really more of a monologue, ended, Dietrich didn't even bother to walk around the campus or look at the academy's facilities before eagerly accepting the job that was offered. It was the beginning of another long association with the academy that culminated with Dietrich's service as headmaster from 1972 to 1981.

Charles Blaker also used his speaking skill from the pulpit of the West Nottingham Presbyterian Church, located at the edge of the campus. At one Christmas service that was held in the church, Blaker read Dickens' *Christmas Carol.* A single spotlight in the darkened church was directed on the headmaster. His strong voice and perfect enunciation seemed to extract for his listeners the deepest meanings from the classic story. When the West Nottingham Church found itself without a pastor, the congregation invited the headmaster, an ordained Presbyterian minister, to fill the pulpit until a permanent pastor could be found. Before the year-long search for a pastor had ended, some of the congregation may have wished that the enthusiastic substitute had never been invited. Blaker expressed himself on a variety of issues from the pulpit, but the sermon that had been roughest on his listeners had been about stewardship; Blaker had urged drastically increased contributions from the members.

Upon his arrival at West Nottingham, Charles Blaker found the curriculum to be "only a skeleton in desperate need of flesh if it were to survive." By Blaker's last year, 1960–61, he had expanded the course offerings to 35, including some of advanced standing for talented students. Expansion of the curriculum was one of the requirements that would qualify the academy for accreditation by the Middle States Association of Colleges and Secondary Schools, which had been lost in 1951. The procedures for gaining accreditation had progressed but were not yet complete when Blaker left in June 1961.

In his early years at the academy, Blaker and the faculty established the "Single-Subject Plan" of study. The idea had originated in the Army during World War II and had been successful in teaching foreign languages. Under the program, a student spent four hours each morning in the intensive study of a single subject. Afternoons were free except for a stipulated period of physical education and athletics. The student covered the equivalent of one year's study of a subject in eight weeks, giving him one credit toward graduation. Because the school year was divided into quarters, the students could gain four credits in four different courses during the year, the same number that would be earned under a traditional system. Ted Wills, a student from 1954–1956, praised the single-subject plan because it was preferable to keeping track of 4 or 5 courses at once. The "Single-Subject Plan" was described in the 1955 and 1956 catalogs, but the *Alumnus* of April 1, 1961, reported that after experimentation and self-study, the academy had put into operation a modification of the original plan in the fall of 1960. The new program provided a weekly schedule of five hours of classroom time for each of three subjects. Classes for each subject met three times a week for two two-hour periods and one one-hour period. Such a schedule approximated a college program, thus giving the student good experience for the future. The program provided enough concentration on separate subjects because there was ample time for laboratory work in the sciences and for debates, research, and panel discussions in the other courses.

By 1958 the curriculum qualified West Nottingham for establishing a local chapter of the National Honor Society, which the academy named the Talisman Club. The first West Nottingham students qualified in 1960 when three girls were recognized: Janet R. Engel, Susan B. Goldmeier, and Nancy V. Roddy. In 1961 the first three boys qualified: Alan Baxter, George H. Derbyshire III, and William N. Thais. Christina Farnlof, daughter of the assistant headmaster, and Jeff Blaker, son of the headmaster, were also early qualifiers.

Ted Wills, a student from Monrovia, California, who graduated in 1956, received a Rhodes Scholarship in September 1960 after graduation from the University of Idaho. He has been the only West Nottingham student to win this prestigious award which provides two or three years of study at Oxford University. Wills commented in retrospect that:

> I credit West Nottingham Academy for laying the foundation and providing me with the mental habits that made this possible ... Most of the classes [at West Nottingham] required essay-style exams ... This was an excellent preparation for college as well as an inducement to integrative understanding.

Enrollment of girls began in the fall of 1953. It had been the academy's policy since 1931 to be a boy's boarding school. Blaker, however, strongly advocated enrollment of girls and found no opposition from the Board of Trustees. To get started, the academy admitted seven girls from Havre de Grace who lived at home but were transported daily to school by an academy bus for $35 a year per girl. The fee did not cover costs, but the headmaster and board were thinking of the long-term advantage to enrollment that would result if the school became coeducational. In September 1954, the first five boarding girls joined the girls from Havre de Grace at the academy. The boarding girls lived in Gayley House with the headmaster and his wife before moving with their housemother, Virginia Bowen, into the Tyson-Sill House which had been renovated for them. As the second year with girl students began, Blaker was enthusiastic about their contribution to the life of the school and regretted that all but two of the first group would graduate that year. Any concern that the girls would not keep coming proved to be needless, however, as shown in the following tabulation:

	Girls	Boys
1952	0	35
1953	7	64
1954	7	56
1955	13	47
1956	23	71
1957	19	76
1958	36	65
1959	28	82
1960	30	96

Blaker suggested varsity sports for the girls, and they formed a basketball team in the winter of 1957 but failed to win a game. The next season, Mrs. Grace Birmingham coached the girls to the first three victories by a girls' team in West Nottingham's history. The team improved its record in 1959 and did still better in 1960, winning 6 and losing 4 under Coach Mary C. Wright in her first year at West Nottingham. Besides basketball, West Nottingham eventually formed girls' teams for baseball, field hockey, and tennis. Blaker's interest in girls' sports was about 20 years ahead of the times. Women's varsity athletic teams were not established in many high schools, colleges, and universities until the 1970s.

The final element in making West Nottingham coeducational was construction of Rowland Hall to house boarding students. The dormitory was dedicated in November of 1958, just six years after the Board of Trustees had asked Blaker, then starting his first year as headmaster, to report on the steps needed to make the academy coeducational. The Tyson-Sill House had been adequate as long as enrollment of boarding girls stayed below 14. The academy's projection of additional growth, however, led to a capital fund effort in 1956 and 1957 to finance construction of Rowland. The single-story brick dormitory consists of 10 rooms, each accommodating two girls; a large student lounge; and a three-room apartment for the dormitory supervisor. Although it was built before the national scarcity of energy became evident in 1974, Rowland is quite energy-efficient with hot water baseboard heating and fiberglass insulation in the ceiling. In conjunction with the construction of Rowland, the academy built a sewage disposal system in 1957 which consists of almost an acre of underground filter beds with automatic chlorination and flow control. The system has the location and capacity to serve Rowland, Hill Top Cottage, and all anticipated construction northwest of the campus lake. The new dormitory was named for J. M. H. Rowland, an academy graduate of 1886 and long the dean of the University of Maryland Medical School. Rowland, Norman Anderson, president of the Board of Trustees, and Sydney J. Venable, board member and former pastor of the West Nottingham Church attended the dedication. The students and faculty, a little chilly in the bright early November weather, heard Anderson, the headmaster, and Sue Castle, a senior student, formally dedicate the first dormitory built at West Nottingham specifically to house girls.

Blaker was engaged in another "first" for the academy in February 1956 when the school admitted Fletcher Morton, a Negro boy from Baltimore. An organization for child care had not given Blaker much notice of the boy's arrival, and the headmaster "gave little thought to possible problems—aside from selecting a roommate with some care." Blaker had already accepted students from the Dominican Republic, Taiwan, and Iran, as well as a couple of African exchange students sponsored by the Presbyterian Church. Although there was some grumbling from a half-dozen students before Fletcher Morton's arrival, there were no ugly incidents afterward. In fact, one white student recalls that "Fletcher was both bright and likeable and became fast friends with nearly everyone." One of the board members, however, was so upset by the prospect of a Negro student that he threatened to resign. He found no support from the other members, and his threat came to nought. Fletcher Morton did not stay long, apparently through lack of funds. The school was shocked to learn a year or two later that he had been killed when he stepped out of a Baltimore store into the middle of a battle between police and gunmen. By the middle 1960s, four to six Negroes, both boys and girls, were attending West Notthingham and a few have continued to attend up to the present time.

After Blaker's first two years, there were generally three to six foreign students at the academy. Most of the students came through personal contact with others who had already come, but the students from Thailand were steered to West Notthingham by the Cultural Attache at the Thai Embassy, who became well-acquainted with Blaker and the academy. The American students welcomed the foreign students, who found life at the academy to their liking. There were only two incidents in which overseas students were harassed. State Police subdued some "town toughs" who were bullying one foreign student. In the other case, a Thai student effectively defended himself with a razor against the attacks of a day student at the academy.

In another move that increased enrollment, Headmaster Blaker revived the junior school, which did not function in Blaker's first year but increased to 11 students by 1956 and averaged well over 10 students annually during the remainder of Blaker's administration. Blaker's addition of girls, foreign students, and junior school students all helped to more than triple the enrollment from 35 to 126 in Blaker's nine-year administration ending in 1961.

A glimpse of the student lunch line in October 1960 is provided by Harry Engel, a reporter for the *Arrow:*

> Conversation does not lag. On the contrary everyone talks at once and the sum total is that one cannot hear what his neighbor is saying but hears a noise similar to Niagara Falls. Seconds creep by until the bell is rung officially opening the dining hall. Then the "line" literally pours down the stairs.
>
> After eating, the gluttons return, go to their respective lounges or their dorms and eagerly wait for the fifth period bell to ring.

In early 1953, Headmaster Blaker faced the rippling effect of Senator Joseph McCarthy's witch hunt for communists in the U.S. Government which had reached West Nottingham in the form of a search for communists by the State of Maryland. In his report to the Board of Trustees at their regular winter meeting of February 20, 1953, Blaker explained that the modest annual support of $500 granted by the State of Maryland had resulted in a request from Annapolis that the academy report action taken to discover and remove subversive persons from its employ. The request was based on the Maryland Subversive Activities Act of 1949 which threatened loss of state aid to any private institution that failed to respond to such a query. Blaker's report attacked the loyalty oaths that would satisfy the state requirements because a witch hunt "results in a suppression of the right of free enquiry which is more damning to the democratic spirit than any amount of Red penetration could ever be." He declared, "As an individual, I will affirm my hatred of Stalinist communism from the housetops. As an educator,

I will steadfastly refuse to sign a loyalty pledge." The headmaster then pointed out to the board that the state grant was "very sorely needed just now" and regretted that his position had the appearance of an ultimatum. However, he concluded, "in good conscience, I cannot do otherwise." The minutes of the meeting simply state that "we back the headmaster in his action with regard to the State Subversive Act which requires a loyalty oath from all employees of the academy." It turned out that no confrontation with the state ensued because Maryland's attorney-general did not insist upon the loyalty oaths at West Nottingham. Nevertheless, the board's prompt support of the headmaster's stand was a proud moment for West Nottingham Academy and consistent with its traditions.

Although most of Blaker's efforts to invigorate the school took effect in a year or two, West Nottingham's athletic fortunes did not follow suit. The new football coach in Blaker's first year, Horace W. Ewing, could not repeat the magic of James L. Buchanan, who had coached winning football and basketball teams between 1948 and 1952 while enrollment declined year after year. Coach Ewing had a winning season in 1954 but departed after the 1955 season. By 1956 things had gotten so bad that for one game only eleven men suited up to play. At the beginning of the same season, Headmaster Blaker, after receiving a request from the football coach for $4,500 for new equipment, recommended to the Board of Trustees that West Nottingham discontinue football. Blaker told the board that four-fifths of the athletic budget went for football uniforms and equipment. The board ignored Blaker's request and continued the football program for another three years without much change or any better results.

Finally in 1959, James (Jim) Spiro, a graduate of Fairmont State College, West Virginia, took over the team and coached it to a record of three wins and four losses. The following spring, Jim Spiro married Mary Wright who was also finishing her first year at West Nottingham, having come as coach of girls' athletic teams. Next year the West Nottingham gridders did even better under Spiro with a 5-2 record that featured a 13-7 victory over Elkton High School and a 54-0 shellacking of Valley Forge Military Academy, usually a pushover for West Nottingham since before World War II.

Meantime the basketball team was also struggling, winning only one game in the 1952–53 season. Some poor and a few good seasons followed under Bud Buck, the guidance counselor, who coached the basketball team until the end of the 1959–60 season. The next season, Jim Spiro added basketball to his coaching duties. If West Nottingham had been heartened by Spiro's first two football seasons, students and faculty had to be astounded by Spiro's first basketball team. Developed in part from Bud Buck's 1960 team which won 11 and lost 11, the 1961 squad started the season with two expected victories, but in its next game found itself 12 points behind at the half against Valley Forge. *Pegé,* the 1961 yearbook, describes what happened in the last half against Valley Forge, "We upset the Cadets . . . by taking complete command . . . throughout the final two periods. Many knew after this game that West Nottingham was capable of beating every team on its schedule." The team did not disappoint these expectations, winning every game to give West Nottingham its first unbeaten basketball season. Skip Hughes from Hollidaysburg, Pennsylvania, led the squad of 10 in scoring with an average of 24 points per game and was named to Maryland's all-state basketball team. The record of 19 victories for the 1960–61 season follows:

West Nottingham Academy		Opponents
61	Northeast	42
80	Patton	29
54	Valley Forge Military Academy	40
54	Stevens Trade	30
54	North Harford	51
69	Perkomen	58
108	Perryville	14
78	Rock Hall	28
50	Williamson	39
64	Patton	33
52	Valley Forge Military Academy	40
75	Rock Hall	21
63	Northeast	38
77	Baltimore Institute	58
72	Williamson	54
48	Stevens Trade	23
58	Perkomen	39
38	Stevens Trade	29

While Headmaster Blaker worked well with the Board of Trustees on the postwar issues of McCarthyism, integration, and admission of girls, he had continuous difficulties with them regarding compensation for teachers, as already mentioned, and money-raising. In his February 1953 message to the board, Blaker had bluntly criticized the trustees for their lack of effort in raising funds with the exception of the three members who had obtained all the recent contributions. A little more than a year later in a report of May 21, 1954, Blaker again chided the board, saying, "Only a few members have done anything about it [finances] . . . [the others only] commiserate with each other over the state of affairs." As a result, the headmaster proposed three courses of action:
  1. To "Muddle along as we have been . . . and finally close the school in five years."
  2. To hire a fund-raising organization and be ready to be prodded into fund-raising activity by the organization.
  3. To place "full responsibility for the task in the headmaster's office and hire an experienced fund-raiser."

While the board and headmaster continued to worry about the school's financial condition, enrollment increased substantially from 76 in September 1955 to 95 in September 1956 and then to 111 in 1957. The headmaster continued to show dissatisfaction by threatening to resign on July 1, 1956 but did not. By early 1957 Blaker believed that he had largely accomplished the work for which he was hired, namely, to bridge the gap between the school and the Baltimore Synod (He was a Presbyterian minister.), to increase enrollment, and "to erase many of the weaknesses in the educational program, noted in the Middle States evaluation of 1952." Satisfied that he had revived the academy, Blaker was determined to resign but was dissuaded by several board members because a fund-raising drive was about to begin. Therefore, Blaker waited until November 1957 to hand his resignation to Norman Anderson, president of the Board of Trustees. Anderson, accustomed to Blaker's efforts to resign, "refused to accept it or believe I could be serious about it," as Blaker recalled. Next month in December 1957, the headmaster offered to remain but only under two main conditions:
  1. Blaker was to retain the title of headmaster and all professional

direction of the faculty. Blaker's salary was to increase from $5,200 to $7,500 because he would do some teaching.

2. A suitable assistant headmaster would be appointed to carry responsibility for office routine, discipline, and partial responsibility for interviewing parents and other casual visitors during the school year.

The board's acceptance of the two main conditions led to the hiring of Norman C. Farnlof as assistant headmaster to start in the fall of 1958.

The advent of Norman Farnlof as assistant headmaster did not resolve the main problem that confronted Headmaster Blaker—namely, working with Norman Anderson who was both president of the Board of Trustees and business manager of the academy. Blaker felt that the crux of the problem was that Anderson as president of the board had the responsibility of supervising Blaker and yet as business manager should be subordinate to Blaker. Because the headmaster and Anderson as business manager could not work together smoothly, the meetings of the Board of Trustees were cluttered with administrative issues. Furthermore, Anderson's dual role probably resulted in over-supervision of Blaker. Over the years, Blaker and Anderson had clashed over compensation of the faculty and Blaker himself. Despite Blaker's dislike for Anderson, Blaker called Anderson the "key to the survival of the Academy" during the 1950s. Anderson owned a lumber, coal, and feed business in Colora, but spent half of his time at the academy, trying "to manipulate the meager income and staggering debt so salaries could be paid and food bought."

After Farnlof arrived as assistant headmaster, enrollment continued to rise while Blaker and Farnlof worked effectively together. The differences between Blaker and Anderson, however, finally led to Blaker's resignation in the spring of 1961. The outgoing headmaster recommended Norman Farnlof as his successor, stating that, "His dynamic leadership and deep concern for the students have been manifest to all and have earned him their bright regard."

16

Continuity with Norman Farnlof and Kenneth Dietrich, 1961–1981

CHARLES W. BLAKER must have felt somewhat discouraged as he made his final departure from West Nottingham after the 1961 spring session. The nine years that he had devoted to the academy seemed to have been a series of struggles: to increase enrollment, to badger the Board of Trustees to raise more money, to prepare the academy for accreditation (completed after he left), and, finally, to try to hold on to valuable faculty members in the face of Norman Anderson's reluctance to raise salaries.

These clashes between Blaker and Anderson do not loom large in comparison to Blaker's achievement in breathing life into the expiring academy and rebuilding its academic quality. Besides Blaker's contributions while in office, his proposal for an assistant headmaster in 1958 had had the fortuitous effect of saving the academy from its recurring inability to find a permanent headmaster. By the time Blaker resigned in 1961, Farnlof, the assistant headmaster, had taken much of the nonacademic load from Blaker's shoulders and was ready to take over as headmaster.

Before coming to West Nottingham in 1958, Norman Farnlof had served five years as head of the junior school at Admiral Farragut Academy. Like Blaker, Farnlof had come to education by way of military service and religion. After serving in the Marine Corps as drill instructor and captain, he had earned a degree from the Episcopalian School of Divinity in Philadelphia.

As Farnlof began his duties as headmaster at West Nottingham, the Board of Trustees also changed its leadership by electing Arthur Stevenson as president. Stevenson defeated Norman Anderson's bid for reelection at the board's meeting on October 22, 1961. Appendix A gives the officers and membership of the board after the October 22 meeting. Anderson continued to serve as board member and business manager of the academy until January 1, 1971 when he died of a heart attack while cleaning snow off his car. Headmaster Farnlof had an easier time dealing with Norman Anderson than Headmaster Blaker because Anderson was no longer president of the board. Furthermore, the academy's improved financial condition eased the relationship between headmaster and board. After Arthur Stevenson's election as president, the board's leadership remained basically the same during the administrations of Headmasters Farnlof and his successor, Kenneth Dietrich (Appendix A).

Farnlof had reason to be pleased as he began his first year as headmaster. The largest student body in history had enrolled, consisting of 123 boarding and 47 day students. The relocation of the administrative offices from Wiley to Magraw made space for the additional boarding students. It was necessary to add two new instructors because of the influx. The desire to attend the academy reached an unprecedented high during the summer when a girl called the new headmaster three times, begging to be admitted even though all the dormitory spaces had been filled. On the final call, she offered to work as a maid in Gayley House in addition to paying full boarding tuition in order to be admitted. Another cause for Farnlof's satisfaction was the opening of Finley Hall.

Finley, constructed during the preceding year, was and is the largest classroom building that West Nottingham has ever had. It contains three laboratories, an assembly room, library, eight classrooms, a dispensary, teachers' lounge, and three restrooms. The structure cost $132,000, and the equipment to furnish the laboratories and classrooms cost $23,000. The Parents' Association paid for the equipment as its first major project. It had been organized in 1960 by Charles W. Dunnett, West Nottingham's first public relations officer. Finley Hall made a change in the daily life of every student because having most classrooms under one roof meant an end to long walks to attend classes in every nook and cranny of the campus, such as the ping pong room where the French class was held.

Later in Farnlof's first year, he appealed to everyone at West Nottingham for cooperation in a matter "of more importance to the Academy even than Finley Hall." He referred to West Nottingham's 10-year effort to gain accreditation by the Middle States Association of Colleges and Secondary Schools. West Nottingham had dropped out of the Middle States Association in 1951 when its fortunes were at a low ebb. In 1952 Headmaster Blaker had begun the necessry expansion of the curriculum to regain accreditation. The required "self-study" had been completed in 1960. The climax of the effort was to be a three-day visit by 15 representatives of the association, beginning March 12, 1962. Farnlof emphasized the crucial role of students in the March issue of *Arrow*, a student publication, as follows:

> The Student Council has already reviewed the part which students will be taking. I hope that you listened carefully in chapel-assemblies when fellow students covered the various items over which you have so much control. Practical matters such as meal line order, campus conduct, the use of facilities, etc. are important. The kind of group impression we make upon the committee depends entirely on the individual responsibility which each of us bears.

In conclusion, the headmaster asked his readers to join him in this daily prayer in preparation for the visitation:

> O God . . . grant to me such respect and loyalty for this historic institution of learning that I may never harm her welfare through thought, word, or deed. As men in this historic place have done before, may I always do my part to advance Nottingham's progress in my time, that she may continue as a monument and witness to sound education, through Jesus Christ, our Lord.

West Nottingham had to wait the better part of a year before Headmaster Farnlof learned the results of the evaluation. Finally, in early December 1963 he sent a "news flash" to each member of the Board of Trustees that concluded, "I am sure that no better news can be passed on to you at this time than this. We can all rejoice together!" It was a bright spot for the West Nottingham community that came soon after saddened students and faculty had honored President Kennedy in prayer services following his assassination on November 22, 1963.

In February 1964, two months after the favorable results of the evaluation were known, Farnlof believed that an all-time high in enrollment activity "at this time of year" was related to the Middle States accreditation which had put the "stamp of approval in the minds of some inquiring parents." The headmaster also happily reported that "our boarding enrollment is at an absolute all-time high of 132." The boarding students plus 33 day students brought the total enrollment to 165 for the year ending in June 1964. The following tabulation shows that enrollment stabilized around 160 for the rest of the decade and that girls had come to make up a sizable proportion of West Nottingham students.

School Year Ending in June of	Girls	Boys	Total
1961	32	95	127
1962	48	112	160
1963	61	106	167
1964	54	111	165
1965	52	100	152
1966	46	112	158
1967	51	108	159
1968	50	99	149
1969	53	116	169
1970	51	90	141
1971	42	91	133
1972	39	72	111
1973	34	82	116
1974	34	65	99
1975	24	70	94
1976	32	62	94
1977	43	78	121
1978	43	73	116
1979	36	89	125
1980	32	85	117
1981	24	64	88

Table XII shows the distribution of students by grade level. As in the 1930s (Chapter XIII) and from 1957 to 1960 (Chapter XV), the number of students in the 11th grade was close to the number of students in the 12th grade the following year. This correlation indicates that most graduating students spent at least their last two years at West Nottingham. For the 1961–81 period, the proportion of the soph-

Table XII
Student Distribution By Grade Level, 1961–1981

School Year Ending in June	Junior High	9	10	11	12	Post Graduates	Total*
1961	19	16	21	26	31	13	126
1962	12	29	25	40	38	16	160
1963	16	16	30	47	46	12	167
1964	16	24	24	44	48	9	165
1965**	10	—	15	42	42	11	152
1966	11	20	35	39	42	11	158
1967	12	27	28	44	40	8	159
1968	0	25	39	43	36	6	149
1969	0	21	37	57	47	7	169
1970	0	12	26	45	55	3	147
1971	0	17	32	39	42	3	133
1972	0	10	32	35	33	1	111
1973	0	16	28	36	36	0	116
1974	0	18	21	24	36	0	99
1975	0	14	23	29	28	0	94
1976	0	14	28	22	30	0	94
1977	0	18	32	35	36	0	121
1978	0	15	31	32	38	0	116
1979	0	17	30	42	35	2	126
1980	0	23	25	34	39	0	117
1981	0	14	13	23	38	0	88

* Second semester of school year
** Distribution data incomplete

omore class to the junior class in the following year was almost always three-fourths or more. This relationship had started in 1941–42 and has generally been maintained to the present. It indicates that perhaps over half of Nottingham graduates have attended for three years or more. After the 1966–67 school year, the academy discontinued junior school because there was no longer enough parental interest in sending children in that age group to boarding school. Table XII shows a plateau of about 40 graduating seniors and 10 post-graduate students per year in the middle 1960s.

Table XIII shows that the number of day students in the student body ranged from less than 20 percent to about 35 percent. The 1960–80 distribution had a larger proportion of day students than the 1930–50 period because no new girls were accepted between 1931 and 1953. From 1940 to 1945, the number of male day students dropped appar-

Table XIII
Approximate Geographical Distribution of Students, 1960–1980*

School Year	Day Md.	PA.	Wash., D.C. Metro****	Boarding N.J.	N.Y.	Del.	Other States or Abroad	Foreign Nationality	Total Boarding	Total**
1959–60***	30	13	22	11	12	12	7	10	2	89	126
1961–62	49	16	37	25	8	7	7	14	4	118	167
1963–64	38	20	32	21	13	11	4	14	7	122	160
1965–66	31	29	31	16	13	10	11	8	2	120	151
1967–68	29	20	31	36	8	4	8	17	4	128	157
1969–70	17	22	29	37	7	5	6	18	1	125	142
1971–72	7	4	1	10	1	2	—	8	1	27	34
1972–73	11	2	2	7	5	0	1	5	3	25	36
1973–74	9	4	5	8	1	1	2	5	1	27	36
1974–75	8	5	7	5	0	0	1	1	1	20	28
1975–76	7	4	3	9	2	—	2	3	—	23	30
1976–77	10	3	5	12	1	—	—	—	5	26	36
1977–78	9	7	9	5	1	1	3	3	1	29	38
1978–79	13	2	4	9	2	1	1	1	3	23	36
1979–80	9	2	8	12	1	1	3	2	1	30	39

* 1971–72 and thereafter, distribution includes seniors and post-graduates only.
** From 1962 until 1972 total includes all students who attended at least part of year.
*** Distribution data incomplete.
**** Includes Washington, D.C.; Northern Virginia suburbs; and Montgomery and Prince Georges Counties in Maryland.

ently because of war conditions but did not pick up in the late 40s after the end of World War II. After the academy again began to admit girls in 1953, the proportion of day students began to rise toward that existing in the late 1920s when girls were being admitted. Table XIII also shows that Maryland and Pennsylvania continued to provide West Nottingham with most of its students, including almost all of its day students and sometimes more than half its boarding students. Washington, D.C., and its environs, which began to send small numbers of students in the 1950s (Table X, Chapter XV), increased its share of the student body to between 10 and 25 percent.

In the middle 1960s, 87 percent of the graduates entered college. In the 1970s, about 80 percent entered college or other schools. The following tabulation shows a wide dispersal of college destinations for the graduates of 1964, 65, 66, and 67:

Delaware 8	South Carolina U 4
Maryville 8	Baldwin-Wallace 4
Clemson 7	Susquehanna U 3
Maryland U 7	Dickinson 3
Penn State 7	124 Other Schools 128
Miami U 4	
Fairleigh-Dickinson 4	Total 183

The fifteen visitors of the evaluation team whose favorable recommendation led to West Nottingham's accreditation were not impressed by the ancient wooden field house used for varsity basketball games. Their comments may have caused the Board of Trustees to consider the state of the academy's athletic plant. The rafters in the old field house hung so low that on one occasion, the West Nottingham team had scored the winning goal in the last seconds of a basketball game with a shot that arched over the rafters and fell cleanly through the basket. At its first regular meeting after the Middle States visitation on May 21, 1962, the board carried a motion to obtain a cost estimate for a new field house. By August 11, 1963, with $80,000 pledged, the board directed the Churchville Construction Company to proceed with construction of the field house. The building was to cost $162,000, plus $38,000 for equipment. The cornerstone was laid after the homecoming football game in the fall of 1963. The spectators shivered a little in the late autumn afternoon, as Sidney Venable, the bespectacled senior member of the Board of Trustees, gave the invocation. After the glee club sang two pieces, Peter Fender, president of the senior class, spoke for the students; Mr. Robert Head spoke for the Parents' Association; and Mr. Edward Rider, Class of 1938, spoke for the alumni. Captain Harry C. Wood, Chaplain USN, Retired, of the Class of 1929, closed with the benediction. The Board of Trustees subsequently named the field house in honor of Mr. and Mrs. John H. Ware, Jr., "in recognition of their generous support of the academy over the years." Ware Field House was ready for use for the West Nottingham summer camp in 1964. It has 62,203 square feet of floor space and contains a basketball court, stage, shower, and locker rooms, two classrooms, and offices for physical education instructors. There is seating for 480 at basketball games and seating for 1,000 when the floor is converted to an auditorium.

The first West Nottingham basketball team to use Ware Field House turned in an 11-3 win-loss record in 1964–65 under Coach Peter Horn, breaking out of a two-year slump in which the Rams had 1-11 and 3-9 records. The Rams' second season in Ware netted only 5 wins in 17 games, setting the stage for the arrival of help in the person of a Princeton graduate, James Brangan. Brangan had been captain of the Princeton 1959–60 basketball team and after graduation joined the investment firm of Janney, Battles, and E. W. Clark in Philadelphia. Brangan stuck it out inside the downtown office for six years before the offer from West Nottingham made him decide to try coaching the sport at which he excelled. Besides coaching basketball and helping coach football, Brangan also taught history and English. The new basketball coach could manage only a 4-11 record his first year; but the following year, the Rams changed it to 11-6. For the next year Brangan accepted an offer to coach basketball at Fair Lawn High School, a large regional school in Fair Lawn, New Jersey, where he stayed for many years.

After Brangan's departure, the obvious choice for coaching the basketball team was James E. Spiro. He had returned to West Nottingham the year before as athletic director after an absence of five years. In his earlier tour of duty, Spiro had coached the West Nottingham basketball team to its only unbeaten season when the Rams gained 19 victories in 1960-61. In his second stint as basketball coach, Spiro's teams compiled the following record through 1979-80.

	Wins	Losses	Remarks
1968-69	12	7	Bob Cameron scored 484 points.
1969-70	16	4	
1970-71	5	12	Rams defeated Perryville (District Champions) 50-49.
1971-72	9	9	Steve Lynch and Larry Carroll made all-Cecil County team.
1972-73	15	5	Rams were 7-1 in Cecil County.
1973-74	20	3	Scott Bogard, Timmy Lockhart, Maceo Leatherwood made all-Cecil County team.
1973-74 (JV)	14	8	Junior Varsity had 10-1 Cecil County record under Coach "Dusty" Miller.
1974-75	17	6	Jake Janney, Steve Chisley, Kevin Corley, Mike Monger, Dave Neville made all-Cecil County team.
1975-76	12	5	Rams lost to Georgetown U. reserves 66-94.
1976-77	8	13	Most games played away from home court because of water damage to floor.
1977-78	16	5	West Nottingham hosted and won first Cecil County Tournament, defeating Rising Sun by one point in final game. Shawn Orr named all-County.
1978-79	14	5	Rams won West Nottingham's second annual Cecil County Tournament by defeating North East and Rising Sun.
1979-80	17	8	Ram Captains were Roger Habershon, Mike Quick, and Jim Spiro. Won West Nottingham's Holiday Tournament, beating Bohemia Manor and John Carroll.

West Nottingham's football team needed even more help than its basketball team when Jim Spiro returned to the campus in the fall of 1967. After his departure in 1962, the gridders had lost all their games in 1962, 1963, and 1965, and had won only one game in 1964. Spiro's best efforts did not yield a winning team in 1967, but the next year's squad had enough boys for Coach Spiro to have separate defensive and offensive teams. The result was a record of 5 wins, 2 losses, and 1 tie, the best since 1960. The 1969 season's record was even better, with 6 wins and 2 losses, although the Rams lost to their ancient rival,

Valley Forge Military Academy. The 1970 team went undefeated, the academy's best season since 1939. The Rams scored an all-time high of 380 points while holding four opponents scoreless and the four others to 40 points. The co-captains were Randy Worthington and Mark Palladinetti. The scores for the 1970 season follow:

West Nottingham Academy		Opponents
36	Carson Long	0
64	Charlotte Hall	6
50	St. James	12
42	Baltimore Friends	0
22	Boys Latin	14
68	Oxford High School	0
34	Severna Prep	8

West Nottingham continued to have successful teams until 1975, which turned out to be the first of a string of losing seasons.

Norman Farnlof was the school's most enthusiastic cheerleader. His participation in a football game started the day before at the pep rally, for which he often wrote original cheers. Although some of the cheers were "pretty awful," there was no escape from using them as the headmaster faithfully attended all of the rallies. If the game was out of town, Farnlof drove a load of students in the school bus. Once the game was underway, the balding, somewhat chubby headmaster ran up and down the sidelines to catch all of the action. In a game against Carson Long Military Academy, Farnlof was back near the West Nottingham goal line where the Nottingham team awaited a Carson kickoff. Noticing the headmaster on the sidelines nearby, Jim Haughey, one of West Nottingham's star backs, promised Farnlof a touchdown on the kickoff return. As chance would have it, the ball came to Haughey who made good on his promise by running through the entire Carson team. Along the sidelines the huffing and puffing headmaster was only a step behind as Haughey crossed the Carson goal.

As mentioned, the construction of Ware Field House had resulted from a deliberate plan to improve the academy's athletic facilities. Several years later two losses forced additional improvements in the school's physical plant. The first occurred when Bird Dormitory, a gray, shingled old farmhouse, was destroyed by fire on March 26, 1968. Most of the eleven boys living at Bird and their dormitory supervisor, Kenneth Dietrich, were in first period class when the attic was reported ablaze at 8:25 a.m. Firemen arrived in a few minutes but were able to save only the first floor from which students rescued the lounge furniture and Dietrich's belongings.

The following month workers started to construct a new dormitory a few yards from the old one. The following fall, boys moved into the modern brickfaced dormitory, which was named in honor of Benjamin Rush, West Nottingham's most eminent graduate. Rush Dormitory has the appearance and design of Rowland, the girls' dormitory; but because it has two floors instead of one, it can house 40 boys and two faculty supervisors instead of the 20 girls and one dormitory supervisor who can live in Rowland. Like Rowland, the large student rooms accommodate two and the interior construction is of cinder block.

The second property loss related directly to a student from Pennsylvania, whom we will call John Doe. John had come to West Nottingham for his junior year in 1967-68 after his psychiatrist had concluded that he no longer needed special schooling. At West Nottingham John was good at chemistry and successful enough in his studies that he was expected to return for his senior year. Nevertheless, John's first year had not been happy because his dormitory mates at Wiley had ignored him and he didn't get along with his dormitory supervisor. Furthermore, the whole West Nottingham community was embarrassed and annoyed when John scrawled, "Ban Red Ink" on blackboards and spelled out the same words with red paint on the walls of various buildings. John's feeling about West Nottingham apparently worsened during the idle weeks of summer. One July morning he set off for the Maryland border on his bicycle. After a long, hot ride, he reached the academy after dark. No one was about as John placed the bomb he had made inside the Old Academy building, now empty but used as the student canteen during school sessions. When John detonated the bomb from outside, the explosion tore off a large section of the roof and broke out large sections of the walls. John then tried to set fires in other buildings, but none of them caused much damage. Emotionally and physically spent, he found a secluded area of the campus and drank what was left of the chemical that he had used in making the bomb. His body was found next day. John Doe's influence on West Nottingham has endured to this day. One of the first things that a new student hears is John's story. Members of the West Nottingham community recall that John's fate had the immediate effect of increased student and faculty awareness of students who might feel left out and unappreciated. To some extent, this awareness has persisted in concert with the perennial retelling of the sad, true story.

Despite the major damage to the Old Academy building, the Board of Trustees decided to restore it to the appearance that had been maintained since its construction in 1864. The Student Canteen Club, which had used Old Academy since 1953, moved to the lobby of the field house until restoration was completed in early 1969. The inside reconstruction provided improved facilities for the canteen as well as a new capability for easy conversion of the building for dances and meetings.

Norman Farnlof had fourteen faculty members when he began his administration, as shown in Table XIV. Of those and the six hired at the beginning of Farnlof's second year, a good proportion served long terms. The Board of Trustees sought to improve the retention of faculty members by authorizing a retirement plan that was put into effect on October 1, 1965. The plan provided for an annual non-taxable contribution of five percent by the teacher that was matched by the academy. A teacher would draw full benefits for retirement at 65 but could retire as early as $59\frac{1}{2}$ at a reduced scale. He could work to the age of 70, but thereafter retirement would be mandatory. In 1961 the board began to offer each faculty member one-half the cost of tuition up to a maximum of $150 for each graduate course approved by the headmaster and successfully completed. In 1962 the board voted to grant automatic $200 annual raises to all faculty members and a minimum salary of $3,000.

Along with Farnlof's success in retaining faculty members, he was eager to help teachers who were down on their luck. On one occasion, he hired a brilliant teacher who had been discharged from the Philadelphia school system for drunkenness. Unfortunately, the teacher could not shake the habit even under Farnlof's benevolent supervision so had to be let go. Another teacher whom Farnlof helped was a recent immigrant from France, Antoni Baranowski, who was a native of Rus-

Table XIV
West Nottingham Faculty, 1961–1971

Service*		Field / Position	Education

a. As of September 1961

1957–72	Carol W. Badenhoop	Social Studies	Wilson A.B., Columbia M.A.
1957–72	Robert E. Badenhoop	Head of English Dept.	Dickinson A.B.
1961–66	Martha T. Darby	Girls' Athletics	Alabama College B.S.
1960–72 1968–72 1972–81	Kenneth E. Dietrich	History / Librarian Assistant Headmaster Headmaster	Dickinson A.B. Pennsylvania A.M.
1946–69	Charles F. Bauer	Head of Language Dept.	Franklin & Marshall A.B. Pennsylvania Ph.D.
1961–72	Antoni Baranowski	Languages	Teachers Colleges, Grodno & Warsaw, Poland Catholic Institute, Paris
1959–68	John L. Gallagher	Head of Science Dept.	Delaware B.S., M.S.
1946–81 1981–Present	C. Herbert Foutz	Head of Mathematics Dept. / Dean of Faculty, Dean Emeritus	Gettysburg A.B. Penn State M. Ed.
1961–62	James E. Griffin	English, Social Studies	Washington College, B.A.
1961–62	Donald B. Irwin	Social Studies	William & Mary B.A.
1959–65	David T. Jones	Head of Junior School	Weaton College B.A.
1961–62	Martin W. Olander	English, Remedial Reading	Phillipsburg A.B.
1961–62 1962–64	Calvin Schutzman	History, Guidance Director	Evansville B.A. Columbia M.A.
1961–65 1968–72	Clarence A. Miller	Science, Mathematics	Lincoln University B.S.
1959–62 1967–82 1982–Present	James E. Spiro	Director of Athletics Football, Basketball, Baseball Coach Director of Admissions	Fairmont State B.A.

b. Faculty additions (1962–1971)

1962–64	Norman K. Smith	English	Temple A.B.
1962–72	Melvin E. Meahl	Mathematics, Head of Science Dept.	Maryland B.S.
1962–65	Edward H. Noll	Mathematics	Dartmouth A.B.
1962–81 1981–Present	Joseph C. Ray	Head of History Dept. Dean of Faculty	Kentucky A.B. Emory M.A.
1962–65	Clarence C. Burley	Physical Education	West Chester State B.S.
1963–67	Katherine M. Holmes	Languages	Indiana A.B.
1962–70	William W. Jones	Social Studies	Haverford A.B., Pennsylvania M.A.

Table XIV (Continued)

Service*	Field / Position	Education
1964–66 Tom Cheetham	English	Pennsylvania B.S.
1965–68 Lena Funk 1969–Present	Mathematics Head of Mathematics Dept.	Locke Haven State B.S.
1965–71 Richard L. Funk	Junior School Mathematics	Lock Haven State B.S. West Chester State M.E.
1972–81 1981–Present	Guidance Director / Assistant Headmaster	
1965–67 Robert P. Reeder	Football Coach / Physical Education	Delaware B.S.
1966–Present Allen B. Yuninger	Religion	Elizabethtown A.B. Princeton Theological Seminary M. Divinity
1966–67 Alan S. Baxter 1969–71	English	William & Mary A.B.
1966–68 L. James Brangan	English, History / Basketball Coach	Princeton A.B.
1966–68 Carol B. Pratt	Physical Education	St. Mary's College
1966–74 Ronald Black 1982–Present	Music, History Choral Music	Elon College A.B. Columbia M.A.

* Start calendar year of fall semester; finish calendar year of spring semester.

sia. Baranowski had been educated in Poland and had taught ten years in Poland and 15 years in French public schools. As a captive of the Nazis in World War II, Baranowski had survived the Auschwitz concentration camp and Buchenwald, another death camp. After the war he taught in France before migrating to the United States. Baranowski told a student reporter from the *Arrow* that he was thrilled with the freedom he enjoyed in America where jobs were open to whoever was qualified. In France a person trying to get citizenship would have to work at the type of job specified by the French Government. The student interviewer concluded by stating that Baranowski "is working here under tremendous odds—he is a foreigner who has trouble communicating, he has no family, and all that he has to work for is a future in America." Baranowski overcame the "tremendous odds" perceived by his interviewer because he taught at the academy for 11 years.

At the start of his second year Farnlof hired Joseph C. Ray, now the head of the history department and dean of the faculty. Ray also has directed all of the annual student dramatic productions since his arrival.

Later in Farnlof's administration, Robert H. von Behr came aboard to teach German and French and stayed 12 years, becoming head of the language department. In 1966 West Nottingham asked Rev. Allen B. Yuninger to teach a course called "Man and Religion" in addition to his main responsibility as pastor of the Rock Presbyterian Church, nine miles east of West Nottingham. One of the earliest pastors of the Rock Church had been Rev. James Finley, brother of Samuel Finley who had founded the academy. The *Arrow* of December 10, 1968, stated that Rev. Yuninger's course was "one of the most interesting" at West Nottingham because "students learn about many of the beliefs and principles that have motivated mankind through history," allowing them to relate "to humanity as a whole." Yuninger also has advised the Chapel Club and a nature appreciation group. The student editors dedicated the 1973 *Pegé* to Yuninger, commenting that his senior students suffered not only because his course was challenging but also because of Yuninger's "daily punning." Yuninger has continued to serve West Nottingham to the present time.

In February 1970, West Nottingham embarked on a new approach for broadening student experience that was based on the special experience or skill of various members of the faculty and administrative staff. Each faculty and administrative participant conducted a three-hour session on Friday morning on a subject of special interest to him. Each student chose one interest group but did not have tests, grades, or homework. Headmaster Farnlof called it the contact program. Although begun on a trial basis, the contact program continued until the spring of 1982. The original list of 20 activities and their leaders follows:

Glass Blowing	Melvin E. Meahl
Concept, Form, and Creation of Fashion	Mrs. Carol Badenhoop
How to Develop a Green Thumb	Richard Funk
Electronics	Richard Hoffman
Painting in Oils	Truman E. Deyo
Fun at the Dump (Finding imaginative uses for discarded objects)	Jessie R. Castle (Nurse)
Guitar Playing	Pearson
Experience with Cinematography	Kenneth Dietrich
Gymnastics	James Spiro

Russian............................	Antoni Baranowski
Simulations (Examination of World and National Problems through Gamelike Exercises).................	Joseph C. Ray James B. Holloway
Fencing............................	Roger B. Heim
Stock Market.......................	C. Herbert Foutz
Woodshop..........................	Clarence A. Miller
Jazz, 1900–1969	Robert E. Badenhoop
Bridge.............................	Mrs. Mary Wright Spiro/ Mrs. Lena Funk
Modern Arab Culture	Robert McClester
The Contemporary Motion Picture ..	Alan S. Baxter
Philosophy	Rev. Allen B. Yuninger
Chess..............................	Craig Thrash

In the late 1960s and in the 1970s, West Nottingham students reached out to help surrounding communities. Under Alan Baxter, a faculty member and West Nottingham graduate, a group of 15 or more students drove into the inner city of Wilmington every Wednesday evening in the fall of 1969 to tutor children one-on-one for about $1\frac{1}{2}$ hours at two downtown churches. The student participants may have learned as much as they taught by getting a first-hand understanding of the problems faced by the children. The Wilmington project continued for a second year with a number of the same West Nottingham students but did not go on to a third year after Alan Baxter left the academy. A few years later, academy students tutored children in the Rising Sun elementary school as part of the contact program. Kenneth Gordon, dean of students, was the sponsor. In addition to getting help with their school work, young children in the West Nottingham area were entertained by the members of the academy's dramatic society in the fall of 1977. Under the direction of Joseph C. Ray, the members of the society rehearsed "Hansel and Gretel" for eight weeks and then performed the play for over 1200 children in a period of two weeks. The Maryland arts council was so impressed by the production that it considered the idea of funding similar West Nottingham productions for children.

"Perry Point" was a project that some West Nottingham students undertook in early 1972, somewhat in the spirit of the Wilmington project. Perry Point functioned as an activity of the contact program and was sponsored by Mrs. Lena Funk, head of the mathematics department. Mrs. Funk started out thinking her main job would be to drive the seven or eight students 10 miles down to the Perry Point Veterans Hospital, wait for three hours, and bring them back. She doubted her own ability to be effective in visiting with the patients, taking walks to the canteen with them, and writing letters for them. With nothing to do for three hours, however, she decided to try to do what the volunteer students were doing so well. It wasn't long before she was looking forward to the weekly trip and three hours in which she completely set aside her own concerns to ease the lives of others. She persuaded her husband, Richard Funk, to go, who likewise spent many hours with the veterans. The Perry Point project ended after the 1980–81 school year when the contact program was dropped because the three hours every Friday took away too much time from the academic schedule.

Besides helping in Wilmington and at Perry Point, the academy cared for one of its loyal workers, Paul Lee, when he became too old to work in 1971 after having been on the maintenance crew since 1942. Long past his prime as a star pitcher in the segregated black baseball leagues when he came to West Nottingham, Lee used his professional knowledge to coach academy pitchers. When he became too weak to care for himself in 1975, the academy arranged for his travel to South Carolina where his relatives could take care of him.

In the spring of 1971, Farnlof's next to last year at West Nottingham, the academy was first forced to confront a dangerous problem that was beginning to plague students throughout America. In early March the administration and faculty were puzzled and then became frightened when students collapsed in class, in the dining room, and on the campus over a period of several days. Intensive questioning and search revealed that a male student from York, Pennsylvania, who was the son of a doctor, had brought 500 tablets of barbiturates back to the campus after a visit home. The academy's investigation resulted in expulsion of 15 students; school closed two weeks early for Easter vacation. Students returning from vacation found state police waiting with dogs to sniff for the presence of drugs in their belongings. The Board of Trustees commended the headmaster, assistant headmaster, and faculty "for the handling in a very effective manner a very critical situation" in the minutes of their May 21, 1971, meeting. The incident did not end the drug problem, which was a persistent annoyance in the 1970s, but it never again reached such magnitude.

Headmaster Norman C. Farnlof saved the greatest surprise of his 14 years at West Nottingham for an all-school meeting at the field house that was announced at breakfast on January 11, 1972, for 9:15 a.m. that morning. Speculation about the reason for the meeting ranged from an outbreak of flu to a build-up of the drug problem. The appearance of Farnlof, Assistant Headmaster Kenneth Dietrich, and Dean of the Faculty C. Herbert Foutz brought silence to the chattering students. The headmaster stepped forward and announced his resignation by reading a letter to that effect to the Board of Trustees. Farnlof's reasons were that the school needed new management after a reasonable period of time and that he had accepted an offer to serve as Dean of Admissions at Admiral Farragut Academy in New Jersey where previously he had headed the junior school. Scott Newman, the student correspondent at the assembly, reported that student reactions to Farnlof's leaving ranged from tears to indifference, but almost everyone was stunned by the resignation because it was so unexpected. Newman recalled Farnlof's "support of the football teams and his genuine love" for the academy. The student reporter also stated:

> Perhaps the headmaster's greatest asset was that of a small-group diplomat; in any given situation he could unify those supporting opposite ends of an argument and immediately chart a course toward . . . solution.

The student editors dedicated the 1972 *Pegé* to Norman Farnlof and his wife Elizabeth. The editors stated that "this husband-and-wife team has worked with diligence and dedication" at the academy for fourteen years, he as assistant headmaster and headmaster and she as bookstore manager. In his farewell in the same publication, Farnlof concluded, "In this parting, we are joined together in real sorrow. But I rejoice forever that I know what it is to be at Nottingham. I hope you, the Class of 72, share in this joy as you move away into a very wide world. Believe me, we all need this magnificent memory." Farnlof's last commencement on June 4, 1972, featured addresses by seniors, Helen E. Hendrickson, P. Scott Newman, and Elizabeth A. Taylor instead of the traditional guest speaker. The diplomas were presented by Farnlof and Dr. Arthur C. Stevenson, president of the Board of Trustees since 1961. After the farewells of commencement, Farnlof had a final part to play in the history the academy. In the latter part of June, he accompanied Kenneth Dietrich, his successor, to a formal meeting of the Presbyterian Synod of the Chesapeake (successor to the Presbyterian Baltimore Synod in its jurisdiction over West Nottingham Academy). After the beginning of West Nottingham's formal association with the Presbyterians in 1916, their support had grown to about $5,000 annually between 1924 and 1950. It had declined to $3,000 by 1970, a considerable reduction when inflation is taken into account. In the summer of 1971, the Chesapeake Synod informed the academy that annual contributions were to end, but the synod was planning to establish a new relationship with the academy. When the synod failed to make any proposals during the winter of 1971-72, the academy suggested that the synod find ten needy students for scholarships each year and share the expense equally with the academy. A committee of the synod approved the proposal in June, but a few days later, at the meeting attended by Farnlof and Dietrich, the synod refused to consider the committee's favorable report. A questioner from the floor asked, "Does this mean we're through with West Nottingham Academy?" The synod executive's answer of "Yes" clearly prevailed over an answer of "No" from the administrative secretary so Dietrich and Farnlof stalked out of the meeting. On the drive home to West Nottingham, Dietrich decided that his first recommendation to the Board of Trustees as headmaster would be to break completely with the synod. The board responded with a unanimous vote to dissolve the academy's relationship with the Presbyterian Church. The synod's reluctance to continue its support was consistent with the national Presbyterian policy of supporting colleges rather than secondary schools.

Kenneth E. Dietrich was "ready and able" to take over as headmaster from Norman C. Farnlof, according to the *Nottingham Alumnus* in its winter issue of 1973. Like Farnlof, Dietrich had served as assistant headmaster for three years (compared to Farnlof's four) before being elected headmaster. Unlike Farnlof, Dietrich had been at the academy for eight years before he became assistant headmaster. Dietrich's introduction to the school was his interview with Headmaster Blaker in

January 1960. The following month Dietrich began as history teacher and dormitory supervisor. After a week of sleeping in the boys' dormitory, the new history teacher was ready to quit. He delayed for a week, however, when he realized that his immediate departure would deprive C. Herbert Foutz, the senior faculty member, of a scheduled recess from dormitory duty. By the time Foutz had returned, Dietrich decided he could handle the job after all.

Eight years later, Dietrich's attitude about being dormitory supervisor had changed considerably. In the spring of 1968, he was supervisor for the eleven boys living in Bird dormitory when it burned almost to the ground. The first idea for lodging the boys was to scatter them in extra rooms in various houses. Because the group wanted to stay together, however, Dietrich arranged for temporary bunking space for all of them in the field house for the rest of the semester. Dietrich's solution showed little concern for the decreased personal comfort that would be entailed for himself. After Dietrich became headmaster and moved to Gayley House, he housed a half-dozen boys upstairs on occasion to improve the school's overall accommodations.

The formal separation of the academy from Presbyterian connections did not lessen religious activities under Headmaster Dietrich. Rev. Allen Yuninger of the Rock Presbyterian Church continued to offer the required course on comparative religion. In a new departure, Dietrich made attendance at Thursday chapel service compulsory for all students and faculty. He dropped the only previous requirement for worship, namely, Sunday evening observance for boarding students.

Unlike his predecessors, Kenneth Dietrich was a bachelor so had more time to give to the students, whom he seemed to consider as members of his family. He invited groups of students to Gayley House for gourmet dinners, giving him occasions to practice his hobby of cooking. He especially liked to treat for dinner the students who had volunteered to be on call to show prospective students around the campus. Dietrich also hosted annual Christmas parties for all students and the faculty. He occasionally practiced his cooking skill in the main kitchen of the academy in making breakfast if some of the kitchen help did not arrive in time. Dietrich's consideration of the students extended to personally opening the student canteen for an hour and a half after classes on week days. On Fridays, the headmaster joined with Joseph Ray, head of the history department, in leading the student photography group in the contact program. On hot days that were outside the stipulated swimming season, the headmaster occasionally would open the pool. For the benefit of the faculty, the headmaster often hosted a dinner off campus early in the school year to help the old and new members become better acquainted.

Dietrich's concern for individual students carried over to the non-achievers. Since Headmaster Blaker had revived the academy in the 1950s, the policy had been to limit the enrollment to students who had the capability to do college work. Arrival on the campus did not necessarily mean that a student would use the capability he had, however. Blaker had weeded out the non-achievers by sending each student a letter each summer that invited him to return or not to return. Only a strong consensus among the faculty and headmaster could produce a negative letter. Headmaster Dietrich in the 1970s likewise used this procedure but almost always left a small crack in the door that indicated to the non-achieving student that a new start might be possible under probation.

One boy who received a very bleak letter was so anxious to return that he and his father visited the campus during the summer of 1972, just after Dietrich had become headmaster. Dietrich appeared very skeptical about the prospect of the boy settling down, declaring that a second chance was possible only with the understanding that a letdown in the student's effort would be quickly followed by permanent expulsion. Dietrich's gamble paid off because the boy graduated that year with a fine academic and extra-curricular record and proceeded to college and a successful teaching career. Dietrich and Richard Funk, whom Dietrich had brought back to West Nottingham as his assistant and guidance director in 1972,* recall that the "gloomy" letter tactic was successful more often than not in getting a student to make a conscientious effort. In fact, Dietrich remembers that at times two or three members of the senior class were in this category although probably not aware of each other's situation.

While trying to keep from losing non-achieving students by the "gloomy" letter tactic, Dietrich was fortunate in retaining a strong group of faculty members (Table XV). Of the nine he inherited, five

---

* Funk interrupted his service at West Nottingham to serve as guidance counselor at the Kennett Square high school, Pennsylvania in 1971–72.

Table XV
West Nottingham Faculty, 1972–1980

a. As of September 1972

Service		Field/Position	Education
1946–Present	C. Herbert Foutz	Head of Mathematics Dept./ Dean of Faculty Dean Emeritus	Gettysburg A.B. Penn State M. Ed.
1962–Present	Joseph C. Ray	Dean of Students/Head of History Department Dean of Faculty	Kentucky A.B.
1972–74	Elizabeth Armstrong	English	San Francisco State B.A.
1972–74	Alan Armstrong	Physics, Physical Science, Mathematics	Santa Clara U.
1966–74 1982–Now	Ronald Black	Music, History Choral Music	Elon College Columbia M.A.
1965–66 1969–Now	Lena Funk	Mathematics Head of Mathematics Dept.	Lock Haven B.S. Lock Haven B.S. West Chester State M.E.
1965–71 1972–81 1981–Present	Richard L. Funk	Mathematics Guidance Director Guidance Director/Assistant Headmaster	
1970–1982	Robert H. von Behr	French, German	New York U.B.A. Delaware M.A.
1970–77	Roger B. Heim	English, Art, History/Head of English Department	Bloomsburg State B.S.
1972–76	Peter Kluk	Spanish, German	University of Madrid M.A., Ph.D.
1972–74	Kenneth G. Gordon	History, English, Public Speaking	Muhlenburg College B.A.

1974–79	James E. Spiro	Dean of Students	Fairmont State B.A.
1959–62		Director of Athletics	
1967–81			
1981–Now		Director of Admissions	
1959–62	Mary Wright Spiro	Girls Athletics	Towson State A.B.
1968–80		Librarian/Girls Physical Education	
1972–82	Ralph E. "Dusty" Miller	History, Sociology, Psychology	West Nottingham 1959 Maryville B.A.
1969–82	Craig M. Thrash	Head of science Department	Catawba A.B.
1966–Present	Allen Yuninger (Pastor of Rock Presbyterian Church)	Religion	Elizabethtown A.B., Princeton B.D.

b. *Faculty Additions (1973–80)*

1973–77	Margaret Wolf	English	Grinnell, Princeton A.B.
1977–Present	Margaret Wolf Wilson	Head of English Dept.	
1974–78	Everett C. Reich	Science, Mathematics	Oklahoma City U. B.A.
1973–75	John H. McKeon	English	Amherst A.B.
1976–79	Kevin L. Campion	German, Spanish	LaSalle B.A.
1975–79	Richard Wilson	Botany	Delaware U.
1976–78	Alan Williams	Art	Salisbury State B.A.
1976–77	Elliot Witkins	English	State University of New York B.A.
1977–78	Richard Yanulaitis	Art	Kutztown State College
1977–78	Jane McMenniman	English	St. Joseph's College (Philadelphia) B.A.
1977–79	Mann Patel	Physics, Mathematics	B.S.
1978–80	Lydia Federov	English	West Chester State B.A.
1978–80	Mike Vicario	English	Syracuse Univ. B.A.

Table XV (Continued)

Service		Field / Position	Education
1978–79	John Taylor	Chemistry, Physical Science	Salisbury State B.A.
1978–80	Mrs. Jackie Geyer	Art	—
1979–80	Glenn Smith	Science, Chemistry, Physics	—
1979–80	Richard Broomfield	Spanish, French	—
1979–80	Mrs. Michaellen Winegrad	Mathematics	—
1979–Present	Victor Maccallum	Dean of Students	West Nottingham 1970, Maryland U. B.S.
1980–82	Paul Uhrig	English	—
1980–81	Curt Mathews	English	—
1980–82	Katherine Emierbrink	German	—
1980–82	David Knee	Chemistry	—
1980–81	Jane Barron	Head of Art Department	—
1980–81	Judy Ziegler	Language	Vanderbilt
1980–84	Roy Money	Mathematics	Delaware U.

are still at West Nottingham, namely, C. Herbert Foutz, Joseph Ray, Lena Funk, Jim Spiro, and Rev. Allen Yuninger. The other four stayed for long periods: Robert von Behr, Roger Heim, Mary Wright Spiro and Craig Thrash. The academy also gained stability from newcomers who started at the beginning of Dietrich's administration and stayed for long periods. These included Richard Funk, now assistant headmaster, Ralph E. "Dusty" Miller, and Kenneth G. Gordon. The following year West Nottingham found a long-term English teacher in Margaret Wolf, and in 1977 she met her husband after the academy hired Richard Wilson to teach botany. Richard left after two years, but Margaret continues as head of the English department.

The West Nottingham student handbook for 1973-74 listed the following clubs and activities:

Organization	Activity	History
Arrow	Student Newspaper. Sponsored by Kenneth H. Gordon.	Replaced *Nottingham News*, published in 1940's and 50's.
Finley Journal	Student literary magazine	Replaced *Literary Advances* which was first issued in 1874.
Canteen	Managed student canteen and campus social activities. Sponsored by C. Herbert Foutz.	Old Academy building has been used as student center and managed by Canteen club since Christmas 1953.
Chapel Club	Opened each class day with morning prayer over loud speaker. Conducts morning worship service once a year at Rev. Allen Yuninger's Rock Presbyterian Church.	Organized by Rev. Allen Yuninger.
Dramatics	Club led in putting on annual school production	Joseph C. Ray has directed since 1962.
Pegé (Greek word for source)	School year book. Shela Sayin the 1974 editor.	First issued by the Class of 1931. It was the idea of John A. Nesbitt, Jr., who was first editor.

Organization	Activity	History
Talisman (Composed of members of National Honor Society)	Helped Headmaster Dietrich with Christmas open house. Provided Christmas tree for dining hall. Sponsored by Mrs. Margaret Wolf Wilson.	West Nottingham joined the National Honor Society in 1958 (Chapt. XV).

There were also clubs for bicycle riding, girls' athletics, riding, photography, and trap shooting. The school's traditional social activities and sponsoring student organizations follow:

    Homecoming Dance—Cheerleaders
    Christmas Dance—Senior Class
    Spring Dance (Junior Prom)—Sophomore Class
    Sports Banquet—Varsity Club
    Commencement Dance (Senior Prom)—Junior Class
    Spring Carnival and Field Day—Student Senate

The following requirements for graduation in 1979–80 had not changed greatly from those in 1941–42 (Table VIII, Chapter XIII).

(1) To graduate, students had to complete four years of English, five years of Mathematics and Science, two years of a foreign language, three years of Social Studies including American History, and one semester of World Religions or Christian Ethics.

(2) Available courses consisted of:

*English (two years)	U. S. History
**French (two years)	Art History
German (four years)	Anthropology
Spanish (four years)	Non-Western Studies
Ancient History	World Religions

    * To complete the English requirement, students in grades 11 and 12 choose from among the following semester electives: American Novelists, Russian Literature, French Literature, Shakespeare, Composition, Creative Writing, Folklore, Playwrights, English Poets, Public Speaking and Logic, Sensory Perception, Developmental English, and Developmental Reading.

    ** Semester courses which make up the third and fourth years of French are French Civilization, French Conversation, French Literature Masterpieces, and French Composition.

Christian Ethics	Health
Introductory Physical Science	American Government
Biology	American Revolution
Advanced Biology	Civil War
Chemistry	English History
Physics	Social Science/Psychology
Botany	Sociology
Zoology	Pre-Algebra
Art	Algebra (two years)
Photography	Geometry
Driver Education	Calculus
Physical Education	Trigonometry

The unusually cold winter of 1976-77 resulted in 18 to 20 inches of ice in the Chesapeake Bay, 26 inches in Northeast Creek, and 15 inches in the Susquehanna River. "To top it all off," Carolyn Cole reported in the *Arrow*, "we have an iceberg on the Eastern Shore floating between Rock Hall and Swan Point." Carolyn advised leaving faucets on just enough to prevent the pipes from freezing and bursting. Unfortunately, the pipes under the floor of the basketball court did burst and prevented its use for the rest of the season. Consequently, the Rams had to play out their schedule at the courts of their opponents. Lacking home crowd support, the Rams could win only 8 games while losing 13. This record contrasted with their 12-5 record the previous season and 16-5 record the following year. Workers repaired the floor temporarily for the 1977 commencement and use by the summer camp. The contractor completed permanent repairs for $10,000, about one-third of the cost of a new floor. Headmaster Dietrich thanked the contributors to the special floor fund and reported in the fall of 1977 that "our athletic and activity programs can return to normal."

To balance the bad luck experienced with the field house floor, more alumni contributed more money in the annual 1976-77 appeal than ever before. Perhaps the 259 contributors were inspired by the nation's bicentennial: they gave $8,636 as compared to the $4,368 given by 122 alumni the year before. The total number of alumni in 1977 was about 1,500, a 50 percent increase from the 1,000 alumni in 1941, the year America entered World War II. Alumni giving increased to a new high for the 1978–79 appeal and increased to another new high of $12,430 for 1979–80.

By the close of the 1979–80 session, Headmaster Dietrich had served the academy for 20 years and began to contemplate some other pursuit. The following fall he informed the Board of Trustees that the 1980–81 session, his ninth as headmaster, would be his last. Dietrich explained his desire to leave as follows:

> The decision . . . is based on the very strong feeling that a change in my life is necessary . . . my feeling is strong that I need another vineyard in which to labor. . . . There have been rough spots, but the happy moments far outweigh the unhappy. If there is a precipitating cause, it would be the increasing pressures of operating a small business (which is essentially what the school is) in difficult times.

Dietrich announced his decision in time for the Board of Trustees to accept his resignation at their regular meeting on October 28, 1980. In response, Arthur C. Stevenson, President of the Board of Trustees, stated that:

> Ken Dietrich caught us by surprise . . . and left us rather unprepared for adjusting to a change in leadership at West Nottingham Academy. As Ken leaves, he also leaves his mark in numerous areas of the school program, e.g., the library, the summer camp, photography and art instruction, a real concern for the welfare of the individual student, and an ongoing recognition of West Nottingham Academy in the Middle Atlantic Association of Secondary Schools and Colleges.

Although Dietrich had surprised the board with his resignation, he had given the trustees ample time to look for a successor by his willingness to stay through the 1980–81 school year. With time available for a careful selection, the Board of Trustees formed a search committee, headed by Robert J. Bruce. The committee received 60 applications for the job of headmaster—a far cry from the embarrassing situation in the early 1950s when the Board of Trustees filled the post with a reluctant acting headmaster for three years. The number of educators who wanted to lead West Nottingham reflected the profound changes that had been effected in 29 years under the leadership of Headmasters Blaker, Farnlof, and Dietrich. In the same period, the Board of Trustees, under the leadership of Norman Anderson and Arthur C. Stevenson, had provided unprecedented improvements in the academy's physical plant. These efforts by the three headmasters and Board of Trustees, in turn, had built upon the determination and success of J. Paul Slaybaugh, who had transformed West Nottingham into a respected boarding school from the tiny day school of 17 students that was West Nottingham Academy in 1924.

Appendix A

Board of Trustees, 1811–1981

1811

George Gale, *President*
Thomas W. Veazy
Robert W. Archer
John Groome
Samuel C. Hall
William C. Miller
Robert Evans
David Patton
John Troy
James Sims
George Kidd
James Maxwell
John Cresswell
Henry W. Physick
James Magraw,* *Secretary*

1852

Samuel Rowland, *President*
Dr. Robert Allen
L. H. Evans
Thomas Gillespie
Rev. John Squier,** *Secretary*
Dr. William B. Rowland, *Treasurer*
Jefferson Ramsay
James L. Maxwell
John Carson
Hugh Steel
Dr. James Turner
William McCullough
Isaac F. Van Arsdale

1865

Rev. Samuel Gayley,* *President,*
  West Nottingham
William B. Rowland, M.D.,
  Treasurer, Rowlandville
Thomas J. Gillespie, Principio
George Gillespie, Principio
James Turner, M.D., Brick
  Meetinghouse

---

* Pastor, West Nottingham Presbyterian Church
** Pastor, Port Deposit Presbyterian Church

211

1865—(Continued)

H. H. Duyckink
Isaac F. Van Arsdale, Zion
James M. Evans, Rising Sun
John P. Evans, Rising Sun
John W. Mount,** Rising Sun
J. Leiper Maxwell, Port Deposit

Hugh Steel, Port Deposit
George P. Whitaker, Principio Furnace
James O. McCormick, Secretary, Woodlawn

1874

Rev. Samuel Gayley,* *President,* West Nottingham
William B. Rowland, M.D., *Treasurer,* Rowlandville
Thomas J. Gillespie, Principio
George Gillespie, Principio

Adam R. Magraw, Colora
James M. Evans, Rising Sun
John W. Mount, Rising Sun
J. H. Rowland, Port Deposit
James O. McCormick, *Secretary,* Woodlawn

1885

Rev. Samuel Gayley,* *President,* West Nottingham
William B. Rowland, M.D., Rowlandville
Henry S. Coudon, Perryville
Adam R. Magraw, Colora
Job Haines, Rising Sun

James M. Evans, Rising Sun
R. E. Bromwell, M.D., Port Deposit
Jacob Tome, Port Deposit
John M. McClenahan, Port Deposit

1887

Jacob Tome, *President,* Port Deposit
A. R. Magraw, *Secretary,* West Nottingham
R. E. Bromwell, M.D., Port Deposit

Samuel A. Gayley,* West Nottingham
John P. Wilson, Rising Sun
William B. Steele, Port Deposit
R. E. McClenahan, Port Deposit

1890

Jacob Tome, *President,* Port Deposit
Job Haines, *Treasurer*
R. E. Bromwell, M.D., Port Deposit

Henry S. Coudon, Perryville
John W. McClenahan, Port Deposit
Samuel C. Rowland

---

* Pastor, West Nottingham Presbyterian Church
** Elected March 15, 1856 to replace Robert Evans who resigned that date

BOARD OF TRUSTEES

1896

Jacob Tome, *President and Treasurer,*
  Port Deposit
Rev. D. E. Shaw,* *Secretary,*
  Colora
John M. McClenahan, Port
  Deposit

Dr. R. E. Bromwell, Port Deposit
William B. Steele, Port Deposit
J. J. Buck, Port Deposit
John P. Wilson, Sylmar
Samuel T. Wiley, Colora
William T. Fryer, Colora

1915 (Until Dec. 27)

James J. Hanna, West Nottingham
William F. Fryer
S. J. Wiley
Rev. F. Harl Huffman,* West
  Nottingham
Charles K. Abrahams
Howard Bryant

H. T. Porter
J. M. Rowland, M.D.
William F. Warburton
Robert F. Cameron
W. B. Steele
Charles S. Pyle

1915 (After Dec. 27)

James J. Hanna, West Nottingham
William F. Fryer
S. J. Wiley
Rev. F. Harl Huffman,* West
  Nottingham
Rev. Paul R. Hickok, Washington,
  D.C.
Charles B. Osborne, Aberdeen,
  Md.
Rev. Henry Rumer, D.D.,
  Darlington, Md.

Rev. William Crawford,
  Wilmington, Del.
Frank Sheppard, Wilmington, Del.
John McKinzie, Baltimore
Judge Stanton J. Peele, Chevy
  Chase, Md.
Rev. John Palmer, D.D.,
  Washington, D.C.
John B. Larner

---

* Pastor of West Nottingham Presbyterian Church

1940

	Residence	Occupation
J. M. H. Rowland,* *President*	Baltimore	Medical Education
Samuel A. Gayley,** *Vice-President*	Philadelphia	Business
George M. Cummings, *Secretary*	Washington, D.C.	Religion
Charles S. Pyle, *Treasurer*	Rising Sun, Md.	—
Jacob France	Baltimore	—
John W. Christie	Wilmington, Del.	Religion
J. H. Mason Knox	Baltimore	Medicine
Joseph T. Richards*	Rising Sun, Md.	—
Stewart M. Ward	Rising Sun, Md.	—
John G. Conner***	Trenton, N.J.	Education, Business
James J. Hanna*	Colora, Md.	Business
John H. Gardner, Jr.	Baltimore	Religion
W. A. Shaw	Oxford, Pa.	—
Joseph R. Sizoo	New York, N.Y.	Religion
William B. Steele*	Port Deposit, Md.	Business
Roger J. Whiteford*	Washington, D.C.	Law
Horace Davis	Berlin, Md.	—
Joseph S. Hamilton	Wilmington, Del.	—
A. Brown Caldwell	Baltimore	Religion
Ernest S. Rowland*	Liberty Grove, Md.	Medicine
Robert L. Swain	Baltimore	Medicine

* Alumnus.
** Grandson and namesake of 19th Century board president.
*** Principal, 1887-1902.

October 28, 1949

	Residence	Occupation
John H. Ware III, *President*	Oxford, Pa.	Business, Politics
Joseph T. Richards,* *Vice-President*	Rising Sun, Md.	—
A. Brown Caldwell, *Secretary*	Baltimore	Religion
Bert S. Thomas, *Treasurer*	Colora, Md.	Accounting
Edwin S. Dorcus	Elkton, Md.	Banking
J. M. H. Rowland*	Baltimore	Medical Education
John W. Christie	Wilmington, Del.	Religion
Sydney J. Venable**	Colora, Md.	Religion
G. Edwin Lawrence	Rising Sun, Md.	Banking
John H. Gardner, Jr.	Baltimore	Religion
R. Allen Brown	Havre de Grace, Md.	Religion
John D. Worthington, Jr.	Bel Air, Md.	Journalism
Norman H. Anderson***	Rising Sun, Md.	Business
Jacob France	Baltimore	—
J. H. Mason Knox	Baltimore	Medicine
J. M. T. Finney	Baltimore	Medicine
John G. Conner****	Trenton, N.J.	Business, Education
Samuel A. Gayley*****	Philadelphia	Business
Richard M. Mussen	Washington, D.C.	Religion
Roger J. Whiteford*	Washington, D.C.	Law
S. K. Dennis	Baltimore	Law

---

* Alumnus.
** Pastor, West Nottingham Presbyterian Church.
*** Appointed Ad Interim, October 28, 1949.
**** Principal of West Nottingham Academy, 1887-1902.
***** Grandson and namesake of 19th Century board president.

October 22, 1961

	Residence	Occupation
Arthur C. Stevenson, *President*	Chadds Ford, Penn.	Business, Science
John H. Ware III, *Vice-President*	Oxford, Penn.	Business, Politics
Frank D. Brown, *Secretary*	Port Deposit, Md.	Business
Norman H. Anderson, *Treasurer*	Colora, Md.	Business
J. Albert Roney Jr.	Elkton, Md.	Attorney, Judge
C. Warden Gass	Wilmington, Del.	Education
E. Lansing Bennett	Salisbury, Md.	Religion
Edwin S. Dorcus	Elkton, Md.	Banking
Sidney J. Venable*	Wilmington, Del.	Religion
John Nesbitt**	Catonsville, Md.	Medicine
Edward M. Rider**	Arlington, Va.	Public Relations
Lloyd G. Ice	Baltimore	Religion
William W. Chase		
Robert Johnston	Baltimore	Florist
Scott S. Bair	Westminster, Md.	Broker
Daniel W. Cauffield		
Robert C. Gerow	Oxford, Penn.	Business
Gerald Wise	Baltimore	Business
Harold Claypool	Columbiana, Ohio	Business
Duane Peterson	Baltimore	Business
Edwin Klaunberg	Baltimore	Business
Charles W. Dunnett	Colora, Md.	Business
Noble McCartney	Washington, D.C.	Law

* Former pastor of West Nottingham Presbyterian Church
** West Nottingham alumnus.

BOARD OF TRUSTEES

1971

	Residence	Occupation
Arthur C. Stevenson, *President* (since 1961)	Chadds Ford, Penn.	Business
John H. Ware III, *Vice-President*	Oxford, Penn.	Business, Politics
Frank D. Brown, *Secretary*	Port Deposit, Md.	Business
J. Albert Roney, *Treasurer*	Elkton, Md.	Attorney, Judge
William P. Chaffinch	Easton, Md.	—
B. N. Waugaman	Wilmington, Del.	—
Earnest N. Cory Jr.	Laurel, Md.	—
John E. Demyan Jr.	Glen Burnie, Md.	Attorney
Edwin S. Dorcus	Elkton, Md.	Banking
C. Warden Gass	Wilmington, Del.	Education
Charles E. Gillespie	Philadelphia, Penn.	Business
Stuart N. Hutchison Jr.	Pittsburgh, Penn.	
Philip R. Magee	Baltimore, Md.	Religion
Robert A. Matteson	Wilmington, Del.	Business
Edward M. Rider*	Chevy Chase, Md.	Business
Rev. Sidney J. Venable**	Wilmington, Del.	Religion

* West Nottingham alumnus.
**Former pastor of West Nottingham Presbyterian Church

1981

	Residence	Occupation
Arthur C. Stevenson, *President* (since 1961)	Chadds Ford, Penn.	Business
John H. Ware III, *Vice-President*	Oxford, Penn.	Business
Frank D. Brown, *Secretary*	Port Deposit, Md.	Business
Robert H. Cameron, *Treasurer*	Rising Sun, Md.	Business
John E. Hartshorn	Wayne, Penn.	Business
John E. Demyan Jr.	Glen Burnie, Md.	Attorney
Robert A. Matteson	Wilmington, Del.	Business
C. Warden Gass	Wilmington, Del.	Education
Ross B. Cameron Jr.*	Asbury Park, N.J	Business
Charles E. Gillespie	Philadelphia, Penn.	Business
William H. Cole*	Rising Sun, Md.	Banking
Mrs. Weston H. Lopez**	Wilmington, Del.	—
Robert J. Bruce	Chester, Penn.	Education
Raymond Crittenden	Wilmington, Del.	Business
Patrick Doordan	North East, Md.	Business
Arthur D. Johnston*	Rising Sun, Md.	Business
Thomas O. Wilson Sr.*	Laurel, Md.	Business

* West Nottingham alumnus.
** The first woman member, elected to board on November 1, 1975.

Appendix B

Former West Nottingham Academy (WNA) Students in World War II Military Service

Last Year at WNA

Adams, William W., Jr. ... 1938
Agnew, James W. 1942
Aikman, E. M. 1942
* Alexander, Richard K. 1940
Allen, J. Gilpin, Jr. 1943
Amick, A. Hammond, III
 1941
Anderson, Walter 1927
Andrews, Philip S. 1940
Aquilani, Joseph L. 1939
Armour, Atlee W. 1942
Armstrong, Guy R. 1943
Armstrong, John E. 1934
Atwood, John W. 1937
* Baden, Michael 1941
Bamberger, Robert J. 1942

Barrett, Arthur G. .... —
Bates, J. Herbert 1943
Baughman, Eugene S., III
 1943
Baughman, Ralph B. 1940
Bayless, William H., II ... 1937
Belleman, William I. 1942
Bennett, Charles L. 1936
Bennett, Rufus J., Jr. 1937
Billingslea, Howell H. 1942
Bliss, Robert 1933
* Bonaventure, Daniel T. ... 1943
Bonoff, William D. 1940
Boone, Robert L. 1944
Bordley, J. Beale 1939
Bortz, John C. 1932

---
* Died in military service.

219

	Last Year at WNA		Last Year at WNA
Bowman, Dewey	—	* Chappell, William H.	1942
Bradley, W. Rolph	1941	Chase, Lovell T.	1938
Braunlein, J. Howard	1938	Christie, J. Watson, Jr.	1944
Brenner, John A.	1940	Coale, Richard Smith	1928
Brodt, William G.	1937	Conner, Morton J.	1940
Brooke, Dandridge	1942	Cooper, Harold R., Jr.	1942
Brousell, Adolph	1941	Conrad, Luther B.	1939
Brown, John	1928	Corner, Avery	1938
Bryant, Charles H.	1911	Cory, Ernest N., Jr.	1933
Buck, George H.	1931	Damon, H. Gilroy, Jr.	1944
Buck, Walter E., Jr.	1939	Davenport, William S.	1942
Burkins, Leonard C., Jr.	1938	Davidson, Marion A.	1944
Burkley, John Kibler, Jr.	1935	Davison, Benjamin D.	1943
Burslem, Bert T.	1937	DeBlassis, Samuel J.	1940
Burslem, William, Jr.	1939	Denny, Ellis M.	1941
Bush, William	1940	Dennis, James B.	1931
Bush, William R.	1943	Dickinson, Morris V.	1938
Bustraan, John	1940	Dilks, Jack H.	1943
Cairnes, George W.	1940	Dinsmore, Herbert	1939
Cameron, Eugene C.	1942	Disbrow, G. Ward	1935
Cameron, George W.	1936	Disbrow, William Stephen, II	1934
Cameron, Merton K., II	1939	Douglas, William S.	1929
Cameron, Walter M., Jr.	1935	Dutcher, Thomas B., Jr.	1941
Cantwell, John A.	1931	Dvorak, Charles	—
Carhart, Leonard	1935	Eby, B. Franklin	1932
Carlson, Allen, Jr.	1944	Eisenberger, Daniel	1934
Carrell, Eugene C.	1942	Emrey, Jay C.	1938
Carson, Clement W.	1943	Evans, Thomas L.	1943
Cauffman, Lewis Bailey	1930	Evans, Standley, Jr.	1943
Cecil, Lawrence	1926	Ewing, G. Garrett	1936
Chandler, David B.	1939	Ewing, H. Wilson	1944
Chandler, J. Merritt	1935		

* Died in military service.

WNA Students in WW II Military Service

Last Year at WNA

Farnum, James R. 1943
Fedor, John A. 1941
Fehr, H. Robert, III 1937
Feltman, David B. 1941
Feltman, Robert F. 1943
Fico, Ralph J. 1943
Finney, Robert L. 1944
Foltz, William 1941
Frazer, Joseph H. 1940
Fritter, Charles Taylor 1928
Fritter, Lee Watson 1934
* Frommhagen, Frederick W.
   .... —
Fullmer, Marvin R. 1942
Fulton, James C. 1938
Funk, George E. 1940
Funk, Stanton C. 1943
Gaines, Clemens W. 1939
Garretson, Peter J. 1942
Gattuso, Leo A. 1941
Gemmill, Lee F. 1939
Gerow, Robert C. 1934
Gessner, Quentin H. 1942
Gibe, Frank A. 1940
Gough, Cecil P. 1940
Grable, Harold 1939
Green, Lyttleton L. 1944
Greenslade, Roger .... —
Hallock, Richard R. 1937
Hanna, Henry Gress 1926
Hanna, James J., Jr. 1926
Hansen, Carl K. 1937

Last Year at WNA

* Happersett, Howard W. .... —
Harding, Robert L. 1932
Harner, Henry C. 1940
Hart, Robert F. 1941
Haven, J. Franklin 1943
Heminway, Bernard 1940
Henderson, John W., Jr. ... 1940
* Hewit, Benjamin H. 1938
Hillis, Richard T. 1944
Hoffman, Robert William
   1928
Hoke, William F. 1939
Holscher, Franz F. S. 1942
Hughes, Lewis E. 1926
Ingram, Elliott 1939
Inman, Murrell D. 1941
Irvine, Don. H. 1942
Jamieson, J. Mitchell 1932
Jefferis, David S. 1930
Jenkins, E. Newell 1935
Jenkins, Malcom B. 1943
Jenkins, Richard 1939
Jenkins, Robert 1942
Jenkins, Walter 1941
Johnson, Gerald E. 1943
Johnston, Albert E., Jr. ... 1939
Jones, Charles R. 1926
Kaldor, Joseph 1939
Kay, Lewis, D. Jr. 1928
Kelly, Peirce C., Jr. 1943
King, Joseph H. 1936
Kitchin, Melville A. 1937

---

* Died in military service.

	Last Year at WNA		Last Year at WNA
Knapp, Robert V.	1943	Mackey, J. William	1943
Kullmar, Malcolm	1936	Metzgar, J. Elvin	1933
Kyle, John T.	1941	Metzgar, John D.	1933
Laird, Edward A.	1943	Metzgar, Robert E.	1937
Leary, Richard C.	1942	Metzgar, William Harold	1930
Lee, Doran M.	1942	Miller, Alan B., Jr.	1939
LeCompte, Walter	—	Miller, Oakley	1930
Liefer, Frederick H.	1943	Miller, Robert R.	1942
Lineweaver, John R.	1943	Minster, J. Davis	1941
Lingenfelter, M. Maney	1942	Mitchell, Vance F.	1940
List, Leonardo J.	1942	Mohlenrich, Philip	—
Little, Glen A., Jr.	1938	Montgomery, George Albert	1935
* Little, Samuel Guy, Jr.	—	Montgomery, William T.	1939
Lowerre, Warren, P.	1935	Moore, William U.	1943
Kayhard, Robert	1935	Moses, John D.	1941
Lynch, H. Dickson	1940	Mowrey, Wayne L.	1937
Lyon, James H.	1942	* Murray, Thomas	1940
McCabe, William	1942	Nesbitt, John A., Jr.	1931
McCarthy, C. Eugene	1940	Newcomb, Albert A., Jr.	1939
McCauley, Barton B.	1943	Newcomb, Edmund	1942
McCauley, Charles O., Jr.	1936	Nissler, C. William	1942
McCauley, C. Newell	1936	Nix, Victor A.	1944
McCloskey, Paul H.	1941	Nuttle, Harry J.	1934
McFadden, Roscoe Isaac	1928	Odell, Edward N.	1933
McGinnis, Warren D.	1942	Otten, Samuel T.	1944
McKeag, Charles C., III	1942	Owings, William Allen	1939
McKnown, James L.	1937	Page, I. Marshall, Jr.	1940
McLain, Paul D.	1944	* Parker, Frank C., Jr.	—
Mackie, Osbourne S.	1935	Patterson, Dale A.	1944
MacMillan, Donald B.	1941		
McVey, George B.	1937		

* Died in military service.

WNA Students in WW II Military Service

	Last Year at WNA		Last Year at WNA
Patterson, James D.	1942	Satterthwaite, Stacy T.	1944
Pattinson, Noel B.	1939	Sandlin, Harry T.	1943
Paul, Walter P., Jr.	1939	Scarborough, J. Gifford	1931
Petersen, Ronald R.	1942	Schloss, Lester	—
Phipps, G. Clark	1939	Schrumpf, H. Allen	1941
Plack, Ralph B.	1943	Scrivener, John W.	1928
Pletts, Donald C.	1940	Seibert, Christian	1941
Poist, Samuel M.	1932	Sheffer, H. Frazer	1941
Preston, Robert N.	—	Shenk, William H.	1944
Price, Gwilyn A., Jr.	1940	Shields, Charles R.	1934
Randall, Richard C.	1940	Shiels, A. Kendall	1942
Rawlings, Addison M.	1936	Sickles, Richard G.	1942
Reese, J. Joseph	1940	Silver, C. Bartol	1941
* Richardson, J. Riale	1936	Sitar, John G.	1939
Rehm, Maurice P.	1936	Skinner, Alan L.	1938
Respass, Robert C.	1937	Skinner, H. Wayne	1939
Reynolds, Delos H.	1943	Smith, Auvan F.	1935
Reynolds, R. Wayne	1942	Kellog-Smith, Donald H.	1941
Rider, Charles J.	1941		
Rider, Edward M.	1938	Smith, Robert H.	1942
Rigler, Robert B.	1942	Smith, Samuel J.	1933
Roak, John C.	1936	Smith, W. Harrington	—
Roberts, Lloyd W.	1940	Smith, William B., III	1933
Rogers, Joseph B.	1936	Smitley, C. Dewey	1938
Ross, Richard R.	1941	Smitley, Elmer H.	1940
Roush, Robert G.	1937	Snow, David R.	1940
* Rowland, John I.	1940	Snyder, Herbert T., Jr.	1938
Rowland, Wallace M.	1934	Sones, John R.	1944
Ruth, Aaron L.	1939	Spaid, Arthur H.	1943
Rutter, Charles C.	1942	Spehnkouch, William E.	1940
Salvaterra, Arnold R.	1938	* Spillane, James E., Jr.	1939
Saltsman, Robert H. W.	1937	Stack, Robert L.	1941

* Died in military service.

	Last Year at WNA		Last Year at WNA
Stahl, E. T. White	1938	Williams, Harry	1944
Steele, Clement C.	1941	Williams, John N.	1939
Stengel, A. H.	—	Williams, Wallace, Jr.	1939
Stevens, Edwin	1941	* Williamson, George T., Jr.	1942
Sullivan, Richard	1942		
Taggert, William N.	1937	Wilson, R. Thomas	1943
Thompson, M. Corthell	1934	Wilson, W. Raymond, Jr.	1938
Thompson, Richard J.	1937		
Tome, C. Barrington	1942	Windisch, Richard G.	1944
Trone, James L., Jr.	1940	Windsor, Clayton	1939
Turner, Arthur G.	1940	Woglom, James	1938
Turner, Philip H.	1943	Wood, Donald B.	1938
Tyson, I. Frank	1935	Wood, Harry, Jr.	1929
Venable, Sidney J., Jr.	1940	Worgan, Malcolm S.	1943
Vincent, Reginald C.	1939	Worthinton, Richard D.	1942
Vogel, Frederick B.	1940	Wysong, Robert D.	1943
Vorhees, Edmund L.	1939	Yerkes, Donald C.	1938
* Ward, Arthur J.	1941	Yerkes, James R.	1938
Warner, John R.	1942	Young, Chester	1943
Watson, Donald C.	1942	Young, J. Forney, Jr.	1936
West, Charles K., Jr.	1941	Young, John W.	1938
Wheeler, Ralph D., Jr.	1938	* Young, Paul T.	—
Williams, Franklin P., Jr.	1943	Zager, James T.	1941
Williams, F. P.	1897		

---

* Died in military service.

Appendix C

Principals and Headmasters of West Nottingham Academy

Principals (until 1924)

Service		Birth	Education**	Birthplace
1744–1761	Rev. Samuel Finley*	1715	Log College	Armagh County, Ireland
1812–1815	Reuben H. Davis	—	—	—
1815–1816	William McCrimmen	—	—	Ireland
1816–1817	Isaac Bird	—	Yale B.A., 1816	New England
1817–1820	Samuel Turney	—	—	—
1820–1835	Rev. James Magraw*	1775	Franklin College	Bart County, Pa.
1835–1840	Samuel Magraw	c.1809	WNA	West Nottingham, Maryland
1840–1850	Rev. George Burrowes*	1811	Princeton; PTS	Trenton, New Jersey
c.1845–1846	Levi Janvier***	—	PTS	—
1850–1851	Edwin Clapp	1849	Amherst B.A., 1849	New England
1852–1855	Rev. Archibald A. Hodge*	1841	Princeton B.A., 1841; PTS, 1847	Princeton, New Jersey
1855–1856	George Duffield & E.F.M. Faehtz	—	—	—
1856–1857	Alfred Yeomans	1852	Princeton B.A., 1852	North Adams, Mass.
1857–1859	William P. Andrews	1853	Lafayette B.A., 1853	Doylestown, Pa.
1859–1862	Rev. Amos H. Sill	1848	Union B.A., 1848; PTS, 1857	New York State
1862–1867	George K. Bechtel	c.1839	Princeton B.A., 1860	New Brunswick, New Jersey

Principals (until 1924) (continued)

Service		Birth	Education**	Birthplace
1867–1872	Rev. Samuel A. Gayley*	1822	Lafayette; PTS	Tyrone County, Ireland
1872–1887	George K. Bechtel	c.1839	Princeton B.A., 1860	New Brunswick, New Jersey
1887–1902	John G. Conner	c.1867	Lafayette B.A., 1887; Lafayette M.A., 1890	—
1902–1908	Clifton C. Walker	—	Hamilton A.B., 1894; Hamilton M.A., 1900	New York State
1908–1911	Horace C. Gillespie	—	WNA, 1892; Johns Hopkins	—
1911–1913	William F.H. Wentzel	—	Penn State MS	—
1913–1914	George B. Pheiffer	—	—	—
1914–1915	Rev. F. Harl Huffman*	—	A.B., A.M.	—
1915–1916	Walter L. Graefe	—	A.B.	—
1916–1917	Rev. F. Harl Huffman*	—	A.B., A.M.	—
1917–1919	Joseph F. Leuthner	—	—	—
1919–1920	T. H. Grim	—	A.M.	—
1920–1922	Frederick A. Torrey	—	Princeton A.M.	—
1922–1923	Dean E. Shull	—	—	—
1923–1924	William A. Cummings	—	B.S., M.A.	—

Headmasters (from 1924)

Service		Birth	Education	Birthplace
1924–1949	J. Paul Slaybaugh	1896	Dickinson B.S.; Pennsylvania M.A.	Mt. Alto, Pa.
1949–1952	Richard W. Holstein (Acting)	c.1912	Lebanon Valley College B.S., 1933	Lebanon, Pa.
1952–1961	Rev. Charles W. Blaker	1918	Pittsburgh Univ. B.S., 1937; Pittsburgh Theological Seminary, 1949	Pittsburgh, Pa.

PRINCIPALS AND HEADMASTERS OF WNA

Service		Birth	Education**	Birthplace
1961-1972	Norman C. Farnlof	1921	Harvard B.A.; Episcopalian School of Divinity, Philadelphia	Waterbury, Conn.
1972-1981	Kenneth Dietrich	1934	Dickinson A.B., Pennsylvania M.A.	Carlisle, Pa.
1981-1983	James Richardson	1942	Duke B.A., Middlebury M.A.	Atlanta, Ga.
1983-1984	Joint Leadership—			
	Richard Funk	1937	Loch Haven B.S., Westchester M.Ed.	Lewiston, Pa.
	James Spiro	1935	Fairmont B.A. in Ed.	Fairmont, W.Va.
	Thomas Varnes	1946	Franklin & Marshall A.B.	Flemington, N.J.
1984-1989	Henry H. Spire	1942	Dickinson B.A., Andover Newton Theological M. Div.	Hershey, Pa.
1989-	Edward J. Baker	1941	Springfield B.S., M.Ed.	Foxboro, Mass.

* Pastor of West Nottingham Presbyterian Church.
** PTS stands for Princeton Theological Seminary.
*** Janvier filled in as principal for Burrowes for a year or less.

Bibliography

Alexander, Archibald, ed. *Biographical Sketches of the Founder and Principal Alumni of the Log College.* Philadelphia: Presbyterian Board of Publication, 1851.
Bode, Carl. *Maryland.* New York: W. W. Norton & Co., 1978.
Cecil Democrat (Cecil County, Maryland). 3 June 1848 and 21 November 1863.
Cecil Whig (Cecil County, Maryland). 13 November 1847 and 26 April 1848.
Cecil County Bicentennial Committee. *Cecil County in the Revolutionary War.* Elkton, Md.: Cecil County Bicentennial Book Committee, 1976.
Comfort, W. W. *The Quakers, a Brief Account of Their Influence on Pennsylvania.* Gettysburg: The Pennsylvania Historical Association, 1948.
Dictionary of American Biography. Allen Johnson and Dumas Malone, eds. New York: Scribners, 1928-37.
Dumschott, F. W. *Washington College.* Chestertown, Md.: Washington College, 1980.
Funk, Henry D. "The Presbyterian Church and Education." *The Influence of the Presbyterian Church in Early American History,* pt. II. *Journal of the Presbyterian Historical Society* (April 1925):152-189.
Gavley, Samuel A. *An Historical Sketch of the Lower West Nottingham Presbyterian Church.* West Nottingham, Md.: Congregation of the West Nottingham Presbyterian Church, 1865.
Gifford, G. E., Jr., ed. *Maryland, 1608-1850, As Seen by Some Visitors, and Several Essays on Local History.* Rising Sun, Md.: George E. Gifford Memorial Committee, Calvert School, 1974.
Hagedorn, Hermann. *Brookings, a Biography.* New York: Macmillan Co., 1936.
Hoffecker, C. E. *Delaware.* New York: W. W. Norton & Co., 1978.
Johnston, George. *History of Cecil County, Maryland.* Elkton, Md.: By the Author, 1881.
Klett, C. S. *The Scotch-Irish in Pennsylvania.* Gettysburg: The Pennsylvania Historical Association, 1948.
Missionary Magazine of the Presbyterian General Assembly, 1805.
Monroe, J. A. *History of Delaware.* Newark, Del.: University of Delaware Press, 1984.

Papenfuse, E. C.; Steverson, G. A.; Collins, S. A.; and Green, L. C., eds. *Maryland, A New Guide to the Old Line State.* Baltimore: Johns Hopkins University Press, 1976.

Persico, Joseph E. "The Great Swine Flu Epidemic of 1918." *American Heritage,* June 1976, pp. 28-32.

Rush, Benjamin. *Travels through Life and Commonplace Book,* ed. George W. Corner. Princeton: Princeton University Press, 1948.

Steiner, Bernard C. *History of Education in Maryland.* Washington, D.C.: U.S. Government Printing Office, 1894.

Wall, Joseph F. *Andrew Carnegie.* New York: Oxford University Press, 1970.

Webster, Richard. *History of Presbyterian Church in America until 1760.* Philadelphia: 1857.

Wertenbaker, T. J. *The Founding of American Civilization, the Middle Colonies.* New York: C. Scribner's Sons, 1938.

Wertenbaker, T. J. *Princeton, 1746-1896.* Princeton: Princeton University Press, 1946.

Wirt, William. *The Letters of a British Spy.* Richmond, Va.: Printed by Samuel Pleasants, Jr., 1803.

Wish, Harvey. *Society and Thought in Early America.* New York: Longmans, Green and Co., 1950.

Work Projects Administration in the State of Maryland. *Maryland, a Guide to the Old Line State.* American Guide Series. New York: Oxford University Press, 1940.

Yuninger, A. B. *A Brief History of the Rock Presbyterian Church, Incorporating the 1872 History by the Reverend John Henry Johns.* Fair Hill, Md.: Rock Presbyterian Church, 1975.

Index*

Accreditation, 124, 171, 179, 183
Admiral Farragut Academy, 181, 198
Alexander, Archibald, 6
Alexander, Joseph, 14
Alexander, Richard "Duke", 140–141, 151
Alumni, 207–208
Alumni Association, 151, 157
Alumnus, 171
American Revolution, 22, 41
Amherst, 63
Anderson, Norman, 156, 168–169, 174, 179–182, 209
Andover Seminary, 49, 51
Andrews, William P., 67, 68
Archer, Henry W., 82
Archer, Jas., 82–83
Archer, John, 26, 27
Archer, Robt. W., 42
Armagh County, 6
Arrow, 175, 183, 195, 207
Athletics, varsity: early teams, 98–100; opponents, 98, 99, 108; 1939 football, 140; "Duke" Alexander, 140–141; 1959 football, 176–177; 1960–1961 basketball, 177–178; 1968–1980 basketball, 189

Balderston, Lloyd, 99n
Baltimore, 7, 43, 57, 74, 94
Baltimore, Lord, 1
Baltimore Sun, 57
Baltimore, Synod of, 110–112, 121, 136
Baynum, George, 118
Baranowski, Antoni, 192
Baxter, Alan, 172, 196
Bayard, John, 26
Bayard, James Asheton, 26
Bechtel, George, 71–90, 91, 93, 114

Bechtel, George Orris, 121
Bechtel, Mrs., 93
Bel Air Academy, 51, 58
Bicentennial, 149–154
Bird Dormitory, 190–191, 200
Bird, Isaac, 45–49, 51
Blair, 4, 5
Blaker, Charles W., 158–181, 208
Blaker, Jeff, 172
Blue Ball Crossroads, 1
Board of Trustees: organization of, 41–42; selected by Synod of Baltimore, 110–112. *See* Appendix A for members, 1811–1981
Bowen, Virginia, 172
Boy Scouts, Catonsville, Md., 113
Brangan, James, 188
Breckinridge, Henry, 154
British: troops, 32, 35; fleet, 43
Brookings Institution, 75, 120, 154
Brookings, Robert S., 74–75, 119, 120, 153
Brookland, 42
Brooks, Nathan C., 54
Bruce, Robert J., 208
Buchanan, Jas. L., 159
Buck, Burdette "Bud", 163, 168
Buildings, 9, 16, 42, 57, 72–73, 76–77, 135. *See also* Magraw Stone Mansion, Residence for principals and headmasters, Wiley, Tyson-Sill, Magraw, Rowland, Bird, Old Academy, Hill Top, Rush, Finley, Ware Field House
Burr, Aaron (Vice-President of U.S.), 26, 46
Burr, Aaron (President of Princeton), 29
Burrowes, Rev. George, 57, 58–60, 63
Buyers, Jas. Armour, 52
Buyers, Rev. William B., 52n

*Does not include many teachers, trustees, and alumni who appear in tabulations, tables, and appendixes but not in the text. It also omits the students in the second illustration of Chapter 15.

231

INDEX

California, Pa., State Teachers College of, 109–110
Calvin, John, xiii, 2, 3, 13
Calvinist doctrines, xiii, 3, 26
Cameron, James, 38
Cameron, William, Sr., 38
Canteen Club, 168, 192
Canteen, (student), 163. *See also* Old Academy
Carson, John, 66
Castle, Sue, 174
Catalogs, Academy, 76–81, 84, 95–97
Cecil County, xiii, 1, 3, 4, 6, 16–18, 36–37, 38, 41, 44, 55, 60–61, 64, 69, 113
Cecil Democrat, 61, 77, 80
Cecil Whig, 60, 61
Charlestown Presbyterian Church, 55, 56
Chesapeake Bay, 9, 46, 55, 207
Chesapeake Synod, 199
Chester Academy, 51
Chester County, England, 10
Childs, 100
Christiana Bridge, 18
Christiana River, 10
Christie, George M., 68
Civil War: and West Nottingham Academy 67–69, 72–73; mentioned, 37, 64, 65, 71, 74, 91, 116, 124
Clapp, Edwin, 58, 63–64
Clarkson, Ann, 18
Clarkson, Dr. Gerardus, 33
Clements, Dr. Rex S., 151–152
Coats, Brother, 77
Cockburn, Admiral Geo., 43
Cochran, Rebekah, 40
Cole, Carolyn, 207
College of New Jersey, xiv. *See* Princeton College
Colora, 38, 83, 179
Columbia, 12, 139
Compromise of 1850, 60–61
Connecticut, 18, 46, 49
Connecticut Assembly, 7, 8
Conner, John G., 91–102, 122–123, 139, 163
Conner, W. S., 92
Conowingo Dam, 117
Contact Program, 195–196

Continental Army, 26
Cooley, John M., 68
Coolidge, President Calvin, 115
Courses of study, 12, 43, 77–79, 95–97, 136–139, 206. *See also* Single-Subject Plan
Cummings, James, 38

Day's Academy, 63
Davies, Samuel, 18–19, 29–30
Davis, Mrs. Juliana B. and son Gabriel, 48
Davis, Reuben H., 51
Declaration of Independence, 10, 26
Deer Creek, 2, 39
Delaware and slavery. *See* Smithers, N.B.
Delaware College, 99
Delaware Gazette, 61
Derbyshire, Geo. H., III, 172
Dickey, Frances R., 93
Dickinson College, 28, 55, 116, 170
Dickinson, Rev. Jonathan, 29
Dictionary of American Biography, 22
Dietrich, Kenneth, 170, 182, 191, 198–209, Appendix C
Donegal, Presbytery of, 15
Dred Scott decision, 61
Duffield, Geo., 64
Dunnett, Charles W., 182

Easton, First Presbyterian Church of, 60
Eby, Franklin, 151, 157
Eckels, Marvin J., 76, 81
Edwards, Jonathan, 3, 7, 29
Edinburgh U. Medical School, 12
Elkton, 42, 47, 49
Elkton Academy, 44
Engel, Harry, 175
Engel, Janet R., 172
English School, 31, 35
Evans, Brother Frank, 77
Evans, Pres. L. H., 64
Evans, Dr. Frederick W., 151
Evans, Robert, 38, 42
Evans, Robt., Jr., 52
Ewing, Horace W., 176

Faber, Russell, 140
Faehtz, E.F.M., 64

INDEX

Faggs Manor Academy, 39
Fairmont State College, 176
Farnlof, Christina, 172
Farnlof, Norman, 169, 179–199, Appendix C
Federal Census. *See* Cecil County
Female teachers, 58, 93
Finley Hall, 182–183
Finley, Mrs. *See* Hall, Sara
Finley, Rev. James, xiv, 6, 11, 18, 36
Finley, Rev. Samuel, xiii, xiv, 5–35, 43, 169
Finney, Rev. William 55
Foreign students, 174–175
Foutz, C. Herbert, 158, 163, 168, 198, 205
Franklin, Benjamin, 4
Franklin College, 39
Freeman, Paul, 122
Fund-raising, 72–73, 76, 161. *See also* Baltimore Synod, Chesapeake Synod, Alumni, J. G. Conner, J. P. Slaybaugh, J. J. Hanna
Fryer, William, 106
Funk, Lena, 197, 205
Funk, Richard, 169–170, 197, 201, 205

Gale, Geo., 42
Garrett, George C., 107
Gayley, Brother, 77
Gayley Hall or House. *See* Residences for principals and headmasters
Gayley, Rev. Samuel A.: arrival as pastor, 65; leadership of West Nottingham Academy, 71–91; historian of academy, 4, 38, 55, 59, 64, 69; and John Conner, 91
Gayley, Samuel A. (grandson of Rev. S. A. Gayley), 120
Gell, William, 156
Gillespie, H., 100
Gillespie, Horace C., 106–109, 114
Gillespie, Rebecca, 93
Girl students, 93, 126, 172–174
Glasgow, Univ. of, 32
"Gloomy" letter tactic, 201
Goldmeier, Susan B., 172
Golibart, Julian, 67
(Golibart), Simon, 68
Gordon, Kenneth G., 205

Graduates, 23–25, 53–54, 68–69, 73–74, 88–90, 101–102
Graham, Rev. Robert, 55, 56
Great Awakening, 2–6, 9, 29
Great Depression, 123–124, 136
Groome, Dr. John, 42, 47–48
Groome, John, 47–48
Groome, Samuel, 47

Hagedorn, Hermann, 71
Haines, Brother, 76
Hall, Jacob, 10
Hall, Sara, 10, 11, 15–16
Hall, Sidney, 82
Hanna, Dave, 100
Hanna, H. Gress, 139
Hanna, J. J., 106, 110, 116, 118, 122, 134
Harford County, 2, 3, 4, 27, 58, 74, 82
Hartshorn, Jonathan, 38
Harvard, 98
Haughey, Jim, 190
Havre de Grace, 43, 112
Hazard, Ebenezer, 27
Head, Robert, 188
Headmasters, 115–209. *See also* Appendix C
Heim, Roger, 205
Hempstead, Joshua, 18
Hendrickson, Helen E., 198
Henry Daniel M., 152
Henry, John, 26
Hill Top Cottage, 174
Hodge, Rev. Archibald Alexander, 64
Hogg, Mrs., 58
Holstein, Richard W., 156–161, Appendix C
Horn, Peter, 188
Huffman, Rev. F. Harl, 112–113

Influenza epidemic, 113–114
Inglis, John A., 54, 67
Ireland, xiii–xvi, 2, 6, 26, 43
Irvine, William Mann, 115–116, 117
Irving Literary Society, 76, 98, 106

James I, VI, xiv–xv
Janvier, Levi, 59

Jenness, Aunt Jane, 75
Johnson, Captain William, 38
Johnston, George, 16, 38, 55
Jones, Hugh, 55n

Kay, Robert H., 94
Kennedy, President, 183
Kerr, Jane, 39
Kidd, Geo., 42, 61, 65
Kidd, George Washington, 42, 61, 65
Kidd, John Carson (J. C.), 65–67
Kilkenny, Ireland, 38
Kirk, Norman, T., 152
Kirkwood, 58–59
Knox, John, xiii, xiv

Log College, xvi, 3, 6
Logan, Jas., xvi
Lafayette College, 59, 63, 67, 71, 91, 92, 100, 139
Law, Jonathan, 7
Lawsing, Albert, 107, 109, 110
Leakin, George A., 68
Lebanon Valley College, 158
Lee, Paul, 197
Lincoln, President, 68
Lincoln University, 99
Literary Advance, 77, 100, 106, 108, 123, 139
Lock Haven State College, 169
Lower West Nottingham Presbyterian Church, 40. *See* West Nottingham Presbyterian Church
Lynch, Gertrude, 116–117, 120

Magraw, Adam R., 80
Magraw, Henry S., 54, 80
Magraw House, 122, 125, 130, 133–134, 169
Magraw, John, 39
Magraw, Rev. James, 39–57, 58, 80, 127
Magraw, Jas. C., 52, 54, 67
Magraw, Robert M., 54, 67
Magraw, Samuel M., 52, 54, 57, 58
Magraw Stone Mansion, 106, 114, 116, 120, 122, 133

Market Street (Philadelphia), 10
Martin, Alexander, 26
Maryland, students from. *See* Student home states
—border dispute with Pa., 1
—and Great Awakening, 3
—House of Delegates, 36
—blacks, 37
—Act of 1810
—requirements for Academy, 44
—and Civil War, 67
—and Subversive Activities Act, 175–176
—subsidy to academy, 43–44,
Maryland U., 141, 151
Mason and Dixon line, 36. *See* Maryland border dispute with Pa.
Maxwell, Esther, 65
Maxwell, Harriet Steele, 57
Meetinghouses. *See* Presbyterians
Mercersburg Academy, 113, 117
Middle States and Maryland, Association of Colleges and Secondary Schools. *See* Accreditation
Milford, Conn., 7
Miller, Ralph E. "Dusty", 205
Miller, Samuel, 38
Milton Academy, Mass., 64
Missouri Compromise of 1820, 61. *See also* Compromise of 1850
Morgan, John, 26
Morgan, Rev. Abel, 7
Morrow, Glenn R., 153
Morton Fletcher, 174
Mount, President P. W., 77

McAuley, Barton B., 148, 149
McCarthy, Senator Joseph, 175
McCrimmen, William, 51
McDowell, T. R., 77, 79
McMinn, Miss, 58, 66–67, 74
McNamee, Albert, 82
McWhorter, Alexander, 22

National Honor Society, 172
Nassau Hall, 29, 32

INDEX

Nesbitt, John A., 98, 113, 119
Nesbitt, John A., Jr., 124
Nesbitt, R., 100
Newark Academy, 75-76
New Brunswick, Presbytery of, 6-7
New Castle, Presbytery of, xiv, 1, 2, 4, 5, 15, 35, 37, 39
New Haven, Conn., Second Society of, 7
New York, Presbytery of, 15
New York, Synod of, xiv, 15
New York and Philadelphia, Synod of, 18
Newman, Scott, 198
Nilsson, K. R., 158, 168
North, adherents of in Civil War, 68
Northern Central Railroad of Md., 67
Nottingham Lots, 1
Nottingham News, 139
Nottinghamshire, England, 1

Octoraro Creek, 1, 2, 3, 9, 37
Old Academy, 72-73, 76-77, 163, 191-192
Orr, Rev. William, 1
Owen, Captain William, 57

Parents Association, 182
Patton, Captain Thomas, 38
Patton, David, 38, 42
Paul, Rev. John, 2
Peale, John R., 93
Pege, 124, 139, 195
Penn family, xvi
Penn, William, 1
Pennsylvania, 10, 39, 40, 58. *See also* Student home states, Maryland border dispute with—, Great Awakening
Pennsylvania Railroad, 94
Pennsylvania U. Medical School, 26
Pennsylvania, University of, 12, 124, 170
Perry Point project, 196-197
Perryville, 42, 83
Pheiffer, George B., 112
Philadelphia, xiv, 1, 6, 7, 9, 12, 33, 46, 94
Philadelphia, Second Presbyterian Church of, 7, 33
Philadelphia, Synod of New York and 16
Philadelphia, Synod of, 16

Pierrepont, Rev., 7
Pittsburg Theological Seminary, 162
Pittsburg U., 161
Polk, Mrs., 110
Polk, Rev. Samuel, 110
Port Deposit, 43, 48, 55, 57, 58, 63, 66, 67, 100, 119, 144
Port Deposit Presbyterian Church, 55, 66. *See also* Squier, Rev. John
Porter, John, 38
Porter, Mrs. Margaret, 94
Porter-Wiley Cottage. *See* Wiley House
Presbyterians, xiii-xvi, 1, 3, 4, 7, 15, 17, 22, 26, 30, 33, 35
—Board of Colleges, 110
—General Board of Education, 119, 122
Princeton College, xiv, 12, 14, 17, 19, 29-35, 58, 71, 83
Princeton, N.J., 29
Princeton Theological Seminary, 58, 59
Principals, 51, 57, 65, 71-87, 104-105, 106-109. *See also* Appendix C
Purinton, Dan, 81

Quakers, xvi, 1, 74

Ramsay, Andrew, 38
Ray, Joseph C., 194-196, 200, 205
Residence for principals and headmasters, 94, 106, 134, 182, 200
Revolutionary War, 22, 26, 32, 35, 37, 43
Rhodes Scholarship, 159, 172
Richards, Dr. G. H., 121
Richardson, D., 76
Rider, Edward, 188
Rising Sun, 1, 5, 9, 40, 69, 75, 100, 119, 122, 196
Robinson, Samuel, 119-120
Rock Presbyterian Church, xiv, 10, 11, 18, 36, 55, 56, 195. *See also* Yuninger, Rev. Allen B.
Roddy, Nancy V., 172
Rodgers, Brother, 77
Rolfe, William J., 58, 63
Roosevelt, Franklin D., 86, 136
Rowland, Brother, 77

Rowland, Isabella, 64
Rowland, John, 5
Rowland, J.M.H., 85, 174
Rowland, Dr. William, 66
Rowland Hall, 173–174, 191
Rules of Government of academy, 44–45
Rush, Banjamin, 10–28, 33, 44, 75, 153, 169, 191
Rush Dormitory, 191
Rush, Jacob, 10
Rush, Mrs., 10
Ruston, Thomas, 14

St. Marks Church Rd., 42
Sample, Nathaniel, 39
Sciple, Carrie Helen, 92
Scotch-Irish, xiii–xvi, 1, 6, 10, 22, 42, 71
Scotland, xiii, xiv, 6, 29, 43
Scots, 32, 39. *See also* Scotch-Irish
Scott, John, D.C., 54
Shaughnessy, Clark, 151
Shippen, William, 26, 31
Shotwell, Amelia, 58
Shotwell, Louise, 58
Sill, Brother, 77
Sill, Mrs., 84, 94
Sill, Rev. A. H., 64, 71, 84
Sims, James, 38, 42
Single-Subject Plan, 171–172
Slaybaugh, Eleanor Jane, 124
Slaybaugh, J. Paul, 65, 81, 83, 85, 106, 112, 113, 115–157, 162–209
Slaybaugh, Jas., 117
Smith, Jonathan Bayard, 26
Smithers, Nathaniel, 68
South, adherents of in Civil War, 67–68
South Carolina and Articles of Secession, 54
Spiro, Jas., 176–178, 188–190
(Spiro), Mary Wright, 176, 205
Spring in West Nottingham, 106
Springer, Brother, 77
Squier, Rev. John, 66, 67
Steiner, Bernard C., 41
Stevenson, Arthur, 170, 181–182, 199, 208–209
Stewart, Jas. A., 81

Stewart, Paul R., 144
Stockton, Richard, 26, 169
Student boarders, 11, 57, 83–84, 86, 94–95, 117
—college entrances, 12, 14, 19, 97, 133–134, 187
—home states, 9, 23–25, 44, 83, 127, 164, 186
—enrollment, 22–25, 53, 73–74, 92–93, 103, 114, 126, 160, 175, 184
—grade levels, 129, 160, 185
—careers, 21–28, 53–54, 88–90, 101–102
—religious affiliations, 128
—veterans, 155
Stump, John, 43
Strain, John, 35
Summer sessions, 124, 125
Susquehanna River, 1, 2, 43, 46, 58, 82, 117, 207
Swain, Robert, 151

Talisman Club, 172
Taney, Chief Justice, 61
Taylor, Elizabeth A., 198
Teachers, 52, 57, 63–64, 81–82, 93, 104–105, 130–132, 158, 165–167, 193–194, 195–196, 202–204
Tennent, Rev. Gilbert, 4, 30
Tennent, William (elder), xvi, 6
Tennent, William (younger), 30
Thais, William, 172
Thrash, Craig, 205
Tilton, James, 26
Tome Institute, 98, 100
Tome, Jacob, 101
Tome, Peter, 83
Tosh, Lawson, 100
Turney, Samuel, 51
Tyrone County, Ireland, 71
Tyson-Sill House, 172

Upper West Nottingham Presbyterian Church, 40, 55, 58

Valley Forge Military Academy, 140

INDEX

Venable, Rev. Sidney, 156, 161, 174, 188
Virdin, William W., 68
Von Behr, Robert H., 195

Waddell, James, 22, 26
Walker, Clifton C., 106
Walker, Eunice, 106
War of 1812, 42
Ware Field House, 187–188
Ware, Mr. & Mrs. John H., Jr., 188
Washington College, 100
Washington, D.C., 75, 127
Washington, D.C., Metro Area, 164, 186
Washington, George, 36, 48
Washington & Jefferson College, 54, 162
Washington University Medical School, 75
Waynesburg College, 144
Webster, Richard, 7
Wentzel, William F. H., 109–110, 112
Wertenbaker, T. J., 21, 30
Wesley Junior College, 158
West Nottingham Presbyterian Church or congregation, 4, 5–19, 35–36, 37, 40, 58–59. *See also* Rev. Jas. C. Magraw, Rev. Geo. Burrowes, Rev. A. A. Hodge, Rev. Samuel Gayley, Rev. Samuel Polk, Rev. Sidney Venable

West Virginia, University of, 81
Western Theological Seminary, 81
Westminster College, 156
Whitefield, George, 4–5, 7
Whitehill, Brother, 77
Wiley, Burton, 121
Wiley, Cora M., 93
Wiley House, 58, 66, 133–134, 191
Williams, Thomas, 38
Wills, Ted, 159, 162, 168, 171, 172
Wilmington project, 196
Wilson College, 116
Wilson, Margaret Wolf, 205
Wilson, President, 75, 153
Wilson, Richard, 205
Wirt, William, 26
Witherspoon, John, 32, 153
Wood, Henry C., 188
Works Progress Administration (WPA), 136
World War I, 113
World War II, 143–149, 154–155, Appendix B

Yale, 46, 98
Yeomans, Rev. Alfred, 66
Yuninger, Rev. Allen B., 195, 200, 205

This book was set in *Palatino* typeface
at Port City Press in Baltimore, Maryland.
William Carter supervised typography.

Book Designer
Ann Feild of the *Baltimore Sun,* recipient
of Award of Excellence for 1984 from the
International Society of Newspaper Designers.

About the Author

Scott A. Mills was born in Des Moines. Before completing his education, he served with the U.S. Navy's amphibious forces in the Pacific. After World War II he graduated from Grinnell College with a history major and earned a masters degree from the School of Advanced International Studies of Johns Hopkins University. His career with the Federal Government has included service with the U.S. Army and the National Aeronautics and Space Administration.